TEN SKILLS
YOU REALLY NEED
TO SUCCEED IN SCHOOL

JOHN LANGAN

Photography by Paul Kowal

TP

Send book orders and requests for desk copies or supplements to:
Townsend Press Book Center
1038 Industrial Drive
West Berlin, New Jersey 08091

For even faster service, contact us in any of the following ways:
By telephone: 1-800-772-6410
By fax: 1-800-225-8894
By e-mail: TownsendCS@aol.com
Through our website: www.townsendpress.com

Credits

Cover design: Larry Didona
Page design: Janet Goldstein and Eliza Comodromos
Photography: Paul Kowal of Cherry Hill, New Jersey (except as noted below)

Photographs of Dr. Ben Carson on pages 8 and 50 by Vince Rodriguez of Baltimore, Maryland.
Photographs of Dr. Ben Carson on pages 25 and 52 by Robert Smith of Baltimore, Maryland.
Photographs of Ryan Klootwyk on pages 35, 48, 64, 66, 69, 91, and 206 by Larry Marcus of Minneapolis, Minnesota.

"Dealing with Feelings" on pages 121–123: Rudolph F. Verderber, *Communicate!* 6th ed., copyright © 1990.
Reprinted with permission of Wadsworth, an imprint of the Wadsworth Group, a division of Thomson Learning.

"Peanuts" cartoon on page 147: Charles Schulz. Reprinted by permission of United Feature Syndicate, Inc.

Story on pages 49–54: Ben Carson, M.D., with Cecil Murphey. From *Think Big*, copyright © 1992
by Benjamin Carson, M.D. Reprinted by permission of Zondervan Publishing House.

Note to Instructors

An Instructor's Manual and Answer Key is available for this book. To receive a copy, call our toll-free number
(1-800-772-6410), or contact us using any of the other methods shown above.

Contents

Introduction to the Book

The transition from high school to college can be overwhelming. Krystal Buhr, one of the students interviewed for this book, remembers her initial one-on-one meeting with her college English professor. "She tore my first paper up as I watched! I was stunned. No one had ever done anything like that to me before."

Krystal Buhr is a student at Bucknell University.

Krystal's experience reminds me of my first college history class with a professor known as Shotgun O'Grady. From the start of the class, he scribbled quickly on the blackboard and fired off a steady stream of ideas, dates, and details. Taken aback, I just listened for several minutes, and then he noticed me sitting there, my arms folded. "I expect you to know all this," he commented. So I started taking notes, lots of them, and halfway through the class my hand was cramped from writing. By the end of the class, I had over ten pages of notes, and I wondered how I would ever study and remember all the material.

John Langan

Krystal Buhr and I, like countless other students, had to do a lot of work developing the writing, reading, and study skills needed to succeed in college. Because we had not mastered or been taught these skills in high school, we had to learn how to learn—at the same time that we were trying to deal with the whole new world of college life. We could have used a book that would teach us the learning skills we needed to know and that would share with us the hard-earned wisdom of other college students. *Ten Skills You Really Need To Succeed in School* will try to be that kind of book for you. Intended for first-year college students as well as for high school students thinking of going on to college, the book provides the know-how needed to achieve academic success.

If You're in College Now

If you're in college now or starting soon and want immediate practical help, you should pay special attention to the following:

Learning how to manage your time (Chapter 4, pages 75–88)

Learning how to take effective classroom notes (Chapter 5, pages 89–104)

Learning how to study and memorize material (Chapter 6, pages 105–118)

Learning how to read and study textbooks (Chapter 7, pages 119–132)

Learning how to be a good test-taker (Chapter 8, pages 133–146)

Learning how to write effective papers (Chapters 9 and 10, pages 147–192)

Also, be sure to read carefully Chapter 1, pages 5–22. Many students in their first year of college must go through a period of adjustment, and if that transition takes too long, it can detract from the time needed for study. Chapter 1 will help you really think about why you are in college and will help you focus on the heart of the matter—which is to work hard at your studies.

If You're in High School Now

If you're in high school, the first chapter you should turn to is Chapter 3. On pages 43–74, you'll see that one college student after another advises high-school students that the key to academic success is regular reading. Also, be sure to read the stories about Dr. Ben Carson, Maria Cardenas, and Ryan Klootwyk, three people who have transformed their lives through the power of reading.

After Chapter 3, you should go on to work through all the other chapters in the book. The chapters teach the skills that you need to become a better student. Chapter 1 may be of special value in helping you gain greater self-knowledge. Many high school students are accustomed to moving passively through the school system. They are more concerned about being like their peers and being liked by their peers than about learning or grades. Lacking a long-term view, they fail to realize that their peers are not going to help them succeed in college or in a career. The key to becoming a serious student is to realize that *you—and you alone—are responsible for your life.*

The Book's Special Features

Ten Skills You Really Need To Succeed in School is a practical book with a special human dimension. It presents as clearly as possible the nuts-and-bolts skills needed for success in school. Using a hands-on approach, it provides a number of activities at the end of each chapter so that you can learn through doing. At the same time, the book personalizes the skills by including photos and testimonials of a number of college students and graduates. Seeing their pictures and reading their comments will give you a better sense that the skills presented are ones that really work. All the students and graduates quoted speak from their own hard-earned experience; all have bridged the gap between high school and college and learned what they need to do well in college.

A Final Thought

Several years ago, my wife and I were vacationing in New Mexico. As we drove into one small town, we suddenly came upon a huge billboard. I was so struck by what it said that I stopped our car and wrote the words down:

If you never have a dream, you'll never make a dream come true.

On the first page of the first chapter, I comment that if you don't have the right attitude, you might as well throw this book in the trash. I'm not kidding. Some students are just pretenders: they talk the talk, but they're not ready to walk the walk. *Ten Skills You Really Need To Succeed in School* will help you "walk the walk"; it will help you master the thinking, reading, study, and writing skills needed to be a success. But the starting point must be a dream inside you—a belief and resolve in your heart that you will achieve a college education. If you decide—*and only you can decide*—that you want a college degree, this book will help you reach that goal.

John Langan

1 / Looking Inside Yourself

RESPECTING YOURSELF

This book is chiefly about the learning skills you need in order to do well in school. But your *attitude* about yourself and about school is even more crucial than any learning skill. Without a good attitude, you might as well take this book and throw it in the trash.

Consider this basic truth about human nature: **we all want to respect ourselves.** We all want to live our lives in such a way that we think well of our behavior and others think well of us. We do not want to be disrespected or thought of as bad people. An equally basic truth is that the only way we can get respect is to earn it. At a certain point in growing up we realize that life doesn't give us something for nothing. What is important and meaningful is what we earn through trying hard and working hard.

Take a moment to think about the following question: Imagine two people. One person has drifted unhappily through life, putting in a minimal effort at a series of jobs and maybe even at times living off others. One morning the telephone rings and someone says to this person, "Congratulations. You have just won a million dollars in the state lottery." The other person works hard and eventually earns a million dollars; that person is well-regarded by others and has a strong sense of accomplishment and self-worth. Which person would you rather be—the one who *won* a million dollars or the one who *earned* a million dollars?

Hopefully you would choose to be the person who takes pride and satisfaction in having earned a good living. If you relate to that person, your attitude would be something like this: "I want to respect myself and have others respect me. To get this respect, I'm going to work hard to succeed. At this stage in my life, that means doing well in school because education is clearly a key to success." And if you've made mistakes in the past (and many of us have), your attitude should be: "I can change my behavior. I'm going to learn to work hard so I can get somewhere and be someone."

On the next page are two people who once had a bad attitude. Joe Davis (on the left) was a high-school dropout and a drug addict. Today he's married, working as a rehabilitation counselor, and also studying for a master's degree, with the hope of starting a new career as a teacher. Rod Sutton (on the right) was an angry, fatherless kid and a bully who was kicked out of more than one school. Today he and his wife have two children, he is teaching at an inner-city school, and he has recently earned a master's degree in education. You will learn more about their stories as well as some of their thoughts about learning in other parts of this book.

Joe Davis is a graduate student at the University of Pennsylvania.
Rod Sutton has a master's degree from Eastern College.

Joe and Rod: "For a long time we just didn't get it."

DOING THE WORK

You need to believe in the saying, "No pain, no gain." The only way to get self-respect and success is to work for them. When I was teaching, I found that among the two hundred or so students I met each year, there was no way of telling at first which students had this attitude and which did not. Some time must pass for people to reveal their attitude by what they do or do not do. What happens is that, as the semester unfolds and classes must be attended and work must be done, some people take on the work and persist even if they hit all kinds of snags and problems. Others don't take on the work or don't persist when things get rough. It becomes clear which students have decided, "I will do the work" and which have not.

The heart of the matter is not the *speed* at which a person learns; the heart of the matter is his or her determination—"I *will* learn." I have seen people who had this quality of determination or persistence do poorly in a course, come back and repeat it, and finally succeed.

For example, I've seen the young woman who wrote the following journal entry as her first assignment in a writing class eventually earn her GED and later a junior college degree:

> Well it's 10:48 and my kid is in bed. I don't know yet what Im going to write about but I hope I think of something before this ten minutes are up. boy I don't even like to write that much. I never send my letters or cards because I dislike writing, may be because I never took the time to sit down and really write, I've always wishes I could, put thing on paper that were in my mind. but my spelling isn't at all good, so when I had to take the time to look up a word, I said to heck with it, but, I can't do that with this any way I don't believ I can write for ten minutes straght, but Im trying to refus to stop until Ive made it. Ive always given my self credit for not being a quiter, so I guess I have to keep fighting at this and every thing else in the future, If I wish to reach my gols wich is to pass my GED and go in to nursing. I know it will take me a little longer then some one who hasn't dropped out of school but no matter how long it takes I'm shure I will be well worth It and I'll be glad that I keep fighting. And Im shur my son will be very proud of his mother some day.

Through knowing people as determined as this young woman, I've come to feel that the single most important factor for school survival and success is *an inner commitment to doing the work*. When the crunch comes—and the crunch is the plain hard work that school requires—the person with the commitment meets it head-on; the person without the commitment avoids it in a hundred different ways.

DISCOVERING THE NEED TO DO THE WORK

I have seen too many students over the years who have acted more like zombies in class than like live people. Such students are their own worst enemies. It's clear they regard themselves as unlikely to succeed in school. They walk into the classroom carrying defeat on their shoulders the way other students carry textbooks under their arms.

I'd look at them slouching in their seats and staring into space and think, "What terrible things have gone on in their lives that they've quit already? They have so little faith in their ability to learn that they're not even trying." These students may suddenly disappear one day, and often no one pays much notice because they have already disappeared in spirit long before.

When I have seen such students with resignation in their eyes, I have wanted to shake them by the shoulders and say, "You are not dead. Be proud and pleased that you have brought yourself this far. Yes, life has probably been very hard, but you can still be someone. Breathe. Hope. Act." Such people should refuse to use self-doubt as an excuse for not trying. They should roll up their sleeves and get to work. They should start taking notes in class and trying to learn. I want to say to them, "Get off the bench. Come onto the playing field. Give it a shot. You'll never learn to succeed if you don't try."

Thankfully, not every such student succumbs to the poison of self-doubt. What I have seen happen is that a spark will ignite. Some students discover possibilities within themselves or realize the meaning that school can have in their lives. As a result, they make the inner commitment to do the work that is essential to academic success.

Here is one student's account of a such a discovery in her first semester in college:

My present feeling about college is that it will improve my life. My first attitude was that I didn't need it. I had been bored by high school where it seemed we spent grades 9 to 12 just reviewing everything we had learned up through grade 8.

When I entered college in January I thought it was fun but that's all. I met a lot of people and walked around with college textbooks in my hand playing the game of being a college student. Some weeks I went to class and other weeks I didn't go at all and went off on trips instead. I didn't do much studying. I really wasn't into it but was just going along with the ball game. Sometimes kids would be going to an early class and I would be walking back into the dorm from an all-night party.

Then two things happened. My sociology class was taught by a really cool person who asked us questions constantly, and they began getting to me. I started asking *myself* questions and looking at myself and thinking, "What's going on with me? What do I want and what am I doing?" Also, I discovered that I could write. I wrote a paragraph about my messy brother that was read in class, and everyone roared. Now I'm really putting time into my writing and my other courses as well.

Just the other day my writing teacher asked me, "What is the point at which you changed? Was there a moment of truth when the switch turned to 'on' in your head?" I don't know the exact moment, but it was just there, and now it seems so real I can almost touch it. I know this is my life and I want to be somebody and college is going to help me do it. I'm here to improve myself, and I'm going to give it my best shot.

Among the present and past students interviewed for this book is Dr. Ben Carson, professor and director of pediatric neurosurgery at the Johns Hopkins Children's Center, the author of several best-selling books, and president of a nonprofit organization, the Carson Scholars Fund.

(The story of how Ben Carson turned his life around from a path that was leading to failure appears on pages 49–54. Dr. Carson is also quoted on pages 48, 79, 115, 141, 204, and 205.)

Dr. Carson talks about his moment of truth in his first semester at Yale:

"Going off to Yale from an inner-city high school in Detroit was an incredible culture shock. I barely had to study in high school. I found myself trying to do that at Yale, and it wasn't working, and I almost had to leave after the first semester. It was that experience, combined with my desire to succeed, that basically made me grab myself by the throat. I said, 'You're going into the stacks in the library where nobody can bother you, and you're going to study every free moment you have.' And that's what turned it around for me, just constantly banging it in, over and over again. Study became crucial for me, like breathing."

➤ Activity: Evaluating Your Attitude toward School

Take a moment to think about your own attitude toward learning. Check off each item that applies to you. (If you agree with some sentences in an item but not others, cross out the ones you do not agree with.)

_____ School has never really turned me on. I feel I can start to study if I need to, but I don't want to. What's wrong with being a bit lazy if life is supposed to be about enjoying yourself and having some fun? I want to take it easy and have as much of a good time as I can for now.

_____ I suppose I am passive about studying, but it's not all my fault. I'm tired of just being told what to do. I'm tired of being force-fed what other people think I need to learn. I can't wait to get out of school and be on my own so I can start living my life.

_____ I'm not ready to take responsibility for learning a lot of stuff that is not going to be of any value to me as far as I can see. Why should I study stuff that has no interest for me?

_____ If I start studying, I'll miss out on the good times that school has to offer. I won't have time to go to games or parties. And I don't want to be alone. If I start studying, some of my friends are going to think twice about hanging out with me.

_____ I want to do more in school, but I'm afraid of really giving it a good effort. What if I try my best and I still get lousy grades? My pals will see this, and they'll just laugh at me. I don't want to look foolish, so I'm probably just going to drift along and not call any attention to myself.

_____ Maybe there is no "take charge of my life" switch inside me. Or if there is, maybe there is no way of turning it on. My feeling is that I just want to cruise along and hope I get lucky. Maybe I will win a lot of money in a lottery. I wish I could work hard, but I want to be honest about that. I just don't think I'm going to do it. I'm just going to keep hanging out with my friends and not doing anything.

_____ I guess I've just been out of it for a long time. There are probably lots of reasons why. I got little encouragement along the way. I pretty much just let things happen to me. I feel like a piece of driftwood tossed about on a stormy sea. I do want to do something and to become someone. I've felt like this for a while, and at times I really want to get serious. But so far I just haven't done so.

_____ I'm not an active student, and I don't do my best all the time. But I'm not a zombie either. I do some studying, just not as much as other people would like me to. I should probably do more, and I'm going to work on that and try to do a better job of taking charge of my studies.

_____ I'm ready to move. I want to be active. I believe that a spark has finally begun to burn inside me. I was dead to learning, and now I'm coming alive. I want to get somewhere, and I'm ready to be a serious student. It's true that some of the stuff I have to study is boring, and some teachers do not care. But I feel now that these are just hurdles that will not stop me. I'm going to do my best to get where I want to go.

_____ I'm on the move, and I have taken charge of my life. There is something inside me that is strong and determined to succeed. I feel in my heart of hearts that nothing is going to stop me. It's my life, and I'm going to work hard, respect myself, and gain success and happiness.

If you have a chance, share your answers with other students. Spend some time talking with each other about what your attitude is and, if necessary, how you can improve it.

RUNNING FROM THE WORK

As a school semester unfolds and the crunch of work begins, students are put up against the wall. Like it or not, they must define their role in school. There are only two roads to take. One road is to do the work: to leave the game table, click off the stereo or television, turn down the invitation to go out, get off the phone, stop anything and everything else, and go off by oneself to do the essentially lonely work that studying is. The other road is to escape the work.

Escape Habits

Here are some of the habits that people practice to avoid doing the hard work that school requires. If you see yourself in any of these situations, you need to do some serious thinking about your behavior. Self-knowledge is power! Once you are aware of a problem, you can begin to deal with it.

"I Can't Do It."

Some people will let themselves be discouraged by bad grades. They'll think, "There's no use trying. I'm just not any good at this." But the only way people will really know that they cannot do something is by first trying—giving it their best shot. They must not let a defeatist attitude keep them from making a real effort.

Do not hesitate to take advantage of a tutoring program or a writing, reading, or math lab. You can often go to your teacher as well. If you think you "can't do it," the reason may be that you have given up far too soon.

"I'm Too Busy."

Some people *make* themselves too busy, perhaps working more hours at a part-time job than they need to. Others get overly involved in social activities. Others allow personal or family problems to become so distracting that they cannot concentrate on their work. There are situations in which people are so busy or so troubled that they cannot do their work. But there are also situations in which people exaggerate conflicts or stress. They create an excuse for not doing what they know they should do.

"I'm Too Tired."

People with this excuse usually become tired as soon as it's time to write a paper or study a book or go to class. Their weariness clears up when the work period ends. The "sleepiness syndrome" also expresses itself as an imagined need for naps during the day and then ten hours or more of sleep at night. Students with this attitude are, often literally, closing their eyes to the hard work that school demands.

"I'll Do It Later."

Everyone tends at times to procrastinate—to put things off. Some students, however, constantly postpone doing assignments and setting aside regular study hours. Time and time again they put off what needs to be done so they can watch TV, talk to a friend, go to the movies, play cards, or do any one of a hundred other things. These students typically wind up cramming for tests and writing last-minute papers, yet they often seem surprised and angry at their low grades.

"I'm Bored with the Subject."

Students sometimes explain that they are doing poorly in a course because the instructor or the subject matter is boring. These students want education to be entertainment—an unrealistic expectation. On the whole, courses and instructors balance out: Some are boring, some are exciting, many are in between. If a course is not interesting, students should be all the more motivated to do the work so that they can leave the course behind once and for all.

"I'm Here, and That's What Counts."

Some students spend their first weeks in college lost in a dangerous fantasy. They feel, "All will be well, for here I am in college. I have a student ID in my pocket, a sweatshirt with the college name on it, and textbooks under my arm. All this proves I am a college student. I have made it." Such students have succumbed to a fantasy we all at times succumb to: the belief that we will get something for nothing. But everyone knows from experience that this hope is a false one. Life seldom gives us something for nothing—and school won't either.

Kenyon Whittington is a student at Hampton College.

Kenyon on "I Can't Do It":

"I had to deal with my own skepticism and self-doubt. Low esteem was a problem for me, and I saw it was a problem for other students. I eventually developed the attitude, 'Just do it. If you don't finish or you don't get a good grade, at least you tried.'"

Tynara on "I'm Too Busy":

"I felt I had to get involved with homecoming, I felt I had to become part of student government, and I just got all involved with extracurricular activities. I also felt I had to run home to be with my boyfriend, who was going through hard times. My grades really began to fall, and I just made myself quit all my activities. I made study the name of the game. Then my grades picked up."

Tynara Chappelle is a graduate of West Chester University.

Kenyon on "I'm Too Tired":

"One can fall into the ridiculous habit of sleeping all the time. Each day can become one big drowsy day. You must take charge!"

Tynara on "I'll Do It Later":

"I reached a point where I was cramming for everything. I became socially involved and just kept thinking I'd be able to handle my studies later. I remember once coming back from a party at five in the morning, and then I had to cram for a test that I was going to have at 8 a.m.! I beat myself up cramming and cramming until I finally realized it just would not work."

Tynara on "I'm Bored with the Subject":

"In any course that was not part of my major, I just did the minimum. My grades suffered until I got the message. I had to be well-rounded and pay attention to those courses. You can't skip studying for a subject just because you don't like it."

Kenyon on "I'm Here, and That's What Counts":

"This is a trap, especially in the first year. You can enjoy yourself, but you also have to take control. Some students think 'I'm here and I'm in college,' but that's not the end reward. The end reward is walking down the aisle to get your college degree. You don't want to be one of those students who can only say, 'I went to such-and-such a school.' You want to be able to say, 'I graduated from that school.'"

➤ Activity: Evaluating Yourself for Escape Habits

Evaluate your own use of the escape habits described above. Check the answers that apply.

"I Can't Do It."

____ Never   ____ Sometimes   ____ Often

"I'm Too Busy."

____ Never   ____ Sometimes   ____ Often

"I'm Too Tired."

____ Never   ____ Sometimes   ____ Often

"I'll Do It Later."

____ Never   ____ Sometimes   ____ Often

"I'm Bored with the Subject."

____ Never   ____ Sometimes   ____ Often

"I'm Here, and That's What Counts."

____ Never   ____ Sometimes   ____ Often

One Student's Escape Story

Here is one student's moving account of the escape pattern in his life and his discovery of it. Gerald (not his real name) had the courage to look at his behavior, to see it for what it was, and to share it with others.

Gerald's Story

Somewhere, a little piece of me is lost and crying. Someplace, deep in the shadows of my subconscious, a piece of my soul has sat down and anchored itself in defeat and is trying to pull me down into the darkness with it. This might sound strange to someone who is not familiar with the inner conflicts that can tear and pull at a person's soul until he begins to stop and sink in his own deep-hollow depths. But sinking doesn't take much. It takes only one little flaw which, left unattended, will grow and grow . . . until, like cancer, it consumes the soul.

I know now, and I have always known, that help comes first from within. I know that if one doesn't come to one's own rescue, then all is lost. I know it is time for me to look at myself, which I would rather avoid. But in order to break free of my own chains, I must look at myself.

I could relate the incidents of youth. I could tell of the many past failures and what I think caused them. But I won't, for one example will show where I'm at. At the beginning of this summer I set my goals. These goals consisted of the college courses I wanted to complete and where I wanted to be physically and mentally when the summer was over. Listed among the goals to be accomplished were courses I needed in writing and accounting. But now here, at the end of July, I am so far behind in both courses it looks as if I will fail them both. I ask myself, "Why?" I know that if I work enough, I can handle the courses. So why have I been so lazy? Why is it that the things I seem to want most I either give up or in some way do not strive for? These are the questions I must try to answer.

I think I've spent too much of my life just waiting for good things to come. I've waited for a magic rainbow to appear in the sky and to drop a pot of gold into my lap. I've been hurt so much in life and now I just want it handed to me.

But it's time for me to stop chasing rainbows. It's time to stop looking into the sky waiting for help to arrive. It's time for me to start scraping the rot out of my mind, to stop dreaming and not acting, before I have nothing left to hope for. I can see now that I've never given it the total effort, that I've always been afraid I would fail or not measure up. So I've quit early. Instead of acting on my dreams, I've laid back and just floated along. I've lived too much time in this world unfulfilled. I've got to make my dreams work. I've suffered enough in this world. I must do this now, and what it takes is the doing. Somehow I must learn to succeed at success rather than at failure, and the time to start is now.

➤ Activity: Gerald's Story

Place a check beside the items you feel seem true about Gerald.

_____   He has been badly hurt in life.

_____   He feels too sorry for himself.

_____   He has moments when he sees himself clearly.

_____   He is completely lacking in self-knowledge.

_____   He fools himself some of the time but not all the time.

_____   He has good intentions but little follow-through.

_____   He is haunted by his failures.

_____   He is very close to taking charge of his life.

_____   He probably escaped by saying, "I'm too tired."

_____   He probably escaped by saying, "I'm bored with the subject."

_____   He probably escaped by saying, "I'll do it later."

_____   He has no regrets.

_____   He probably dropped out of school at some point after writing this essay.

_____   He probably went on to pass his courses and to get a degree.

If you have a chance, discuss your answers with other students. Also, take time to think about the questions below.

1. What do you think Gerald means by saying he "just floated along"?

2. What do you think he means by saying he has "waited for a magic rainbow"?

3. What does Gerald mean when he says that it's time for him to "break free of . . . chains" and "to stop chasing rainbows"?

4. Have you any answers for these questions that Gerald asks himself: "So why have I been so lazy? Why is it that the things I seem to want most I either give up or in some way do not strive for?"

5. Have you or has anyone you know ever resembled Gerald? In what ways?

We have probably all known students like Gerald. They are students who never really determine to try their best. They know what they should do but never do it. They make excuses; they escape. They fool themselves, time and time again. They try to have as much fun as they can, and they keep saying, "Tomorrow. Tomorrow I will get serious. Tomorrow I will start working hard." There is often a terrible hurt deep inside them. And for some reason deep inside them a switch never turns on, a spark of determination never ignites. They are individuals who are unable to take charge of their own lives, unable to work hard, and, as Gerald puts it, unable "to succeed at success."

TWO SUCCESS STORIES

Here are the accounts of two students determined to meet the challenges of learning:

Zamil's Story

Zamil Ortiz is a student at
Haverford College.

Zamil Ortiz is a small person with a shy smile and a soft, polite voice. But on the topic of education—of being the best person that one can be—she speaks out boldly.

"Whatever obstacles stand between you and school, you can overcome them," she says. "If you have to go to school without breakfast because there's no food in the house, then you do that. If you have no money to continue, then work for a semester or a year and earn enough to go back, but go! There's no excuse for giving up. Don't just stay home and watch TV."

Zamil knows the difficulties that she's talking about. Growing up poor after her father abandoned his family, she often heard her mother say, "You know, when you make it through college and have a good job, your father will come around and want to be part of your life again."

"And if that happens, I will be ready," says Zamil proudly. "I'll say to him, 'We did this, Mom and me, all by ourselves.' My success will be my gift to my mother."

Zamil talks more about the personal commitment one must make to oneself: "You have to believe in your inner worth. Don't let anybody stop you. Remember, this is *your* life. Don't follow somebody else around. Don't think, 'Oh, but if I go to college I might lose my girlfriend, might lose my boyfriend.' Excuse me? Is that person living your life, or are you? Get your head on straight!"

Ginger's Story

Ginger Jackson is a student at
Muhlenberg College.

Ginger Jackson, a second-year student at Muhlenberg College, wants to make a difference by becoming a teacher some day. She loves being in college and says, "All I have to do when I get discouraged is remind myself that if I don't keep making good grades, I'll have to leave. That's enough to get me back on track."

Ginger shrugs off any difficulties about college life. "Yeah, I have to work hard, but that's why I'm here," she says. In her opinion, the difference between a successful and an unsuccessful school experience is a student's attitude and sense of focus. "I see a huge difference between kids who really want to be in college and kids whose parents have said, 'You're going.' To succeed in school—or anywhere else—you have to really want to be where you are."

Hanging above the desk in Ginger's room is a poster announcing in giant letters, "DON'T QUIT." Every time Ginger glances at it, she remembers the words that guide her, and that she will share with her own students some day: "Where there's a will, there's a way. Your goal may seem very far away at first, but if you keep going a step at a time, you'll reach it."

FINAL THOUGHTS

1   If you have not yet taken charge of your life, this chapter is the most important one in the book for you. A statement at the beginning of the chapter bears repeating: If your attitude is not a hopeful and determined one, you might as well take this book and toss it in the trash.

2   Here is another final thought for you to consider:

    In your heart of hearts, you know that all the following words are true. The truth is that school, like life, is demanding. The truth is that to become someone and to get somewhere, we must be prepared and able to make a solid effort. We must accept the fact that little can be won or achieved or cherished in life without hard work. The decision that each of us must make is the commitment to do the hard work required for success in school—and ultimately in life. By making such a decision, and acting on it, we assume control of our lives. By not acting, by waiting for good things to drop into our laps, we run the terrible risk of waking up some day and knowing that we have wasted our lives. Please don't let this happen. Wake up to the possibilities and the power within you. Have faith and a brave heart and begin working to succeed in your life.

FINAL ACTIVITIES

1   Check Your Understanding

To check your understanding of the chapter, answer the following questions.

1. The most crucial factor needed for one to do well in school is
    a. the ability to learn quickly.
    b. respect for teachers.
    c. involvement in extracurricular activities.
    d. a commitment to doing the work.

2. Which of the following is *not* one of the escape habits outlined in the chapter?
    a. "I'm too disorganized."
    b. "I'll do it later."
    c. "I'm bored with the subject."
    d. "I'm too tired."

3. According to the chapter, students who tell themselves "I'm here, and that's what counts" believe that
    a. it is up to them to work hard in college.
    b. they have already proved their worth merely by getting into college.
    c. God has put them on earth for a special purpose.
    d. attending class faithfully is the key to success in school.

4. The student named Gerald
    a. always made the right choices in college.
    b. succumbed to his feelings of defeat and withdrew from college.
    c. finally realized that he must actively work to succeed.
    d. will never find the inspiration to succeed in school.

5. Which of the following is *not* one of the truths we must accept in order to succeed in school?
    a. School, like life, is demanding.
    b. Good things come to those who wait for them to happen.
    c. We must be prepared to make a solid effort in order to achieve our goals.
    d. Little can be accomplished without hard work.

2   Questions for Writing or Discussion

You may find it helpful to think about and write out your answers to the following questions. Or your instructor may put you in a small group or pair you with another student and have you discuss the questions with each other.

1. An opening statement in the chapter is that "we all want to respect ourselves." Describe someone you know who you feel respects himself or herself. How can you tell?

    Then describe someone you know who does not respect himself or herself. Again, how can you tell?

    Finally, think about how much you do or do not respect yourself. What steps do you need to take to respect yourself even more than you may now?

2. The author says that "the single most important factor for school survival and success is *an inner commitment to doing the work*." Do you feel you have this commitment? If not, or if it is not as strong a commitment as you want, what do you think you need to do to create a strong commitment?

3. Do you know any students like the ones described on page 7 who are "more like zombies in class than like live people"? How do they behave? What do you think can be done to help them change?

4. Do you have any of the escape habits described on pages 10–11? Which is your favorite habit? Do you think this habit has been harmful to you as you pursue goals in life? What would be your advice to yourself?

5. In light of the amount of respect you have for yourself, your attitude about school, the choices you make between working hard and having fun, and the escape habits you may practice, how would you rate your chances of success in school? Be as honest as you can in doing this!

___ 100%   ___ 75%   ___ 50%   ___ 25%

What are your reasons for how you rate your chances?

3   Reacting to a Reading

Read the following essay, and then write about or discuss the questions that follow.

The Fist, the Clay, and the Rock

The best teacher I ever had was Mr. Gery, who taught twelfth grade English. He started his class with us by placing on the front desk a large mound of clay and, next to it, a rock about the size of a tennis ball. That got our attention quickly, and the class quieted down and waited for him to talk.

Mr. Gery looked at us and smiled and said, "If there were a pill I could give you that would help you learn, and help you want to learn, I would pass it out right now. But there is no magic pill. Everything is up to you."

Then Mr. Gery held up his fist and kind of shook it at us. Some of us looked at each other. What's going on? we all thought. Mr. Gery continued: "I'd like you to imagine something for me. Imagine that my fist is the real world—not the sheltered world of this school but the real world. Imagine that my fist is everything that can happen to you out in the real world."

Then he reached down and pointed to the ball of clay and also the rock. He said, "Now imagine that you're either this lump of clay or the rock. Got that?" He smiled at us, and we waited to see what he was going to do.

He went on, "Let's say you're this ball of clay, and you're just sitting around minding your own business and then out of nowhere here's what happens." He made a fist again and he smashed his fist into the ball of clay, which quickly turned into a half-flattened lump.

He looked at us, still smiling. "If the real world comes along and takes a swing at you, you're likely to get squashed. And you know what? The real world will come along and take a swing at you. You're going to take some heavy hits. Maybe you already have taken some heavy hits. Chances are that there are more down the road. So if you don't want to get squashed, you're better off if you're not a piece of clay.

"Now let's say you're the rock and the real world comes along and takes a swing at you. What will happen if I smash my fist into this rock?" The answer was obvious. Nothing would happen to the rock. It would take the blow and not be changed.

He continued, "So what would you like to be, people, the clay or the rock? And what's my point? What am I trying to say to you?"

Someone raised a hand and said, "We should all be rocks. It's bad news to be clay." And some of us laughed, though a bit uneasily.

Mr. Gery went on. "OK, you all want to be rocks, don't you? Now my question is, 'How do you get to be a rock? How do you make yourself strong, like the rock, so that you won't be crushed and beaten up even if you take a lot of hits?'"

We didn't have an answer right away, and he went on, "You know I can't be a fairy godmother. I can't pull out a wand and say, 'Thanks for wanting to be a rock. I hereby wave my wand and make you a rock.' That's not the way life works. The only way to become a rock is to go out and make yourself a rock.

"Imagine you're a fighter getting ready for a match. You go to the gym, and maybe when you start you're flabby. Your whole body is flab and it's soft like the clay. To make your body hard like a rock, you've got to train.

"Now if you want to train and become hard like the rock, I can help you. You need to develop skills, and you need to acquire knowledge. Skills will make you strong, and knowledge is power. It's my job to help you with language skills. I'll help you train to become a better reader.

I'll help you train to be a better writer. But you know, I'm just a trainer. I can't make you be a fighter.

"All I can do is tell you that you need to make yourself a fighter. You need to become a rock. Because you don't want to be flabby when the real world comes along and takes a crack at you. Don't spend the semester just being Mr. Cool Man or Ms. Designer Jeans or Mr. or Ms. Sex Symbol of the class. Be someone. Be someone."

He then smashed that wad of clay one more time, and the thud of his fist broke the silence and then created more silence. He sure had our total attention.

"At the end of the semester, some of you are going to leave here, and you're still going to be clay. You're going to be the kind of person that life can smush around, and that's sad. But some of you, maybe a lot of you, are going to be rocks. I want you to be a rock. Go for it. And when this comes"—and he held up his fist—"you'll be ready."

And then Mr. Gery segued into talking about the course. But his demonstration stayed with most of us. And as the semester unfolded, he would call back his vivid images. When someone would not hand in a paper and make a lame excuse, he would say, "Whatever you say, Mr. Clay" or "Whatever you say, Ms. Clay." Or if someone would forget a book, or not study for a test, or not do a reading assignment, he would say, "Of course, Mr. Clay." Sometimes we would get into it also and call out, "Hey, Clayman."

Mr. Gery worked us very hard, but he was not a mean person. We all knew he was a kind man who wanted us to become strong. It was obvious he wanted us to do well. By the end of the semester, he had to call very few of us Mr. or Ms. Clay.

Questions on the Reading

1. What does Mr. Gery mean by saying that fists will come along in life? Give an example of a time you experienced a fist, or someone you know experienced a fist.

2. What does Mr. Gery mean by "clay"? What is the danger of being clay?

3. What does Mr. Gery mean by "rock"? How does one best become a rock?

4. How would you describe yourself—as clay, or as rock? What steps might you need to take to make yourself a rock?

4 Writing a Paragraph

A *paragraph* is a short paper of 150 to 200 words. It consists of an opening **point** followed by a series of sentences supporting that point. Write a paragraph in which you provide supporting details for one of the points below.

Point: Several experiences have helped me realize that I must start acting responsibly in everyday life.

Point: My attitude about school has begun to change.

Point: At times I fall into some of the escape habits described on pages 10–11 of this chapter.

After you have chosen your point, provide **supporting details or examples** to back up your point. For instance, if you have decided to support the first point above, you might say in part:

> When my parents got divorced, I became aware that my father could not do everything to take care of me. I had to stop acting like a child and start behaving more like an adult. For example, I started pulling together the dirty clothes and sheets and doing the laundry.

Or if you decided to support the second point above, you might say in part:

> I didn't really study much for my first test in biology this semester. When I got the test back, it was full of red X's and at the bottom was an "F" written so big that it took up half the page. I was embarrassed by the grade and quickly hid the paper so others would not see it. But I was also angry at myself for doing so poorly.

Or if you decided to support the third point above, you might say in part:

> For one thing, I tell myself "I'm too busy." But often all I mean by this is that I would rather talk on the phone and hang out with friends or watch TV than do any real studying.

When writing your paragraph, use examples and details that are based on your actual experience.

5   Speaking about Motivation and Commitment

Imagine that you have been asked to give a speech about self-respect, motivation, and commitment to a class of students who will be entering college in the fall. Prepare a talk full of practical advice that really communicates with them. Imagine that the students have been told beforehand that you will be as stiff and dry as a board and that your talk will have little relevance or value. You have two goals, then: 1) to use language and images that really connect with students, and 2) to pack your talk with lots of truly helpful information. Your speech should be five to ten minutes long.

2 / Thinking Clearly

THE BASICS OF CLEAR THINKING

What do you need to do to become a better thinker? In a nutshell, you need to understand the relationship between a point and its support. The **point** is the main idea that a person is making. The **support** is the evidence that is given to back up this idea.

The two most important things you must do as a speaker or writer are to

1 Make a point.

2 Support the point.

The two most important things you must do as a reader are to

1 Recognize the point.

2 Recognize the support for the point.

An Example of a Point and Its Support

Point: You should not put your hand into that box.

Now, is there support for this point? In other words, is the person who made it thinking clearly and logically? Let's say the person then goes on to provide the following details:

1. A flesh-eating spider as big as a small turtle just crawled in there.

2. There are freshly cut leaves of poison ivy within.

3. A mousetrap is loaded inside, ready to spring.

As you can see, the details provide solid support for the point. They give us a basis for understanding and agreeing with the point. In light of the details, we probably won't be putting a hand anywhere near that box.

We see here a small example of what clear thinking is about: making a point and providing support that truly backs up the point.

Another Example of a Point and Its Support

One person interviewed for this book is Dr. Ben Carson, professor and director of pediatric neurosurgery at the Johns Hopkins Children's Center, the author of several best-selling books, and president of a nonprofit organization, the Carson Scholars Fund. In his latest book, *The Big Picture*, he tells about the role his mother played in his life. One point that he makes is:

Point: My mother was one tough lady.

Our question again can be: Is there support for this point? Is Dr. Carson thinking clearly and logically, or is he just being a polite son? Let's look at some of the supporting details that Dr. Carson provides to back up his point:

1. Immediately after making the above statement about his mother being a tough lady, he writes:

   "I remember a day when, as a boy, I was riding in the car with her. The traffic stopped suddenly, and a tailgating driver bumped us from behind. The man quickly drove away without even getting out of the car. My mother chased him clear across Detroit before he finally gave up, pulled over, and got out to exchange insurance information."

2. He describes how his father left home, taking the modest nest egg his mother had managed to save. Unwilling to depend on welfare, his mother worked two and sometimes three jobs as a domestic to keep herself and her two sons independent.

3. He goes on to tell how his mother decided to deal with her sons' low grades in school. She limited them to two television shows a week and required them to read and write reports on two library books a week. Her insistence that he become a regular reader changed Dr. Carson's life, as you'll see when you read an excerpt from his book *Think Big* on pages 49–54.

4. He tells of how his mother would at times cope with stress and depression by checking herself into a hospital just long enough to get her emotional strength back. She would leave her sons in the care of a loving woman from her church, and she never failed to return to her sons on the day she said she would.

5. He relates how his mother so believed in the power of education that after she had gotten her sons into college, she went back and earned her GED and then eventually graduated from junior college.

All this evidence, and much more, overwhelmingly supports Dr. Carson's point that his mother is "one tough lady." He has proved himself to be—not surprisingly!—a clear and logical thinker.

The Importance of Logical Support for a Point

When you look at the support provided for a point, you want to make sure that the support truly backs up the point. The support, in other words, must be logical and relevant. Suppose someone made the following point:

Point: My dog Otis is not very bright.

Dr. Ben Carson poses with his mother, Sonya Carson,
who inspired him to succeed.

Suppose as well that this person offered the following support for the point. Look closely at the support, and you will see that only three items really support the point. The other items are not relevant to the point. See if you can circle those three items.

1. He is five years old and doesn't respond to his name yet.

2. He is sad when I leave for work every day.

3. He always gets excited when visitors arrive.

4. He often attacks the backyard hedge as if it's a hostile animal.

5. He gets along very well with my neighbor's cat.

6. I often have to put food in front of him because he can't find it by himself.

Now read the following comments on the six items to see which ones you should have circled and why.

1. Most dogs know their names, so Otis's not knowing his own name does suggest that he is not too bright. You should have circled the number of this item.

2. This item does not support the point. A loving dog will be sad when its companions leave the house.

3. This item as well does not support the point. Both bright and not-so-bright dogs are excited to see old and new human friends.

4. The inability to distinguish between a bush and an animal does suggest a lack of intelligence. You should have circled number four.

5. This item does not support the point. Dogs of all degrees of intelligence have been known to be friendly with cats.

6. Most dogs have no trouble knowing when food is nearby. Otis's inability to find food suggests that he is not the brightest dog on the block. You should also have circled the number of this item.

More about Logical Support

Let's look now at another example:

Point: Our meal in that new restaurant was unpleasant.

Is there support for this point? Is the person thinking clearly and logically? Let's say the person then goes on to provide the following details:

1. Our meal took forty-five minutes to arrive.

2. The chicken we ordered was tough, and the rice and vegetables were cold.

3. The dessert choices were limited to stale cake and watery Jell-O.

All these details provide solid, logical support for the point. They give us a basis for understanding and agreeing with the point. In light of the details, we would not be eager to eat at that restaurant.

But what if the person had provided these reasons for saying that the meal at the restaurant was unpleasant?

1. We had to wait fifteen minutes for the food to arrive.
2. The chicken we ordered was too juicy, and the vegetables were buttery.
3. The dozen dessert choices did not include my favorite, carrot cake.

We might question whether these are good reasons for not liking the restaurant. To have to wait fifteen minutes is not so bad. Many people would like their chicken juicy and their vegetables buttery, and they would appreciate having a dozen dessert choices.

When evidence is provided, we have a chance to be both logical and critical thinkers: to decide for ourselves whether there is enough valid, relevant evidence in support of a point. If the second set of reasons above were the only ones given, we might decide to try the restaurant for ourselves.

Point and Support in Everyday Life

In everyday life, people are constantly making points and providing support for those points. Here are some examples:

*   A **lawyer** states, "So and so is guilty," and then tries to provide evidence to support his point. Another lawyer says, "So and so is not guilty," and attempts to back up her statement.

*   An **advertiser** tries to convince us that something is "a great product."

*   A **political candidate** offers reasons why he or she is the person to vote for.

*   **Textbook authors or teachers** advance all kinds of points and then supply evidence on behalf of their ideas.

*   **Reviewers** offer their thoughts about why a given book, movie, TV show, or restaurant is good or bad.

- **Editorial writers or magazine columnists** express their opinion on one issue or another and then argue on behalf of it.

- **All of us** in everyday conversation make points such as the following:

    "Everyone likes that instructor."

    "I hate my job."

    "She is a good friend."

    "You should help that person."

    "That boy is trouble."

    "She is the best teacher in the school."

They will also offer reasons and details to support their points, and on the basis of the evidence they provide, we can decide whether or not we agree with them.

In sum, all around us is a mix of points and support. If the points were always clearly stated and logically supported, the world would be in pretty fine shape. Mr. Spock, the spokesman for reason and logic in the original *Star Trek* series, would be most impressed with us all. Unfortunately, many people are not skilled in clear thinking. The ideas they advance often lack reasonable support.

PRACTICE IN POINT AND SUPPORT

Chances are that you, like most people, will benefit greatly from sharpening your thinking skills. By learning to constantly ask, "What is the point?" and "What is its support?" and "How logical is that support?" you can become an effective one-person jury.

Such questions may seem simple, but learning to use them will not happen overnight. You must train your mind to think in terms of clear points and logical support. Your practice can start with the activities that follow.

1 Recognizing Point and Support

This activity will sharpen your sense of the difference between a point and its support. Remember that a point is a general idea; support is the specific information that backs up the point. Look at the following group of items. It is made up of a point and three statements that logically support the point. See if you can write P in front of the point and S in front of the three supporting statements.

_____ a. The roof on this house is leaking.

_____ b. The house is not in good shape.

_____ c. There are signs of termites in the basement.

_____ d. The furnace is constantly breaking down.

Explanation:

Sentence *a* states a major problem with the house. Sentences *c* and *d* also state significant problems with the house. In sentence *b*, however, no one specific problem is named. The statement "The house is not in good shape" is a general statement about problems with the house. Therefore sentence *b* is the point. The other sentences support that point by providing specific examples.

➤ Activity 1: Recognizing Point and Support

In each of the following groups, one statement is the point, and the other statements are support for the point. Identify each point with a P and each statement of support with an S.

1. _____ a. Some parrots can be trained to count.

   _____ b. Parrots are intelligent pets.

   _____ c. Parrots have been taught to recognize shapes and colors.

   _____ d. Most parrots can learn to speak—as many as two hundred words.

2. _____ a. Sharp pieces of broken glass are scattered near the swing sets.

   _____ b. Large stray dogs wander through the park, growling at people who walk near them.

   _____ c. Our neighborhood park is not a safe place to play.

   _____ d. The park has been the site of gang violence on several occasions recently.

3. _____ a. The authors do not define the new terms they use in each chapter.

   _____ b. The book has few illustrations and no index.

   _____ c. The sentence are long and hard to understand, and the material does not seem well organized.

   _____ d. That chemistry textbook is not very helpful.

4. _____ a. Hearing can be damaged by a number of common sounds.

   _____ b. Listening to loud music through headphones can cause hearing loss.

   _____ c. Machinery, such as lawn mowers and leaf blowers, can contribute to deafness.

   _____ d. The noise level of many buses and trucks is high enough to damage hearing permanently.

5. _____ a. Requiring kids to wear uniforms to school is a good idea.

   _____ b. Studies show that students work better when they are dressed in uniforms.

   _____ c. Uniforms costs less than store-bought clothes.

   _____ d. Uniforms stop kids from teasing each other about the clothes they wear.

2   Identifying Logical Support I

Once you identify a point and its support, you need to decide if the support really applies to the point. The critical thinker will ask, "Is this support logical? Or is it beside the point?" In their enthusiasm to advance a point, people often bring up support that does not apply. For example, a student may wish to make the point that her English instructor is a poor teacher. To support that point, the student may say, "He speaks so softly I can hardly hear him. In addition, he wears ridiculous clothes." A critical thinker will realize that although a soft voice may in fact interfere with an instructor's effectiveness, what the instructor wears has nothing to do with how well he teaches. The first reason for disliking the English teacher is logical and relevant support, but the second reason is beside the point.

This activity will sharpen your ability to decide whether evidence truly supports a point. It will help you become a critical reader who can ask and answer the question, "Is there logical support for the point?" Read the following point and the three items of "support" that follow. Then circle the letter of the one item that provides logical support for the point.

Point: That woman in the news was courageous.

Support:

a. She collected bags of canned and boxed food for months and then brought it to the Golden Door Soup Kitchen to be used for Thanksgiving. Thanks to her efforts, the soup kitchen was able to feed five hundred more people this year than last. That number includes over a hundred children.

b. She had at hand all the facts and figures to back up her statements, citing three different studies by experts in the field. She handled the reporter's questions with ease and confidence.

c. When she saw the child being attacked, she went to his aid without a moment's hesitation. She ran up shouting "Let him go!" and then kicked the ferocious pit bull as hard as she could. When the dog released the child, she grabbed the boy and pushed him to safety, even as the dog turned on her.

Explanation:

a. The information here tells us that the woman on the news was kind and generous with her time. However, nothing she did required her to face danger, so no courage was required. You should not have chosen this item. It is about generosity, not courage.

b. The woman described here showed mastery of her subject and skill in being interviewed, but neither demands great courage. You should not have chosen this item either.

c. The woman referred to here put herself in danger to help a child. Clearly, to do so, she had to be courageous. If you circled the letter of this item, you were correct.

➤ Activity 2: Identifying Logical Support I

Below is a point followed by three clusters of information. Put a check (✓) next to the one cluster that logically supports the point.

1. **Point:** Greg is irresponsible.

    ____ a. He gives up his bus seat to elderly commuters. When he sees people carrying heavy packages or struggling with squirming children, he rushes to open doors to help them out.

    ____ b. He never pays his bills on time. When he borrows things, he returns them damaged, or not at all. He is usually late for appointments, if he even remembers them at all.

    ____ c. No matter how much trouble I'm having with my English assignment, he refuses to do any of it for me. He says that between his own homework and his job, he doesn't have time. But he always gets B's, and I have trouble getting C's. Furthermore, when I need someone to cover for me at work so that I can see my girlfriend, he's always too busy with something else to help me out.

2. **Point:** That child is very curious.

    ____ a. He was reciting the alphabet when he was only three years old. By age seven, he was doing math at a fourth-grade level. He skipped third and fifth grades.

    ____ b. His favorite word is "No!" He doesn't start picking up his toys until the fifth or sixth time he is told. Mealtime is a battle to get him to eat properly.

    ____ c. He has taken apart all the clocks in the house to see how they work. He borrowed his father's hammer to break rocks because he "wanted to see what they looked like inside." He is forever asking how and why.

3. **Point:** Lola is self-centered.

    ____ a. She'll avoid a party invitation to stay home and curl up with a good book. At times, she's so quiet, people forget she's there. When her best friend tried out for the lead in the play, Lola was content to work quietly behind the scenes.

    ____ b. Any time we talk, I hear all about her life, but she never even asks what's new with me. She makes her boyfriend take her to dance clubs and sci-fi movies, but she'll never go to hockey games with him. Every year she throws a birthday party for herself, yet she never even sends her best friends a card on their birthdays.

    ____ c. She spends much of her time assisting her grandparents. Several days each week, she takes a bus to their home to help them clean and take care of their house. Many days, she cooks them dinner and talks to them about times when her mother was a child.

4. **Point:** Our biology teacher is lazy.

    ____ a. He has his top students present the lessons to the class so he doesn't have to do anything. If someone is having trouble in class, he tells him or her to get help from one of the other students. So he doesn't have to grade papers, he allows us to grade each other's homework and test papers, even midterm and final exams.

____ b. His favorite saying is, "There is no such thing as partial credit. Either the answer is right or it isn't." We can expect at least two hours of biology homework every night, and more on weekends and holidays. Even the best students in class have trouble finishing his tests before the end of the period, and the average grade for his class is C-minus.

____ c. He presents his lessons in a monotone. He reads word for word out of the textbook and never offers his own insights. Class is conducted the same way every day—we never break up into small groups or have team competitions, as we do in other classes.

5. **Point:** The teenage boys at the dance were much more shy than the girls.

____ a. They yelled and laughed out loud, drawing attention to themselves. One of them complained, "This sounds like music my grandmother would dance to!" Many hung around the punch bowl and made fun of the way some of the girls were dancing. Then, they left with their friends to go to a nearby party.

____ b. They all gathered at one end of the room, away from the girls. They looked nervously at the girls who were dancing. When a group of girls approached them, they got quiet and pretended not to notice. Several girls had to drag them out in order for them to dance.

____ c. They walked right up to a group of girls and introduced themselves. They smiled broadly and asked the girls to dance. Before they left at the end of the night, they asked the girls for their phone numbers.

3   Identifying Logical Support II

This activity will also develop your skill in thinking clearly about logical support for a given point. Below is a point followed by five statements. Three of the statements logically support the point; two of the statements do not. In the spaces provided, write the letters of the **three** logical statements of support.

Point: English 102 was the hardest course I ever took.

a. The course included a research paper, five essays, three oral reports, and two major exams.

b. The course was required for my major.

c. The teacher called on students without warning and deducted points when they didn't know an answer.

d. The teacher has been at the school for over twenty years.

e. On average, I had to do at least three hours of homework for every hour in class.

Items that logically support the point: _____ _____ _____

Now read the following comments on the five statements to see which ones you should have chosen and why.

Explanation:

The fact that a course is required doesn't make it more difficult, so answer *b* does not support the point. Answer *d* does not support the point either—how long a teacher has been at a school has nothing to do with how hard the course is. So you should have chosen answers *a, c,* and *e.* Each one tells about a different difficulty experienced in taking the course.

➤ **Activity 3: Identifying Logical Support II**

Each point is followed by three statements that provide logical support and two that do not. In the spaces, write the letters of the **three** logical statements of support.

1. **Point:** I'm a perfect example of someone who has "math anxiety."

   a. Fear of math is almost as widespread as fear of public speaking.

   b. I feel dread every time I sit down to take our Friday math quiz.

   c. During the math midterm, I "froze" and didn't even try to answer most of the questions.

   d. I also have a great deal of anxiety when I sit down to write a paper.

   e. I turned down a job as a salesclerk because I would have had to figure out how much change customers should get back.

   Items that logically support the point: _____ _____ _____

2. **Point:** My kids are getting into the spirit of Halloween.

   a. Today I found a plastic spider in my soup.

   b. Last night there was a bloody rubber hand on my pillow.

   c. Today a cardboard tombstone with my name on it appeared in the back yard.

   d. My kids also like to decorate the house on Thanksgiving.

   e. The other day, my oldest daughter said she was too old to go trick-or-treating.

   Items that logically support the point: _____ _____ _____

3. **Point:** Planting a flower garden in that vacant lot would benefit the neighborhood.

   a. Farming was one of the earliest activities of civilization.

   b. Flowers provide beauty that everyone can enjoy.

   c. People would not dispose of garbage in a garden, as they do in a vacant lot.

   d. Planting a garden would bring young and old people together, promoting harmony.

   e. There are many types of flowers that could be planted in this climate.

   Items that logically support the point: _____ _____ _____

4. **Point:** Schools should eliminate the summer vacation.

   a. It costs too much money for school buildings to remain empty in the summer months.

  b. Children have more energy than adults.

  c. Year-round school can better prepare students for year-round work in the adult world.

  d. During summer classes, schools should be air-conditioned.

  e. Children will learn more if they attend school twelve months a year.

 Items that logically support the point: _____   _____   _____

5. **Point:** By today's standards, early automobiles were uncomfortable and difficult to operate.

  a. The introduction of the factory assembly line made the price of the Model T drop from $440 in 1915 to $290 in 1925.

  b. Hard, high-pressure tires on early cars made for very bumpy rides.

  c. Early cars were open on top, so driving on unpaved roads left riders choking on dust and dirt.

  d. During World War II, numerous cars and trucks were manufactured for military use.

  e. A driver had to start the car's engine by cranking it by hand, and the crank sometimes sprang back and broke the driver's thumb.

 Items that logically support the point: _____   _____   _____

4 Generating Your Own Point and Support

➤ **Activity 1**

The best way to sharpen your sense of point and support is to generate material yourself. Choose one of the following points and see if you can provide three separate items of support for it.

 I could tell I was coming down with a bad cold or flu.

 The (*choose one*) breakfast / lunch / dinner I had yesterday was a terrible meal.

 (*Name a person*) _____ can be a mean person at times.

 Mr. (*or* Ms.) _____ is the best teacher I ever had.

 The (*choose one*) living room / bathroom / kitchen was not very clean.

 My (*choose one*) apartment / house / room is in need of repairs.

 I was very busy over the weekend.

Point you have chosen: _____

Support for that point: (Make sure each of your supporting items is different from and does not overlap with the others.)

  1. _____

  2. _____

  3. _____

➤ **Activity 2**

Generate material for another of the points above.

Point you have chosen: _____

Support for that point: (Make sure each of your supporting items is different from and does not overlap with the others.)

1. _____

2. _____

3. _____

➤ **Activity 3**

Now see if you can create a point of your own as well as three items of support for that point.

Your point: (Make sure that your point expresses your attitude or point of view about your topic—that it is good or bad in some way.)

_____

Support for your point:

1. _____

2. _____

3. _____

POINT AND SUPPORT IN WRITING AND READING

Here are final thoughts to keep in mind as you do the writing and reading required in school.

In Writing

When you are asked to write papers in school, what you must do, in a nutshell, is to make a point and to support that point. Whether your paper is a paragraph or a several-paragraph essay, your goal will be to make a point at the start of the paper. The point is called a *topic sentence* in a paragraph and a *thesis statement* in an essay.

You'll then be expected to develop and support that point in the rest of the paper. If you understand the concept of point and support, you understand the two most basic steps needed for competent writing. Chapters 9 and 10 in this book explain what else you need to know to write effectively.

In Reading

When you read, what you must do, in a nutshell, is to look for authors' main points (commonly known as *main ideas*) as well as their support for those points. Chapter 7 in this book explains what you need to know to find and take study notes on an author's main ideas.

Caren Blackmore is a student at
Oberlin College.

Caren: "*Again and again, I'll get papers back from professors who say, 'You make a good point, but you haven't backed it up with support.' I'm gradually getting better at providing that support. As I read my textbooks, I see how writers have to back up the points that they've made.*"

Michelle: "*Making a point and supporting a point come naturally to us when we speak. If I say 'I like her,' I automatically go on and give some reasons why I like her. But I learned that when we write, we need to be even more careful to give real support. And when I read my textbooks, I'm aware all the time of the way good writers back up their points with support.*"

Michelle Miller is a student at
Temple University.

Terry Oakman is a student at
Temple University.

Terry: "*If I write a paper, I try to support my point, my thesis. When you read a book, you might get ideas at the beginning in a preview or abstract. Then you read the chapter to see the support for those ideas. When you're reading, you should always be looking for ideas and the support for those ideas.*"

Ryan: "*When I entered college, it really got to me that there is a close connection between reading and writing. What you read and what you write have the same structure—it is like the frame of the house. The house needs a main idea or roof and strong supports for that roof. When reading an essay, you're looking at the way an author has framed the house. When you write something, you try to frame your own house by providing point and support. The more you read and the more you practice writing with that structure in mind, the better off you are.*"

Ryan Klootwyk is a graduate of
Grand Valley State University.

FINAL ACTIVITIES

1   Check Your Understanding

Answer the following questions to check your understanding of the chapter.

1. The key to becoming a better thinker is
   a. expressing your opinions immediately.
   b. understanding what a supporting detail is.
   c. understanding the relationship between a point and its support.
   d. recognizing points in your reading.

2. In order to truly back up a point, support must be
   a. logical.
   b. lengthy.
   c. complicated.
   d. general.

3. To become a one-person jury, we must learn to constantly ask
   a. "What is the point?"
   b. "What is the support for the point?"
   c. "How logical is the support for the point?"
   d. all of the above.

4. Which of the following does *not* back up the point that a restaurant meal was unpleasant?
   a. The meal took forty-five minutes to arrive.
   b. The chicken was tough.
   c. The rice and vegetable were cold.
   d. The dessert choices did not include carrot cake.

5. When you are writing an essay, what do you call the main point that begins the essay?
   a. A topic sentence
   b. A paragraph
   c. A thesis statement
   d. Logical support

2   Questions for Writing or Discussion

You may find it helpful to think about and write out your answers to the following questions. Or your instructor may put you in a small group or pair you with another student and have you discuss the questions with each other.

1. Describe a person you know who is very good at supporting his or her points. That person should be someone who can express ideas clearly and then offer convincing reasons for those ideas. Also describe a person you know who may do a lot of talking but who seldom seems to offer solid evidence to back up his or her statements or ideas.

2. In what professions do you think it would be especially important for a person to back up the points he or she was making with support? Give examples of situations in which such a person would need to support his or her points.

3. Of the supporting details that Dr. Carson provides to show that his mother was "one tough lady," which do you think is most effective? Why?

4. Get together with a partner. Each of you should then do the following:

   a. Think of a person you know well and describe him or her in one word by completing this statement: "_____ is a very _____ person."

   b. On a piece of paper, list several examples of the person's behavior that demonstrate why you describe him or her as you do.

   c. Discuss your list with your partner, who will select the one or two examples that best support your point.

3 Writing a Paragraph with Logical Support

Write a paragraph in which you take special care to make sure that all your examples and details clearly and logically support your point. Begin your paragraph with one of the **points** below.

Point: _____ is a very _____ person.

Point: _____ was the worst job (*or* chore) I ever had.

Point: I had a very busy (or inactive) day yesterday.

After you have chosen your point, provide **supporting details or examples** to back up your point. Double-check to be sure that all your support is *on target*, truly relating to your opening point. For example, if you write about a worst job and mention that the job was convenient to get to, that detail would not be logical support for your point. Every detail you provide must be evidence about how unpleasant the job was.

4 Speaking about Clear Thinking

Imagine that you have been asked to give a speech on the basics of clear thinking to a class of students who will be entering college in the fall. Prepare a talk full of practical advice that really communicates with them. Imagine that the students have been told beforehand that you will be as stiff and dry as a board and that your talk will have little relevance or value. You have two goals, then: 1) to use language and images that really connect with students, and 2) to pack your talk with lots of truly helpful information. Your speech should be five to ten minutes long.

5 Added Practice in Clear Thinking

Following are a series of activities to give you added practice in thinking clearly. The more practice you have, the sharper a thinker you can become.

➤ Activity 1

In each of the following groups, one statement is the point, and the other statements are support for the point. Identify each point with a P and each statement of support with an S.

Group 1

____ 1. My husband is a vegetarian.

____ 2. My mother, who lives with us, can't digest certain vegetables.

____ 3. One of my children is allergic to milk, wheat, and eggs.

____ 4. My family is difficult to cook for.

Group 2

____ 5. Each year, Americans spend billions of dollars buying cold medications.

____ 6. Colds cause American businesses to lose millions of hours of work every year.

____ 7. The average child misses a week of school each year because of colds.

____ 8. The common cold has a powerful effect on the nation.

Group 3

____ 9. Nearby kids threw a football onto the table, spilling all the drinks.

___10. Dozens of angry bees attacked people sitting at the picnic table.

___11. A rain shower made all the food soggy and wet.

___12. The picnic was a disaster.

Group 4

___13. Before underground plumbing, city people dumped raw sewage out of their windows and into the streets.

___14. In the days when city vehicles were horse-drawn, manure was piled high in the roadways.

___15. Cities of the past were very dirty.

___16. Before trash collection was available, pigs were set loose in city streets to eat the garbage thrown there.

Group 5

_____ 17. Roaches are a major cause of the increase in asthma cases.

_____ 18. Insects play a major role in the spread of certain diseases.

_____ 19. The worst disease in history—the Black Death—was spread by fleas living in the fur of rats.

_____ 20. Malaria, a disease affecting millions of people each year, is often carried in the mouth of a mosquito.

➤ **Activity 2**

A. Each point is followed by three statements that provide logical support and two that do not. In the spaces, write the letters of the **three** logical statements of support.

1–3. **Point:** Mel's new restaurant has a good chance of succeeding.

    a. Another restaurant at the same location did not do well.

    b. The menu offers delicious dishes at reasonable prices.

    c. The restaurant itself is bright, clean, and attractive.

    d. Mel is a good host who makes customers feel welcome and special.

    e. The weekly specials at the restaurant change every Thursday.

Items that logically support the point: _____   _____   _____

4–6. **Point:** I do not trust my sister's new boyfriend.

    a. He likes one of my favorite bands very much and has seen it in concert three times.

    b. He refuses to give my sister his phone number, saying that he'll call her.

    c. When anyone asks what he does for a living, he just says, "I have a lot of projects going on."

    d. My sister met him at the video store where she works.

    e. When I saw him in a restaurant with another girl, he acted very embarrassed and left before I could say hello.

Items that logically support the point: _____   _____   _____

7–9. **Point:** People should be careful when buying used cars.

    a. Many used cars do not come with a guarantee, so you will have to pay if something breaks.

    b. Used cars are much cheaper than brand-new ones.

    c. A used car may have serious mechanical problems and still look fine on the outside.

    d. Some used cars come with a guarantee and are nearly as reliable as new cars.

    e. Used cars whose past owners did not take care of them are more likely to develop problems.

Items that logically support the point: _____   _____   _____

B. (10.) Below is a point, followed by three clusters of information. Put a check (✓) next to the one cluster that logically supports the point.

Point: Neil is a hypocrite, often saying one thing but meaning another.

____ a. He spent forty-five minutes talking and laughing with someone yesterday, then later confided to me, "I can't stand that man!" He lectures his son about the dangers of drug addiction, then sits down to watch the ball game with a case of beer and a carton of cigarettes.

____ b. He waits until December to put in winter storm windows, and his Christmas tree is still up in March. He usually pays his bills a few days after they are due, and he does not get his car's 10,000-mile checkup until the car has gone 25,000 miles.

____ c. After thirty-seven years of marriage, he still writes love letters to his wife. He took early retirement so he could stay home and care for her when an illness left her bedridden. He never leaves the house without bringing home something special for her.

➤ **Activity 3**

A. In each of the following groups, one statement is the point, and the other statements are support for the point. Identify each point with a P and each statement of support with an S.

Group 1

____ 1. The only character we liked was killed halfway through the film.

____ 2. The movie we saw last night was not very good.

____ 3. We were able to figure out the ending long before the movie was over.

____ 4. The most exciting scene was filmed with so little light that we could not see what was happening.

Group 2

____ 5. The storm caused the creek to overflow, flooding the basements of several homes.

____ 6. The recent storm did a lot of damage to the neighborhood.

____ 7. Storm winds knocked down a large tree, which broke through the roof of one house.

____ 8. The storm knocked down wires, leaving many houses without electricity for two days.

B. (9.) Below is a point followed by three clusters of information. Put a check (✓) next to the one cluster that logically supports the point.

Point: That roller coaster is dangerous.

___ a. It is slower than any other roller coaster in the state. The curves of its track are so wide and the hills are so shallow that a ride on this roller coaster seems like a drive in the country. People don't scream when they ride it. Instead, they look at the view they have of the rest of the park.

___ b. It is known as one of the best roller coasters in the country. People will wait in line for hours just to try it. At certain points it reaches the same speeds as cars do on highways. The track is so tall and long that you can see it miles away.

___ c. Last year, it broke down several times, leaving people stranded in their cars sixty feet off the ground. In most cars, the seat belts are torn and don't always buckle properly. One area of the track shakes and makes a strange grinding sound whenever a car passes over it.

C. (10.) Below is a point, followed by three clusters of information. Put a check (✓) next to the one cluster that logically supports the point.

Point: Margo is a very rude worker.

___ a. She can barely stay awake while at work. Almost every day, she arrives at the store a half hour late. Her lunch breaks usually last twenty minutes longer than anyone else's. She apologizes each time she does something wrong, but she never improves.

___ b. She keeps customers waiting while she talks with a coworker. When someone asks her about a sale item, she snaps, "If it isn't on the shelf, we don't have it!" When her boss isn't watching her, she answers the telephone by saying, "Yeah, what do you want?"

___ c. She can answer the phone, ring up a customer's purchases, and count large amounts of money all at the same time. She often volunteers to help customers bring their bags to their cars. She does not mind taking time to answer a customer's question or help someone stock a shelf.

➤ Activity 4

A. Each point is followed by three statements that provide logical support and two that do not. In the spaces, write the letters of the **three** logical statements of support.

1–3. **Point:** Raising the speed limit on America's highways is a bad idea.

a. Raising the speed limit will make traffic accidents more severe, since cars will be hitting each other at higher speeds.

b. Cars traveling at higher speeds produce more pollution.

c. By traveling faster, people can get where they are going in less time.

d. Cars get poorer gas mileage at higher speeds than at lower speeds.

e. The higher speed limit will apply only to open highways, not to roads that are heavily crowded.

Items that logically support the point: _____   _____   _____

4–6. **Point:** People should get rid of their credit cards.

    a. Many credit-card companies charge high yearly fees—even if the card is never used.

    b. Having only one credit card keeps people from charging too much.

    c. Having credit cards encourages people to spend more money than they have, resulting in high debts.

    d. Not everyone is approved to get a credit card.

    e. The interest rate on many credit cards is so high that people end up paying a lot more than the purchase price for what they buy.

Items that logically support the point: _____   _____   _____

7–9. **Point:** Some wild animals do very well living around human beings.

    a. Pigeons enjoy living in areas with lots of people, particularly big cities.

    b. Coyotes have adjusted to human environments and are increasing their numbers in populated suburban areas.

    c. Most animals move further into wooded areas when people move nearby.

    d. Urban and suburban areas alike are packed with squirrels, and the numbers are increasing almost daily.

    e. Many animals are struck and killed each year by vehicles.

Items that logically support the point: _____   _____   _____

B. (10.) Below is a point followed by three clusters of information. Put a check (✓) next to the one cluster that logically supports the point.

Point: The meal I cooked for my girlfriend was horrible.

____ a. The chicken took an hour to prepare and two hours to cook. I had to travel for twenty miles to find a produce store that sold the vegetables I wanted. In order to make all this food, I had to buy a whole new set of pots and pans. Afterward, it took me hours to clean the kitchen and wash the dishes.

____ b. My girlfriend's car would not start when she wanted to come over. By the time she arrived, she was two hours late and very angry. As we sat down to eat, all she could talk about was how much it would cost to have her car fixed. When I tried to change the subject, she said I never listen to her, so I apologized. Then she accused me of apologizing too much. We both got so mad that we hardly touched dinner.

____ c. The chicken came out so tough and dry that I could barely cut it with a steak knife. I overcooked the fresh vegetables so much that they changed from a bright green to the color of an army jeep. The cake I tried to bake collapsed into itself, turning into a shapeless chewy mass that resembled a giant cookie.

3 / Reading for Pleasure and Power

WHY READ?

Recently I was at a conference where a panel of first-year college students were asked, "If you could give just one bit of advice to high-school kids, what would it be?" One student answered, "I can answer that in one word: **Read.** Read everything you can. The more you read, the better off you're going to be." Up and down the panel, heads nodded. No one disagreed with this advice.

All these students agreed because they had learned the truth about reading—that it is the very heart of education. They had been in college long enough to realize that the habit of regular reading is the best possible preparation for college and for success in life.

Here are four specific reasons why you should become a regular reader:

1 **Real Pleasure.** Chances are that you have done little reading for pleasure in your life. You may be an unpracticed reader who has never gotten into the habit of regular reading.

   Perhaps you grew up in a home like mine, where a television set dominated the household. Perhaps you got off to a bad start in reading class and never seemed to catch up. Or maybe you were eager to learn about reading when you began school but then soured on it. If you were given uninteresting and irrelevant material to read in school, you may have decided (mistakenly) that reading cannot be rewarding for you.

   The truth is that reading can open the door to a lifetime of pleasure and adventure. If you take the time to walk through that door, chances are you will learn that one of the great experiences of life is the joy of reading for its own sake.

2 **Language Power.** Research has shown beyond any question that frequent reading improves vocabulary, spelling, and reading speed and comprehension, as well as grammar and writing style. If you become a regular reader, all these language and thinking abilities develop almost automatically!

3 **Job Power.** Regular reading will increase your chances for job success. In today's world more than ever before, jobs involve the processing of information, with words being the tools of the trade. Studies have found that the better your command of words, the more success you are likely to have. *Nothing will give you a command of words like regular reading.*

There are hundreds of stories about people who went on to distinguished careers after developing the reading habit. One is the story of Ben Carson, who as a boy believed that he was "the dumbest kid" in his fifth-grade class. After he started reading two books a week, at his mother's insistence, his entire world changed. Within two years he had moved to the head of his class, and he was later to become Dr. Benjamin Carson, a world-famous neurosurgeon at Johns Hopkins University Hospital. His story appears later in this chapter on page 49. In addition, Dr. Carson was interviewed for this book, and his comments about study skills appear in other chapters.

4 **Human Power.** Reading enlarges the mind and the heart. It frees us from the narrow confines of our own experience. Knowing how other people view important matters helps us decide what we ourselves think and feel. Reading also helps us connect with others and realize our shared humanity. Someone once wrote, "We read in order to know that we are not alone." We become less isolated as we share the common experiences, emotions, and thoughts that make us human. We grow more sympathetic and understanding because we realize that others are like us.

A Personal Story about the Value of Reading

Many people have their own personal stories of how they became regular readers. In my own case, I read mostly comic books up until my junior year in high school. But what gave me the most pleasure was watching television. I developed a routine after school: get my homework done, do any household chores, eat dinner, and then spend the evening watching the tube.

Fortunately, something happened in the summer before my junior year that changed my life. The country was in the middle of a recession, so I was not able to get a job. I felt too old to spend the summer playing back-alley baseball with neighborhood buddies, and there was thankfully not enough on daytime TV (this was before cable) to hold my interest. Except for a once-a-week job of cutting my aunt's grass, I had nothing to do and felt restless and empty.

Then, sitting on my front porch one day in early June, I saw a public service message on the side of a bus that was rumbling noisily down the street. I remember the exact words: "Open your mind—read a book." Such messages had always annoyed me. On general principle I never liked being told what I should do. I also resented the implication that my mind was closed just because I didn't read books. I thought to myself, "For the heck of it, I'm going to read a book just so I know for sure there's nothing there."

That afternoon I walked to the one bookstore in town, browsed around, and picked out a paperback book—*The Swiss Family Robinson*—about a family that had been shipwrecked on an island and had to find a way to survive until rescue came. I spent a couple of days reading the story. When I was done, I had to admit that I had enjoyed it and that I was proud of myself for actually having read an entire book.

But in the perverse frame of mind that was typical of me at age fifteen, I thought to myself, "I just happened to pick out the one story in the world that is actually interesting. Chances are there aren't any more." But the more reasonable part of me wondered, "What if there are other books that wouldn't waste my time?"

I remembered that upstairs in my closet were some books that my aunt had once given me but I had never read. I selected one that I had heard of and that seemed to have some promise. It was *The Adventures of Tom Sawyer*, by Mark Twain, and it was a hardbound book now so old that its binding cracked when I opened it up. I began reading, and while the activities of Tom were interesting enough, it was his girlfriend Becky Thatcher who soon captured my complete attention. My adolescent heart raced when I thought of her, and for a while I thought about her night and day. For the first time in my life, I had fallen in love—incredibly enough, with a character in a book! The character of Becky helped show me what power a book can have.

Tom had a friend named Huck Finn, about whom Mark Twain had written another book. So when I finished Tom's story, I went to the library, got a library card, and checked out *The Adventures of Huckleberry Finn*. I figured this book might tell me more about Becky. As it turned out, it didn't, but by pure chance I wound up reading one of the great novels of American literature.

If Becky had made my blood race, the story of Huck Finn and the trip that he and his friend Jim took on a raft down the Mississippi River caught me up in a different but equally compelling way. While I could not express what happened at the time, the book made me look at people in a new light. I saw a whole stage of characters who felt very human and whose stories seemed very real. Some of these characters were mean and stupid and cowardly and hateful, others were loyal and courageous and dignified and loving, and a few were a blend of good and evil. By the time I finished Huck's story, I knew that books could be a source of pleasure, and I sensed also that they could be a source of power—that they could help me learn important things about the world and the people around me. I was now hooked on books. By the end of the summer, I had read over twenty novels, and I have been reading ever since.

HOW TO BECOME A REGULAR READER

How, you might be wondering, does one become a regular reader? The key, as simple as it might sound, is to do a great deal of reading. The truth of the matter is that reading is like any other skill. The more you practice, the better you get. In his book *The Power of Reading: Insights from the Research,* the reading scholar Stephen Krashen surveys a large number of studies and concludes that reading itself is the "way that we become good readers." The value of regular reading is a point about which common sense and research are in complete agreement.

The following suggestions will help you make reading a part of your life. Remember, though: These suggestions are only words on a page. You must decide to become a regular reader, and you must follow through on that decision. Only then will reading become a source of pleasure and power.

- Set aside a half hour or hour for reading in your daily schedule. That time might be during your lunch hour, or in the late afternoon before dinner, or in the half hour or so before you turn off your light at night. Find a time that is possible for you and make reading then a habit. The result will be both recreation time and personal growth.

- Subscribe to a daily newspaper and read the sections that interest you. Keep in mind that it is not *what* you read that matters—for example, you should not feel obliged to read the editorial section if opinion columns are not your interest. What does matter is *the very fact that you read.* Feel perfectly free to read whatever you like: the sports page, the fashion section, movie reviews, front-page stories—even the comics.

- Subscribe to one or more magazines. Browse in the magazine section of your library or a local bookstore; chances are you'll find some magazines that interest you. You may want to consider a weekly newsmagazine, such as *Newsweek* or *Time;* a weekly general-interest magazine, such as *People;* or any number of special-interest monthly magazines, such as *Glamour, Sports Illustrated, Essence,* or *Health and Fitness.*

    You'll find subscription cards inside most magazines; and on many school bulletin boards, you'll see display cards offering a wide variety of magazines at discount rates for students.

- Read aloud to children in your family, whether they are younger brothers or sisters, sons or daughters, or nephews or nieces. Alternatively, have a family reading time when you and the children take turns reading.

- Read books on your own. This is the most important step on the road to becoming a regular reader. Reading is most enjoyable when you get drawn into the special world created by a book. You can travel in that world for hours, unmindful for a while of everyday concerns. In that timeless zone, you will come to experience the joy of reading. Too many people are addicted to smoking or drugs or television; you should try, instead, to get hooked on books.

    What should you read? Select anything that interests you. That might be comic books, fantasies and science fiction, horror and mystery stories, romances, adventure and sports stories, biographies and autobiographies, or how-to books. To select a book, browse in a bookstore, library, or reading center. Find something you like and begin reading. If you stick to it and become a regular reader, you may find that you have done nothing less than change your life.

Kenyon: "*Read as much as possible. Read the paper every morning. Read books that appeal to you. Read self-help books about a positive attitude. Reading is first and foremost because reading stimulates thought. Reading will make you think.*"

Kenyon Whittington

Terry Oakman

Terry: "If you asked me for advice I'd give to high school students, I'd say 'Read.' The most important thing you can do in high school is to read all kinds of books and novels and whatever grabs you. If you read a lot, it will make you a better writer, too. It will also broaden your vocabulary tremendously."

May: "The main thing is to read. Read everything you can. If you're used to reading, you can handle all the reading you'll have to do in college."

May Lam is a student at Temple University.

Paul Blocker is a student at Villanova University.

Paul: "Do a lot of reading is the first thing I would say. Read stories, biographies, and nonfiction books to make you think."

Jasmin: "Read and write a lot. In every class in college you'll have to be able to read and write well."

Jasmin Santana is a student at Drexel University.

Floyd Allen is a graduate of Wilkes College.

Floyd: "Reading is a key: the more you read in high school, the more you're going to be prepared for college. All the reading that I did in high school helped me get into college, and then it helped me stay in college."

Dr. Ben Carson

Dr. Carson: "*Reading is critical for becoming ready for college and for life. It's critical because all of the information that humans have ever known is written down, and we have access to it. Reading and learning are how you program the incredible computer that is your brain. Reading is active work in which you exercise and develop your brain; watching TV is completely passive.*"

Dr. Carson became a regular reader when he was in fifth grade. His story appears in this chapter starting on page 49.

Maria: "*I strongly recommend that high school students prepare themselves for college by doing a lot of reading. With lots of reading, students can increase speed and comprehension and really improve their vocabulary. College instructors may assign several chapters to read per course, per week, so if you're taking several courses in one semester, the reading really adds up. The one habit a student should pick up in school is the reading habit.*"

Maria became a regular reader when she was a married woman in her twenties. Her story appears in this chapter starting on page 56.

Maria Cardenas

Ryan Klootwyk

Ryan: "*The most important advice I would give to younger students is to read what you enjoy, what gets your interest and truly grabs you. The more you read, the more you'll develop your reading and writing skills.*"

Ryan became a regular reader when he was six years old. His story appears in this chapter starting on page 64.

ACTIVITIES

Following are the personal stories of three real-life people for whom books and reading have played a major role in life.

➤ Activity 1: The Power of Reading for Dr. Ben Carson

Preview

Ben Carson was convinced he was "the dumbest kid in fifth grade." His report card seemed to say so, too. Then Ben's mother came up with a simple plan that changed his life. Today Ben Carson is a world-famous surgeon at the Johns Hopkins Children's Center in Baltimore, Maryland, This chapter from his autobiography *Think Big* tells how a "dummy" became a brilliant student.

1   "Benjamin, is this your report card?" my mother asked as she picked up the folded white card from the table.

2   "Uh, yeah," I said, trying to sound casual. Too ashamed to hand it to her, I had dropped it on the table, hoping that she wouldn't notice until after I went to bed.

3   It was the first report card I had received from Higgins Elementary School since we had moved back from Boston to Detroit, only a few months earlier.

4   I had been in the fifth grade not even two weeks before everyone considered me the dumbest kid in the class and frequently made jokes about me. Before long I too began to feel as though I really was the most stupid kid in fifth grade. Despite Mother's frequently saying, "You're smart, Bennie. You can do anything you want to do," I did not believe her.

5   No one else in school thought I was smart, either.

6   Now, as Mother examined my report card, she asked, "What's this grade in reading?" (Her tone of voice told me that I was in trouble.) Although I was embarrassed, I did not think too much about it. Mother knew that I wasn't doing well in math, but she did not know I was doing so poorly in every subject.

7   While she slowly read my report card, reading everything one word at a time, I hurried into my room and started to get ready for bed. A few minutes later, Mother came into my bedroom.

8   "Benjamin," she said, "are these your grades?" She held the card in front of me as if I hadn't seen it before.

9   "Oh, yeah, but you know, it doesn't mean much."

10   "No, that's not true, Bennie. It means a lot."

11   "Just a report card."

12   "But it's more than that."

13   Knowing I was in for it now, I prepared to listen, yet I was not all that interested. I did not like school very much, and there was no reason why I should. Inasmuch as I was the dumbest kid in the class, what did I have to look forward to? The others laughed at me and made jokes about me every day.

14   "Education is the only way you're ever going to escape poverty," she said. "It's the only way you're ever going to get ahead in life and be successful. Do you understand that?"

15   "Yes, Mother," I mumbled.

16   "If you keep on getting these kinds of grades you're going to spend the rest of your life on skid row, or at best sweeping floors in a factory. That's not the kind of life that I want for you. That's not the kind of life that God wants for you."

17   I hung my head, genuinely ashamed. My mother had been raising me and my older brother, Curtis, by herself. Having

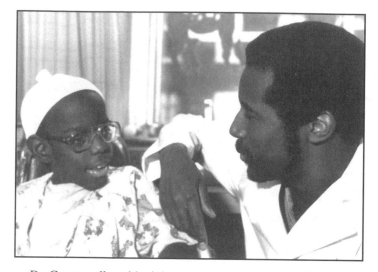

Dr. Carson talks with eight-year-old patient Dontae Sample.

only a third-grade education herself, she knew the value of what she did not have. Daily she drummed into Curtis and me that we had to do our best in school.

18   "You're just not living up to your potential," she said. "I've got two mighty smart boys and I know they can do better."

19   I had done my best—at least I had when I first started at Higgins Elementary School. How could I do much when I did not understand anything going on in our class?

20   In Boston we had attended a parochial school, but I hadn't learned much because of a teacher who seemed more interested in talking to another female teacher than in teaching us. Possibly, this teacher was not solely to blame—perhaps I wasn't emotionally able to learn much. My parents had separated just before we went to Boston, when I was eight years old. I loved both my mother and father and went through considerable trauma over their separating. For months afterward, I kept thinking that my parents would get back together, that my daddy would come home again the way he used to, and that we could be the same old family again—but he never came back. Consequently, we moved to Boston and lived with Aunt Jean and Uncle William Avery in a tenement building for two years until Mother had saved enough money to bring us back to Detroit.

21   Mother kept shaking the report card at me as she sat on the side of my bed. "You have to work harder. You have to use that good brain that God gave you, Bennie. Do you understand that?"

22   "Yes, Mother." Each time she paused, I would dutifully say those words.

23   "I work among rich people, people who are educated," she said. "I watch how they act, and I know they can do anything they want to do. And so can you." She put her arm on my shoulder. "Bennie, you can do anything they can do—only you can do it better!"

24   Mother had said those words before. Often. At the time, they did not mean much to me. Why should they? I really believed that I was the dumbest kid in fifth grade, but of course, I never told her that.

25   "I just don't know what to do about you boys," she said. "I'm going to talk to God about you and Curtis." She paused, stared into space, then said (more to herself than to me), "I need the Lord's guidance on what to do. You just can't bring in any more report cards like this."

26   As far as I was concerned, the report card matter was over.

27   The next day was like the previous ones—just another bad day in school, another day of being laughed at because I did not get a single problem right in arithmetic and couldn't get any words right on the spelling test. As soon as I came home from school, I changed into play clothes and ran outside. Most of the

boys my age played softball, or the game I liked best, "Tip the Top."

28   We played Tip the Top by placing a bottle cap on one of the sidewalk cracks. Then taking a ball—any kind that bounced—we'd stand on a line and take turns throwing the ball at the bottle top, trying to flip it over. Whoever succeeded got two points. If anyone actually moved the cap more than a few inches, he won five points. Ten points came if he flipped it into the air and it landed on the other side.

29   When it grew dark or we got tired, Curtis and I would finally go inside and watch TV. The set stayed on until we went to bed. Because Mother worked long hours, she was never home until just before we went to bed. Sometimes I would awaken when I heard her unlocking the door.

30   Two evenings after the incident with the report card, Mother came home about an hour before our bedtime. Curtis and I were sprawled out, watching TV. She walked across the room, snapped off the set, and faced both of us. "Boys," she said, "you're wasting too much of your time in front of that television. You don't get an education from staring at television all the time."

31   Before either of us could make a protest, she told us that she had been praying for wisdom. "The Lord's told me what to do," she said. "So from now on, you will not watch television, except for two preselected programs each week."

32   "Just *two* programs?" I could hardly believe she would say such a terrible thing. "That's not—"

33   "And *only* after you've done your homework. Furthermore, you don't play outside after school, either, until you've done all your homework."

34   "Everybody else plays outside right after school," I said, unable to think of anything except how bad it would be if I couldn't play with my friends. "I won't have any friends if I stay in the house all the time—"

35   "That may be," Mother said, "but everybody else is not going to be as successful as you are—"

36   "But, Mother—"

37   "This is what we're going to do. I asked God for wisdom, and this is the answer I got."

38   I tried to offer several other arguments, but Mother was firm. I glanced at Curtis, expecting him to speak up, but he did not say anything. He lay on the floor, staring at his feet.

39   "Don't worry about everybody else. The whole world is full of 'everybody else,' you know that? But only a few make a significant achievement."

40   The loss of TV and play time was bad enough. I got up off the floor, feeling as if everything was against me. Mother wasn't going to let me play with my friends, and there would be no more television— almost none, anyway. She was stopping me from having any fun in life.

41   "And that isn't all," she said. "Come back, Bennie."

42   I turned around, wondering what else there could be.

43   "In addition," she said, "to doing your homework, you have to read two books from the library each week. Every single week."

44   "Two books? Two?" Even though I was in fifth grade, I had never read a whole book in my life.

45   "Yes, two. When you finish reading them, you must write me a book report just like you do at school. You're not living up to your potential, so I'm going to see that you do."

46   Usually Curtis, who was two years older, was the more rebellious. But this time he seemed to grasp the wisdom of what Mother said. He did not say one word.

47   She stared at Curtis. "You understand?"

48   He nodded.

49   "Bennie, is it clear?"

50   "Yes, Mother." I agreed to do what Mother told me—it wouldn't have occurred to me not to obey—but I did not like it. Mother was being unfair and demanding more of us than other parents did.

51   The following day was Thursday. After school, Curtis and I walked to the local branch of the library. I did not like it

much, but then I had not spent that much time in any library.

52   We both wandered around a little in the children's section, not having any idea about how to select books or which books we wanted to check out.

53   The librarian came over to us and asked if she could help. We explained that both of us wanted to check out two books.

54   "What kind of books would you like to read?" the librarian asked.

55   "Animals," I said after thinking about it. "Something about animals."

56   "I'm sure we have several that you'd like." She led me over to a section of books. She left me and guided Curtis to another section of the room. I flipped through the row of books until I found two that looked easy enough for me to read. One of them, *Chip, the Dam Builder*—about a beaver—was the first one I had ever checked out. As soon as I got home, I started to read it. It was the first book I ever read all the way through even though it took me two nights. Reluctantly I admitted afterward to Mother that I really had liked reading about Chip.

57   Within a month I could find my way around the children's section like someone who had gone there all his life. By then the library staff knew Curtis and me and the kind of books we chose. They often made suggestions. "Here's a delightful book about a squirrel," I remember one of them telling me.

58   As she told me part of the story, I tried to appear indifferent, but as soon as she handed it to me, I opened the book and started to read.

59   Best of all, we became favorites of the librarians. When new books came in that they thought either of us would enjoy, they held them for us. Soon I became fascinated as I realized that the library had so many books—and about so many different subjects.

60   After the book about the beaver, I chose others about animals—all types of animals. I read every animal story I could get my hands on. I read books about wolves, wild dogs, several about squirrels, and a variety of animals that lived in other countries. Once I had gone through the animal books, I started reading about plants, then minerals, and finally rocks.

61   My reading books about rocks was the first time the information ever became practical to me. We lived near the railroad tracks, and when Curtis and I took the route to school that crossed by the tracks, I began paying attention to the crushed rock that I noticed between the ties.

Dr. Carson and his wife, Candy, are photographed at home with their sons (from left to right), Murry, Rhoeyce, and B.J., and Dr. Carson's mother.

62   As I continued to read more about rocks, I would walk along the tracks, searching for different kinds of stones, and then see if I could identify them.

63   Often I would take a book with me to make sure that I had labeled each stone correctly.

64   "Agate," I said as I threw the stone. Curtis got tired of my picking up stones and identifying them, but I did not care because I kept finding new stones all the time. Soon it became my favorite game to walk along the tracks and identify the varieties of stones. Although I did not realize it, within a very short period of time, I was actually becoming an expert on rocks.

65   Two things happened in the second half of fifth grade that convinced me of the importance of reading books.

66   First, our teacher, Mrs. Williamson, had a spelling bee every Friday afternoon. We'd go through all the words we'd had so far that year. Sometimes she also called out words that we were supposed to have learned in fourth grade. Without fail, I always went down on the first word.

67   One Friday, though, Bobby Farmer, whom everyone acknowledged as the smartest kid in our class, had to spell "agriculture" as his final word. As soon as the teacher pronounced his word, I thought, *I can spell that word.* Just the day before, I had learned it from reading one of my library books. I spelled it under my breath, and it was just the way Bobby spelled it.

68   *If I can spell "agriculture," I'll bet I can learn to spell any other word in the world. I'll bet I can learn to spell better than Bobby Farmer.*

69   Just that single word, "agriculture," was enough to give me hope.

70   The following week, a second thing happened that forever changed my life. When Mr. Jaeck, the science teacher, was teaching us about volcanoes, he held up an object that looked like a piece of black, glass-like rock. "Does anybody know what this is? What does it have to do with volcanoes?"

71   Immediately, because of my reading, I recognized the stone. I waited, but none of my classmates raised their hands. I thought, *This is strange. Not even the smart kids are raising their hands.* I raised my hand.

72   "Yes, Benjamin," he said.

73   I heard snickers around me. The other kids probably thought it was a joke, or that I was going to say something stupid.

74   "Obsidian," I said.

75   "That's right!" He tried not to look startled, but it was obvious he hadn't expected me to give the correct answer.

76   "That's obsidian," I said, "and it's formed by the supercooling of lava when it hits the water." Once I had their attention and realized I knew information no other student had learned, I began to tell them everything I knew about the subject of obsidian, lava, lava flow, supercooling, and compacting of the elements.

77   When I finally paused, a voice behind me whispered, "Is that Bennie Carson?"

78   "You're absolutely correct," Mr. Jaeck said, and he smiled at me. If he had announced that I'd won a million-dollar lottery, I couldn't have been more pleased and excited.

79   "Benjamin, that's absolutely, absolutely right," he repeated with enthusiasm in his voice. He turned to the others and said, "That is wonderful! Class, this is a tremendous piece of information Benjamin has just given us. I'm very proud to hear him say this."

80   For a few moments, I tasted the thrill of achievement. I recall thinking, *Wow, look at them. They're all looking at me with admiration. Me, the dummy! The one everybody thinks is stupid. They're looking at me to see if this is really me speaking.*

81   Maybe, though, it was I who was the most astonished one in the class. Although I had been reading two books a week because Mother told me to, I had not realized how much knowledge I was accumulating. True, I had learned to enjoy reading, but until then I hadn't realized how it connected with my schoolwork. That day—for the first time—I realized that Mother had been right. Reading is the way out of ignorance, and the road to achievement. I did not have to be the class dummy anymore.

82   For the next few days, I felt like a hero at school. The jokes about me stopped. The kids started to listen to me. *I'm starting to have fun with this stuff.*

83   As my grades improved in every subject, I asked myself, "Ben, is there any reason you can't be the smartest kid in the class? If you can learn about obsidian, you can learn about social studies and geography and math and science and everything."

84   That single moment of triumph pushed me to want to read more. From then on, it was as though I could not read enough books. Whenever anyone looked for me after school, they could usually find me in my bedroom—curled up, reading a library book—for a long time, the only thing I wanted to do. I had stopped caring about the TV programs I was missing; I no longer cared about playing Tip the Top or baseball anymore. I just wanted to read.

85   In a year and a half—by the middle of sixth grade—I had moved to the top of the class.

Dr. Carson finds time between surgical operations to deliver motivational talks to groups of schoolchildren.

Here are two activities to help deepen your understanding and appreciation of the selection.

Comprehension Check

1. Which sentence best expresses the central point of the selection?
   a. Children who grow up in single-parent homes may spend large amounts of time home alone.
   b. Because of parental guidance that led to a love of reading, the author was able to go from academic failure to success.
   c. Most children do not take school very seriously, and they suffer as a result.
   d. Today's young people watch too much television.

2. Which sentence best expresses the main idea of paragraph 56?
   a. Bennie's first experience with a library book was positive.
   b. The first book that Bennie ever checked out at a library was about a beaver.
   c. The librarian was very helpful to Bennie and Curtis.
   d. At first, Bennie could not read most of the animal books at the library.

3. To get her sons to do better in school, Mrs. Carson insisted that they
   a. stop watching TV.
   b. finish their homework before playing.
   c. read one library book every month.
   d. do all of the above.

4. We can conclude that the author's mother believed
   a. education leads to success.
   b. her sons needed to be forced to live up to their potential.
   c. socializing was less important for her sons than a good education.
   d. all of the above.

5. From paragraphs 70–80, we can infer that
   a. Bennie thought his classmates were stupid because they did not know about obsidian.
   b. Mr. Jaeck knew less about rocks than Bennie did.
   c. this was the first time Bennie had answered a difficult question correctly in class.
   d. Mr. Jaeck thought that Bennie had taken too much class time explaining about obsidian.

Critical Thinking and Discussion

1. Why did Bennie consider himself "the dumbest kid in the class"? How did his image of himself affect his schoolwork?

2. The author recalls his failure in the classroom as an eight-year-old child by writing, "Perhaps I wasn't emotionally able to learn much." Why does he make this statement? What things in a child's home or social life might interfere with his or her education?

3. Part of Carson's mother's plan for helping her sons to improve their schoolwork was limiting their television watching to two programs a week. How much of a role do you think this limit played in the success of her plan? Do you agree with her that unrestricted television watching can be harmful to children?

4. Reading on a regular basis helped turn Carson's life around. Think about your daily schedule. If you were to read regularly, where in your day could you find time to relax for half an hour and just read? What do you think would be the benefits of becoming a regular reader?

➤ Activity 2: The Power of Reading for Maria Cardenas

Preview

The life of a migrant worker is rarely easy. For migrant worker Maria Cardenas, it was often a nightmare. Her childhood was an exhausting time of backbreaking labor, constant moves, and family violence. Remarkably, Maria continued to cling to her dream of a better life. This selection from *Groundwork for College Reading* tells the story of Maria's journey from the fields to the college classroom where she is today.

Maria is shown picking oranges in Florida.

1   As I walk into the classroom, the teacher gazes at me with her piercing green eyes. I feel myself shrinking and burning up with guilt. I go straight to her desk and hand her the excuse slip. Just like all the other times, I say, "I was sick." I hate lying, but I have to. I don't want my parents to get in trouble.

2   I'm not a very good liar. She makes me hold out my hands, inspecting my dirty fingernails and calluses. She knows exactly where I've been the past several days. When you pick tomatoes and don't wear gloves, your hands get rough and stained from the plant oils. Soap doesn't wash that out.

3   In the background, I can hear the students giggling as she asks her usual questions: "What was wrong? Was your brother sick, too? Do you feel better today?"

Of course I don't feel better. My whole body aches from those endless hot days spent harvesting crops from dawn to dusk. I was never absent by choice.

4   That year, in that school, I think my name was "Patricia Rodriguez," but I'm not sure. My brother and I used whatever name our mother told us to use each time we went to a new school. We understood that we had to be registered as the children of parents who were in the United States legally, in case Immigration ever checked up.

5   My parents had come to the States in the late '60s to work in the fields and earn money to feed their family. They paid eight hundred dollars to someone who smuggled them across the border, and they left us with our aunt and uncle in Mexico. My five-year-old brother, Joel, was the oldest. I was four, and then came Teresa, age three, and baby Bruno. The other kids in the neighborhood teased us, saying, "They won't come back for you." Three years later, our parents sent for us to join them in Texas. My little heart sang as we waved goodbye to those neighbor kids in Rio Verde. My father did love us!

6   My parents worked all the time in the fields. Few other options were open to them, because they had little education. At first, our education was important to them. They were too scared to put us in school right away, but when I was eight, they did enroll us. I do remember that my first-grade report card said I was "Antonietta Gonzales." My father made sure we had everything we needed—tablets, crayons, ruler, and the little box to put your stuff in. He bragged to his friends about his children going to school. Now we could talk for our parents. We could translate their words for the grocer, the doctor, and the teachers. If Immigration came by, we could tell them we were citizens, and because we were speaking English, they wouldn't ask any more questions.

7   In the years to come, I often reminded myself that my father had not forgotten us like the fathers of so many kids I knew. It became more important for me to remember that as it became harder to see that he loved us. He had hit my mother once in a while as I was growing up, but when his own mother died in Mexico in 1973, his behavior grew much worse. My uncles told me that my father, the youngest of the family, had often beaten his mother. Maybe it was the guilt he felt when she died, but for whatever reason, he started drinking heavily, abusing my mother emotionally and physically, and terrorizing us kids. The importance of our education faded away, and now my papa thought my brother and I should work more in the fields. We would work all the time—on school vacations, holidays, weekends, and every day after school. When there were lots of tomatoes to pick, I went to school only every other day.

8   If picking was slow, I stayed home after school and cooked for the family. I started as soon as I got home in the afternoon. I used the three large pots my mother owned: one for beans, one for rice or soup, and one for hot salsa. There were also the usual ten pounds of flour or *maseca*, ground corn meal, for the tortillas. I loved this cooking because I could eat as much as I wanted and see that the little kids got enough before the older family members finished everything. By this time there were three more children in our family, and we often went to bed hungry. (My best subject in school was lunch, and my plate was always clean.)

9   Other than lunchtime, my school life passed in a blur. I remember a little about teachers showing us how to sound words out. I began to stumble through elementary readers. But then we'd move again, or I'd be sent to the fields.

10   Life was never easy in those days. Traveling with the harvest meant living wherever the bosses put us. We might be in little houses with one outdoor toilet for the whole camp. Other times the whole crew, all fifty or one hundred of us, were jammed into one big house. Working in the fields meant blistering sun, aching muscles, sliced fingers, bug bites, and my father yelling when we didn't pick fast enough to suit him.

11   But we were kids, so we found a way to have some fun. My brother and I would make a game of competing with each other and the other adults. I never did manage to pick more than Joel, but I came close. One time I picked 110 baskets of cucumbers to Joel's 115. We made thirty-five cents a basket.

12   Of course, we never saw any of that money. At the end of the week, whatever the whole family had earned was given to my father. Soon he stopped working altogether. He just watched us, chatted with the field bosses, and drank beer. He began to beat all of us kids as well as our mother. We didn't work fast enough for him. He wanted us to make more money. He called us names and threw stones and vegetables at us. The other workers did nothing to make him stop. I was always scared of my father, but I loved him even though he treated us so badly. I told myself that he loved us, but that alcohol ruled his life.

13   I knew what controlled my father's life, but I never thought about being in control of my own. I did as I was told, spoke in a whisper, and tried not to be noticed. Because we traveled with the harvest, my brothers and sisters and I attended three or four different schools in one year. When picking was good, I went to the fields instead of school. When the little kids got sick, I stayed home to watch them. When I did go to school, I didn't understand very much. We spoke only Spanish at home. I don't know how I got through elementary school, much less to high school, because I only knew how to add, subtract, and multiply. And let's just say I got "introduced" to English writing skills and grammar. School was a strange foreign place where I went when I could, sitting like a ghost in a corner alone. I could read enough to help my mother fill out forms in English. But enough to pick up a story and understand it? Never. When a teacher told the class "Read this book, and write a report," I just didn't do it. I knew she wasn't talking to me.

14   In 1978, my mother ran away after two weeks of terrible beatings. Joel and I found the dime under the big suitcase, where she had told us it would be. We were supposed to use it to call the police, but we were too scared. We stayed in the upstairs closet with our brothers and sisters. In the morning, I felt guilty and terrified. I didn't know whether our mother was alive or dead. Not knowing what else to do, I got dressed and went to school. I told the counselor what had happened, and she called the police. My father was arrested. He believed the police when they said they were taking him to jail for unpaid traffic tickets. Then the police located my mother and told her it was safe to come out of hiding. My father never lived with us again, although he continued to stalk us. He would stand outside the house yelling at my mother, "You're gonna be a prostitute. Those kids are gonna be no-good drug addicts and criminals. They're gonna end up in jail."

15   My father's words enraged me. I had always had a hunger for knowledge, always dreamed of a fancy job where I would go to work wearing nice clothes and carrying a briefcase. How dare he try to kill my dream! True, the idea of that dream ever coming true seemed unlikely. In school, if I asked about material I didn't understand, most of the teachers seemed annoyed. My mother would warn me, "Please, don't ask so many questions."

16   But then, somehow, when I was fourteen, Mrs. Mercer noticed me. I don't remember how my conversations with this teacher started, but it led to her offering me a job in the Western clothing store she and her husband owned. I helped translate for the Spanish-speaking customers who shopped there. I worked only Saturdays, and I got paid a whole twenty-dollar bill. Proudly, I presented that money to my mother. The thought "I can actually do more than field work" began to make my dreams seem like possibilities. I began to believe I could be something more. The month of my sixteenth birthday, Mrs. Mercer recommended me for a cashier's job in the local supermarket. I worked there for six weeks, and on Friday, January 16, 1981, I was promoted to head cashier. I was on top of

Maria is shown on the day she graduated with honors
from Edison Community College.

the world! I could not believe such good things were happening to me. I had a good job, and I was on my way to becoming my school's first Spanish-speaking graduate. I thought nothing could go wrong, ever again.

17   But that very night, my dreams were shattered again—this time, I thought, permanently. The manager let me off at nine, two hours early. I didn't have a ride because my brother was not picking me up until 11:00 p.m. But I was in luck! I saw a man I knew, a friend of my brother's, someone I had worked with in the fields. He was a trusted family friend, so when he offered me a lift, I said, "Of course." Now I could go home and tell everybody about the promotion.

18   I never made it home or to my big promotion. The car doors were locked; I could not escape. I was abducted and raped, and I found myself walking down the same abusive road as my mother. My dreams were crushed. I had failed. In my old-fashioned Mexican world, I was a "married woman," even if I wasn't. To go home again would have been to dishonor my family. When I found I was pregnant, there seemed to be only one path open to

me. I married my abductor, dropped out of tenth grade, and moved with him to Oklahoma.

19   "My father was right," I thought. "I am a failure." But dreams die hard. My brother Joel was living in the same Oklahoma town as I was. He would see me around town, my face and body bruised from my husband's beatings. But unlike the workers in the fields who had silently watched our father's abuse, Joel spoke up. "You've got to go," he would urge me. "You don't have to take this. Go on, you can make it."

20   "No!" I would tell him. I was embarrassed to have anyone know what my life had become. I imagined returning to my mother, only to have her reprimand me, saying, "What's the matter with you that you can't even stay married?"

21   But Joel wouldn't give up. Finally he told me, "I don't care what you say. I am going to tell Mother what is going on."

22   And he did. He explained to our mother that I had been forced to go with that man, that I was being abused, and that I was coming home. She accepted what he told her. I took my little girl and the

clothes I could carry, threw everything into my car, and left Oklahoma for Florida. My husband taunted me just as my father had my mother: "You'll be on food stamps! You can't amount to anything on your own!" But I proved him wrong. I worked days in the fields and nights as a cashier, getting off work at midnight and up early the next day to work again. I don't know how I did it, but I kept up the payments on my little car, I didn't go on food stamps, and I was happy.

23 But as Antonietta grew up and started school, I began to think my little triumphs were not enough. I was thrilled to see her learning to read, doing well in school. And when she would bring me her simple little books and trustingly say, "Read with me!" it filled me with joy. But I realized the day would come, and come soon, that I would be unable to read Antonietta's books. What would she think of me when I said, "I can't"? What would I think of myself?

24 Teaching myself to read became the most important goal in my life. I began with Antonietta's kindergarten books. I thought sometimes how people would laugh if they saw me, a grown woman, a mother, struggling through *The Cat in the Hat*. But with no one to watch me, I didn't care. Alone in my house, after my daughter was asleep, I read. I read everything we had in the house—Antonietta's books, cereal boxes, advertisements that came in the mail. I forced myself through them, stumbling again and again over unfamiliar words. Eventually I began to feel ready to try a real story, a grown-up story. But my fears nearly stopped me again. We lived near a library. Antonietta had asked again and again to go there. Finally I said "all right." We walked in, but panic overwhelmed me. All those people, walking around so briskly, knowing where to find the books they wanted and how to check them out! What was someone like me doing there? What if someone asked me what I wanted? Too intimidated to even try, I insisted that we leave. I told Antonietta to use the library at her school. I struggled on in private, eventually earning my GED.

25 The years passed, and I married a wonderful man who loved me and my daughter. He was proud that I had some real education, and he knew that I wanted more. But I couldn't imagine that going on in school was possible.

26 Then, in 1987, I was working for the Redlands Christian Migrant Association. They provided services for migrant children. One day, in the office, I spotted something that made my heart jump. It was a book called *Dark Harvest*. It was filled with stories about migrant workers. Although my reading skills had improved, I had still never read a book. But this one was about people like me. I began reading it, slowly at first, then with more and more interest. Some of the people in it had gone back for a GED, just as I had! Even more—some had gone on to college and earned a degree in education. Now they were teaching. When I read that book, I realized that my dream wasn't crazy.

27 My husband and I took the steps to become legally admitted residents of the United States. Then, my husband found out about a federal program that helps seasonal farm workers go to college. I applied and found I was eligible. When I took my diagnostic tests, my reading, English, and math levels turned out to be seventh-grade level. Not as bad as I thought! The recruiter asked if I would mind attending Adult Basic Education classes to raise my scores to the twelfth-grade level. Mind? I was thrilled! I loved to study, and in spite of a serious illness that kept me out of classes for weeks, my teacher thought I was ready to try the ABE exams early. Her encouragement gave my confidence a boost, and I found that my scores had zoomed up to a 12.9 level.

28 Then, in the fall of 1994, I took the greatest step of my academic life. Proud and excited, I started classes at Edison Community College in Florida. Of course, I was also terrified, trembling inside almost like that scared little girl who used to tiptoe up to the teacher's desk with her phony absence excuses. But I'm not a scared little kid anymore. My self-confidence is growing, even if it's growing slowly.

29   I laugh when I look back at that day I fled in terror from the library. My family and I might as well live there now. We walk in with me saying, "Now, we have other things to do today. Just half an hour." Three hours later, it's the kids saying to me, "Mom, are you ready yet?" But it's so exciting, knowing that I can learn about anything I want just by picking up a book! I've read dozens of how-to books, many of them about gardening, which has become my passion. I can't put down motivational books, like Ben Carson's *Gifted Hands* and *Think Big*. I love Barbara Kingsolver's novels. One of them, *The Bean Trees*, was about a young woman from a very poor area in Kentucky whose only goal, at first, was to finish school without having a child. I could understand her. But my favorite author is Maya Angelou. Right now, I'm rereading her book *I Know Why The Caged Bird Sings*. She writes so honestly about the tragedy and poverty she's lived with. She was raped when she was little, and she had a child when she was very young. And now she's a leader, a wonderful writer and poet. When I see her—she read a poem at President Clinton's inauguration—I am very moved. And I can't talk about my life now without mentioning Kenneth and Mary Jo Walker, the president of Edison Community College and his wife. They offered me a job in their home, but so much more than that: they have become my friends, my guardian angels. I am constantly borrowing books from them, and they give me so much encouragement that I tell them, "You have more faith in me than I do myself."

30   Sometimes I have to pinch myself to believe that my life today is real. I have a hard-working husband and three children, all of whom I love very much. My son Korak is eleven. Whatever he studies in school—the Aztecs, the rain forest, Mozart—he wants to find more books in the library about it, to learn more deeply. Jasmine, my little girl, is seven and is reading through the *Little House* books. Like me, the children have worked in the fields, but there is little resemblance between their lives and mine as a child. They are in one school the whole year long. They work at their own pace, learning the value of work and of money—and they keep what they earn. Antonietta, who inspired me to begin reading, is seventeen now. Although she's only a junior in high school, she's taking college calculus classes and planning to study pre-med in college, even though her teachers have encouraged her to become a journalist because of her skill in writing.

31   And guess what! My teachers compliment my writing too. When I enrolled in my developmental English class at Edison, my teacher, Johanna Seth, asked the class to write a narrative paragraph. A narrative, she explained, tells a story. As I thought about what story I could write, a picture of a scared little girl in a schoolroom popped into my head. I began writing:

32   *As I walk into the classroom, the teacher gazes at me with her piercing green eyes. I feel myself shrinking and burning up with guilt. I go straight to her desk and hand her the excuse slip. Just like all the other times, I say, "I was sick." I hate lying, but I have to. I don't want my parents to get in trouble.*

33   I finish my narrative about giving my phony excuses to my grade-school teachers and hand it in. I watch Mrs. Seth read it and, to my horror, she begins to cry. I know it must be because she is so disappointed, that what I have written is so far from what the assignment was meant to be that she doesn't know where to begin to correct it.

34   "Did you write this?" she asks me. Of course, she knows I wrote it, but she seems disbelieving. "You wrote this?" she asks again. Eventually I realize that she is not disappointed. Instead, she is telling me something incredible and wonderful. She is saying that my work is good, and that she is very happy with what I've given her. She is telling me that I can succeed here.

35   And now I know she's right. I'm graduating from Edison as a member of Phi Theta Kappa, the national academic honors society for junior colleges. I'll

enroll in the fall at Florida Gulf Coast University to finish my degree in elementary education. I will spend the summer working, maybe picking crops once again. But in the fall, when my children return to school, so will I. I have a goal: to teach migrant children to speak English, to stand on their own two feet, to achieve their dreams. In helping them, I will be making my own dream come true.

Maria and her children (from left to right), Antonietta, Korak, and Jasmine.

Here are two activities to help deepen your understanding and appreciation of the selection.

Comprehension Check

1. Which sentence best expresses the central point of the entire selection?
   a. Maria's goal is to graduate from college and teach migrant children to achieve their dreams.
   b. With hard work and courage, Maria was able to overcome great difficulties to build a wonderful family and go to college.
   c. Some books are filled with inspirational stories that can help us all.
   d. Maria showed us that certain skills are necessary if we want to succeed in college.

2. Which sentence best expresses the main idea of paragraph 16?
   a. One of Maria's teachers offered Maria a job at a Western clothing store.
   b. One of Maria's teachers and her husband owned a Western clothing store.
   c. Thanks to a kind teacher and her own good work, Maria began to believe she could be more than a field worker.
   d. At the age of sixteen, Maria became a supermarket cashier and soon was promoted to head cashier.

3. Which sentence best expresses the main idea of paragraph 26?
   a. In 1987, Maria worked for the Redlands Christian Migrant Association.
   b. The book *Dark Harvest* convinced Maria that her dream for a better education wasn't crazy.
   c. The Redlands Christian Migrant Association provided services for migrant children.
   d. The book *Dark Harvest* contained stories about migrant workers, including some who had gone on to college and became teachers.

4. Maria's father began to drink heavily and abuse his wife more than ever after
   a. he lost his job.
   b. his children began going to school.
   c. Immigration came to the house.
   d. his mother died.

5. You can conclude from paragraph 18 that
   a. Maria's "old-fashioned Mexican world" offered freedom and choice for women.
   b. Maria often wished to be part of the "old-fashioned Mexican world."
   c. The "old-fashioned Mexican world" was very strict about sex and marriage.
   d. Maria was glad that her abductor wanted to marry her.

Critical Thinking and Discussion

1. Maria's children work in the fields, as their mother had. In what ways are those children's lives different from Maria's life when she was a child working in the fields?

2. Why do you think Mrs. Seth cried upon reading the narrative about Maria giving phony excuses to her grade-school teachers? Why do you think Maria thought that Mrs. Seth was disappointed with what she had written?

3. What do you think Maria means when she says she wants to teach migrant children to "stand on their own two feet"?

4. Like Ben Carson, Maria has been deeply affected by books. Which books does she say have been particularly meaningful to her? Why do you think these books meant so much to her?

➤ Activity 3: The Power of Reading for Ryan Klootwyk

Preview

Ryan Klootwyk's childhood was torn apart by drugs, alcohol, and violence. He had no one to turn to for help. But as a little boy, he discovered a safe place he could always go when times were hard. That place was the world of books. Ryan's story, taken from the book *Ten Steps to Building College Reading Skills*, shows how a love of reading can carry a person through painful experiences.

Ryan Klootwyk today outside his home in Muskegon, Michigan.

1   "Drink it. It will make a man out of you."

2   Ryan Klootwyk jerked his head away from the cup of beer that his stepfather Larry was shoving in his face. "But I don't like how it smells," he pleaded. For a moment, Larry just glared drunkenly at the eight-year-old boy, his bloodshot eyes like two cracked windows. Then he raised the cup high in the air and poured the contents on Ryan's head. As Larry stormed out of the room, Ryan sat quietly at the table drenched in the stinking fluid. He was relieved. Larry could have done much worse; he usually did.

3   Nearly twenty years later, Ryan remembers that moment as if it were yesterday. He tells the story, sitting at another table—his own—with his wife and two young sons. Watching his kids play, Ryan thinks how different their childhood is from his own. "My children will never have to go through what I went through," he says, shaking his head. "Never."

4   Ryan's childhood home was shattered by heroin. Both his parents were addicts. When Ryan was six years old, his father died, an apparent drug-related suicide. Alone and vulnerable, his mother soon brought a new man into their home. This was Larry.

5   When Larry first entered Ryan's life, he seemed friendly. He took Ryan and his brother Frank fishing. He bought new furniture for the house, and his mother told the kids to call him "Dad." The two lonely young boys started to accept Larry in his

new role. But Larry was keeping a secret from the family. Underneath his pleasant exterior, Larry was a monster.

6   Ryan's first glimpse into Larry's true nature occurred a few months after he had moved in with the family. Ryan's dog—one that had belonged to Ryan's father—had an accident on the carpet. High and drunk, Larry announced he was going to kill the dog. Horrified, Frank shouted for him to stop. "That's my dad's dog! That's my dad's dog!" he screamed.

7   Larry ignored Frank's screams, but when their mother heard the commotion and yelled, "Larry, what are you doing?" he snapped. Seven-year-old Ryan watched in helpless horror as Larry beat her, hitting her face with his fists. "My childhood ended that night," Ryan says today. "I hid behind the table and watched him. I had no idea why he acted that way. I only knew I was scared that he would kill one of us." Ryan, Frank and their mother fled into the boys' bedroom. Immediately, Larry cornered them there and issued a stern warning. "Don't you ever, *ever* mention your father to me again," he hissed. Terrified, the little boys could only stare.

8   As Larry wandered away, Ryan felt emptiness and terror threaten to overwhelm him. There was nowhere to go; there was no one to turn to. But a comforting thought broke through his despair. Reaching under his bed, he pulled out a battered copy of his favorite book, *The Five Chinese Brothers*. Crawling into bed, he quickly lost himself in the familiar pages. Thoughts of Larry's brutality, of fear, of pain, of humiliation faded as he read the story of the brave, clever little brother who saved everyone. Ryan was only seven, but he had already found the lifeline that would keep him afloat through the horrifying years ahead. He had discovered books.

9   Larry supported himself by robbing nearby households and businesses. With the police constantly trailing him, he had to keep moving. The moves would often occur without notice. "I would come home from school, and we'd be out the door," Ryan remembers. Traveling from motels to shelters, from friends' houses to apartments, Ryan lived in six different states and passed through fifteen separate schools, never staying in one place more than a year and a half. The constant moving took its toll. "I wanted to be a normal kid," he says, "but transferring from school to school made that impossible. The only people that were constant in my life were my mother and my brother. They were the only ones who knew how bad things were. My biggest fear as a child was that I would lose them, that I would be totally alone."

10   When Ryan was eight years old, that fear almost came true. This time, the family was in Texas. Even drunker and angrier than usual, Larry began kicking and stomping on Ryan's mother. Frank, now nine years old, made a desperate effort to protect her. When he stepped between Larry and his mother, shouting "Don't hit her!" Larry turned on the boy. He kicked him in the face with his heavy black boots. Frank crumpled to the floor.

11   For the rest of that evening, little Ryan watched over his brother and tried to comfort him. "I could see that his eye was swollen shut, and pus and fluid were oozing out of it," he recalls. "Nothing Larry ever did hurt me inside more than when he hurt my brother like that," says Ryan, his voice wavering. Alone in the darkness with his silent, wounded brother, Ryan quietly sobbed through the night.

12   The next day Frank was a little better, and his mother took him to the hospital. Ryan went along. Larry instructed the boys to lie about what had happened. "Tell them you were playing baseball and Frank got hit in the head with the bat," Larry said. The boys and their mother obediently lied, but the injury still made people at the hospital suspicious. A police officer questioned the kids, but they stuck to Larry's story.

13   "I wanted to tell the truth, but we were so afraid of Larry," says Ryan. He still feels the frustration of those days. "We knew what would happen if we told the truth. They would take him away, he would be in jail for a short time, and then he would come out and get us, and he would kill Mom." Without the boys' cooperation,

Ryan meets with Paula Doctor, his former writing instructor at Muskegon Community College.

the police could do nothing. And a few weeks later, Larry, aware of the watchful eye of the police, decided to move the family again. In yet another state and another school, the beatings continued.

14   Amazingly, amidst the constant abuse at home, Ryan did well in school. "School was the one safe place in my life. When I was in school, I was away from Larry. I was free from threats to my family. I could pretend to be a normal kid," recounts Ryan.

15   As a third-grader, Ryan won a school reading contest. The prize was a copy of *Charlotte's Web*. The book quickly became a new favorite. In it, a little runt pig, Wilbur, has his life saved twice: first by a kind little girl, and then by a clever and loving spider, Charlotte. Charlotte's first word to Wilbur is "Salutations!" Like Wilbur, Ryan had no idea what the word meant. He appreciated Charlotte's explanation to Wilbur: "Salutations are greetings," she said. "When I say 'salutations,' it's just my fancy way of saying hello." Ryan loved Charlotte for her friendship and kindness to lonely little Wilbur.

16   Charlotte and Wilbur joined the five Chinese brothers and Ryan's other favorite characters as pieces in a shield between him and the horrors of his home life. "Reading was a way I could forget about everything," he said. "It was the only thing that was completely in my control. I am not sure if I would have survived without it." He looked for things to read the way a hungry child might look for food that others had overlooked. "Once I even found some old history textbooks in the school trash can. To someone, those old books were trash, but to me they were a treasure. I took them home and read them cover to cover."

17   Ryan's success at school had no effect on his troubled home. Each time he transferred to a new school, he concealed the painful truth of his home, of his mother's addiction, of the constant moves, and of Larry. Ryan's strong grades and good adjustment to school were all his teachers saw. Outwardly he seemed to be doing well. Inwardly, he was begging for help. "Sitting in all those classrooms, I remember thinking 'Why doesn't anyone do something about what is happening?'" Ryan remembers. "I desperately wanted someone to ask about us, to investigate, to care. I was incapable of asking for help. I

was ashamed about what was happening to us, ashamed at what Mom allowed to go on, ashamed that I couldn't do anything about it. And, on top of all that, I was afraid that if someone found out about our family, they might separate my mother and brother and me. I was so scared, I just kept it all inside," he explains. In silence, Ryan endured years of abuse, violence, and intimidation at the hands of Larry. "I just hoped that we would run away from Larry one day. That is what kept me going."

18   When Ryan was ten years old, his dream almost came true. His mother took the two boys and fled to Michigan, not letting Larry know where they were going. For three months, Ryan was free of the constant threat of violence. But the freedom did not last. Ryan returned from school one day to find Larry sitting on the couch with a smile on his face. "Hi," he said smugly.

19   Ryan could barely speak. "My soul dropped. I just wanted to cry. It was as if something inside me died." Again the cycle of terror began. This time, Ryan's mother sought legal help. A judge granted her a restraining order that barred Larry from being near her home. Larry's response was to stalk the family. Lying in bed one night soon after the order had been issued, Ryan heard a window break. When he went to investigate, he found Larry punching his mother. She managed to call the police, but Larry ran away before they arrived. For three more years the family ran from Larry, moving from town to town and from school to school.

20   As Ryan grew up, so did his tastes in reading. Instead of make-believe heroes like Charlotte and the clever Chinese brother, Ryan was drawn to real-life stories of brave men and women. He read biographies of Abraham Lincoln, once a poor boy who would walk miles to borrow a book. He read of Frederick Douglass, a former slave who became a fiery speaker for human rights. Larry's stalking continued until Ryan's mother became involved with a new boyfriend. The two men got into a fight in the street outside

Larry's house, and Larry was almost killed. At last, he disappeared from Ryan's life.

21   At the age of thirteen, Ryan felt that life was starting at last. His mother overcame her drug addiction and moved into a nicer apartment. For the first time in his life, Ryan was able to attend the same school for more than a year. He began to put down roots, make friends, feel at home. The future looked bright—briefly. Then Ryan's mother announced she could no longer afford the apartment they were living in. They were going to move again.

22   The news that he would have to uproot his life once again shocked Ryan. This time, he rebelled. "I was thirteen, and I had *had* it," he remembers. "I did not want to move any more. For the first time in my life, I had gotten a chance to have a normal healthy life, and now someone was going to take it away again." Ryan begged and pleaded for his mother to stay, but she refused. "When we moved, something inside me snapped. It is sad to say, but in ninth grade I just stopped caring. I figured no one ever seemed to care about me, so why should I?"

23   Ryan's grades reflected his changing attitude. In just months he went from a B+ student to a student who got D's and F's. "I started skipping school, hanging out with the wrong crowd, and then using drugs. I just gave up. All the anger that had built up inside all those years was coming out, and nobody could do anything to stop me." A low point occurred when a cousin called, asking Ryan if he knew someone who would buy stolen jewelry. Ryan arranged the sale. After he and his cousin spent the eighty dollars they'd made on drugs and whiskey, Ryan asked who owned the jewelry. The cousin had stolen it from his own parents, Ryan's aunt and uncle.

24   Because of Ryan's poor performance in school, he was sent to a high school for troubled young people. There he was surrounded by students who spent much of their time trying to find a way to smoke marijuana in class. Fights were common. Far more attention was given to discipline than to learning. Once again, overwhelmed

by the surrounding violence, Ryan retreated to the one safe place he knew— the world of books.

25   "I cut school to go to the public library and read," he remembers. "At school, it was clear that the teachers had given up on the students. They were more like baby sitters than anything else. But at the library—away from the dangers of school —I could read and learn about anything I wanted." By this time, he was drawn to stories from the pages of military history books. He read about prisoners of war who survived long years of unspeakable torture. One book in particular, *The Forgotten Soldier*, moved him. It told the story of a man fighting his own personal war against himself as World War II rages around him. The author had been a prisoner. Ryan thought of himself as a kind of prisoner, too. But unlike Ryan, the author had pulled himself out of his prison and into a better life. Ryan was still locked inside his own private jail.

26   Somehow, despite poor grades and a complete lack of direction, Ryan managed to graduate from high school. He went to work as an industrial painter. While working long hours at manual labor, Ryan had time to think about his life since Larry disappeared. "I realized that I had lost control of my life. I asked myself, 'Is this what I want? Is this all there is?'" In order to cope with his own dissatisfaction, Ryan continued reading. "I worked all day and read all night," says Ryan. "I read true stories about people who overcame incredible obstacles, about people who survived wars and concentration camps. I would get depressed because I'd read about people doing amazing things, and I wasn't doing anything except complaining."

27   Ryan's constant reading and the drudgery of his work forced him to re-think the choices he had made. "I said to myself, 'How did I get here? What am I doing? Where am I taking my life?'" His self-examination was painful. "I became aware of how I had hurt myself, how I had wasted time and made poor choices. But I could not see anything in my future except

more of the same. It all seemed like a big nothing. I grew very depressed."

28   Then things got worse. On the job one day, Ryan slipped off a pedestal and shattered his wrist. He couldn't work. His wife was pregnant, and now she had to work more hours to support their household. Feeling scared and sorry for himself, Ryan went to see his brother Frank.

29   "I was looking for sympathy when I went over there," Ryan admits. "I told him I had no income, no food, no money to buy food, no way to support my wife." But Frank didn't want to listen to Ryan's complaints. Instead, Frank gave Ryan the best advice he could think of. With disgust in his voice, Frank said, "Why don't you go back to school and get an education so you can be somebody when you *do* grow up?"

30   "I wanted to punch his lights out," Ryan says. "I had come over to find a friendly, supportive brother, and instead I found someone telling me what to do." Angry and frustrated, Ryan barged out of his brother's home. Yet Frank's words lingered with him. "The more I thought about it, the more I realized that what Frank said was right. I needed to take charge of my life, and I needed to hear someone say it. Today I thank Frank for telling me the truth."

31   One of the next books to make an impression on Ryan was *Embattled Courage*. In that book, soldiers who fought the long-ago American Civil War spoke of what the war had done to them and their innocent dreams. "Once again, I realized that people who go through hell *can* learn to cope with life."

32   These long-dead soldiers were in Ryan's mind a year later when he enrolled in Muskegon Community College in Michigan. He was the first one in his family to go to college. The transition was not easy.

33   "The first day I set foot on campus, I was terrified," he says. "I looked around and saw that I was ten years older than most of my fellow students, and I thought, 'What am I doing here?' I was sure that everyone in the school was looking at me, thinking I was stupid for being so old. Sometimes I still feel that way," he admits.

With Ryan on the shore of Lake Michigan are his wife Ronda
and their two sons, Reid and Ryan Richard.

34   "But worse than anything was my fear of failure. I was afraid that I wasn't prepared for the demands of college, since my high school years had been such a waste. I thought if I failed, then I would be a complete failure in life, that I wouldn't amount to anything, that everything that happened years earlier would have beaten me."

35   Over the course of his first semester, Ryan's fear faded. His constant reading over so many years had done more than help him to survive: it had helped prepare him for college. Ryan quickly became one of the strongest students in his classes. His love of learning had been buried under the years of abuse and poor choices, but it had not died. "I had given up on school for so long, but when I stepped into college, my mind woke up again," Ryan says. "It was like being reborn." Today, after two years in community college, Ryan is a solid A student.

36   His college work inspired Ryan to decide on a direction for his life. "For years, I survived because I read books about people who kept on fighting, who kept on struggling in the face of horror. At college, I realized that I could teach these same stories to others. It became clear to me that what I wanted to do with my life was to be a history teacher."

37   Ryan is making his goal a reality. In a few months, he will transfer from a school one more time, and this time the move will be his choice. He will attend a four-year university to study history.

38   "When I read books about extraordinary people, when Larry was hurting us or when I was depressed, I would say to myself, 'If they can survive, so can I,'" says Ryan. "Today, there are people everywhere—kids and adults—who are fighting to survive just as I was. Abuse, drugs, violence—the problems are still out there; they aren't going away. But if just one person can learn to make it, from my story or the ones I teach, then all that I have been through is worthwhile," he says. "You have to learn from the past to build your future. That is the lesson of history."

39   "I have another mission too," he says, watching his two sons playing nearby. His older boy, Ryan Richard, is five years old; Reid, his second son, is three. "It is to be something for them that I never had. . . ." He pauses for a moment, picks up Ryan

Richard, and gives him a warm hug. "A dad," he says, cradling his son. His eyes are moist when he puts Ryan Richard down. Reid doesn't notice his father coming over to hug him. He is engrossed in his favorite book—*Goodnight Moon*—one which has been read to him so many times that he can recite the words from memory. Ryan puts his big hand gently on Reid's small shoulder and embraces him. "They are what I live for most," Ryan says, drying his eyes. "When I look in their faces, when I see them looking back at me—safe, secure, and loved—I know why I am here. And despite all my anger and resentment for so many years, I feel thankful."

40   He sits on the floor with Reid. "Can we read, Daddy?" Reid asks hopefully.

41   "Yeah, but you have to start," Ryan replies.

42   Reid's childish voice carefully recites the book's first line: *In the great green room there was a telephone and a red balloon . . .*

43   Ryan smiles. He is writing his own kind of book, the book of his life. A painful chapter has ended, and a new one filled with promise and possibilities has begun.

Here are two activities to help deepen your understanding and appreciation of the selection.

Comprehension Check

1. Which sentence best expresses the central point of the selection?
   a. Ryan Klootwyk was abused as a child.
   b. A love of reading helped Ryan Klootwyk escape abusive treatment at home and problems in school.
   c. Ryan Klootwyk, who loves reading, is a straight-A student in college.
   d. Inspired by books, Ryan Klootwyk overcame child abuse and poor choices and has become a success both as a college student and as a parent.

2. Which sentence best expresses the main idea of paragraph 17?
   a. Although Ryan did well at school, he was inwardly miserable.
   b. Each time Ryan transferred to a new school, he hid the truth of his home situation.
   c. Ryan was afraid to ask for help.
   d. Ryan put up with years of abusive treatment from Larry.

3. When Ryan was in third grade, he
   a. ran away from home.
   b. finally told someone about what a monster Larry was.
   c. won a copy of *Charlotte's Web* as a prize in a school reading contest.
   d. did all of the above.

4. We can conclude that Ryan's brother Frank
   a. liked Larry more than Ryan did.
   b. lent Ryan money after Ryan injured his wrist in an accident.
   c. wanted Ryan to be independent and self-reliant.
   d. did all of the above.

5. From paragraphs 39–43, we can infer
   a. that Ryan is a much better father to his children than his father and Larry were to him.
   b. that Ryan Richard is Ryan's favorite child.
   c. that Ryan Richard has problems with reading.
   d. all of the above.

Critical Thinking and Discussion

1. As a child, Ryan used books as a "lifeline" to escape his troubled home life. When you are troubled or stressed, what do you like to do to make yourself feel better? Does your "lifeline" work as well for you as books worked for Ryan? Explain.

2. Ryan's favorite book was *The Five Chinese Brothers*. Later, he found a new favorite: *Charlotte's Web*. Judging from his story, why do you think these two books appealed so much to Ryan? If you also had a favorite book when you were younger, why did you like it so much?

3. Ryan tells about a "low point" in his life when he helped a cousin sell stolen jewelry and then spent the proceeds on drugs and liquor. Yet he managed to reject such behavior and eventually turned his life around. Have you or has anyone you've known come back from a similar low point in life? Describe the experience and its lessons.

4. "You have to learn from the past to build your future," Ryan says. What lessons has Ryan learned from the past? What lessons from the past do you think can help you build *your* future?

FINAL ACTIVITIES

1 Check Your Understanding

Answer the following questions to check your understanding of the chapter.

1. Which of the following statements best describes the main idea of this chapter?
   a. Reading can increase a person's vocabulary, spelling, and comprehension.
   b. More than ever before, today's jobs require the skillful processing of information.
   c. More than any other single skill, reading prepares one for success in school and in life.
   d. Reading helps us feel connected to other members of the human family.

2. The key to becoming a regular reader is to
   a. read difficult materials.
   b. read frequently.
   c. avoid newspapers and magazines and read only books.
   d. read in school only.

3. Besides watching less television and doing homework before going out to play, Benjamin Carson's mother required him to read
   a. a book every day.
   b. a book every week.
   c. two books every week.
   d. two books every month.

4. Maria Cardenas was inspired to become a better reader by
   a. her mother.
   b. her little daughter.
   c. her employer at the Western clothing store.
   d. the president of Edison Community College.

5. When Ryan would cut classes at his high school for troubled young people, he would
   a. go to the library and read.
   b. steal jewelry and sell it.
   c. get into fights with his brother.
   d. attend classes at Muskegon Community College.

2 Questions for Writing or Discussion

You may find it helpful to think about and write out your answers to the following questions. Or your instructor may put you in a small group or pair you with another student and have you discuss the questions with each other.

1. Was reading a priority in the home where you grew up? If so, tell how reading was emphasized. If not, describe what seemed to be the attitude toward reading in your home. How did your family's attitude (positive or negative) about reading affect your development as a reader?

2. When you were growing up, what role did school play in encouraging or discouraging you to read? Describe experiences in school that made you feel positive or negative about reading.

3. Whose story did you find most interesting: Ben Carson's, Maria Cardenas's, or Ryan Klootwyk's? Why? If that person had not become a regular reader, what do you think are some ways his or her life might be different today?

4. Of the five suggestions that appear in the section in this chapter entitled "How to Become a Regular Reader," how many do you follow now? What is an additional one that you could adopt without too much trouble?

3   Writing about a Book

Read a book that you choose on your own, or a book from the short book list on the next page. Then write a paragraph about one of the following:

1. The main character in the book. Provide supporting details and examples to back up your idea that the main character was likable and perhaps even admirable—or not so.

2. The main conflict or conflicts presented in the book. The conflict is often between the leading character and another character, or between the leading character and a larger force (such as peer pressure or racial attitudes); sometimes the conflict may involve different choices within the main character's mind.

3. The relevance of the book to everyday life. How is the book related to your life, experiences, feelings, and ideas? How has the book reinforced or changed or expanded your own attitudes?

Here are examples of **points** that could start a paragraph:

Point about a main character: In *Gifted Hands*, Ben Carson is an appealing and admirable person.

Point about a conflict: In *Lord of the Flies*, the conflict is between the good and bad sides of human nature.

Point about the relevance of a book: The idea in *Man's Search for Meaning* that all of us need meaningful work or meaningful relationships helps me understand the behavior of people I know.

After you have chosen your point, provide **supporting details or examples** to back up your point. For instance, if you have decided to support the first point above, you might say in part:

One quality I admire is Ben Carson's desire for self-improvement. He describes the time his bad temper led him to the brink of stabbing a neighborhood friend in his neighborhood. As a result of that experience, he determined that he would never again let his temper control him.

A Short Book List

Following is a brief book list that includes descriptions of some appealing books. You should be able to find any one of these books at a good bookstore or at your library.

Autobiographies and Nonfiction

The Diary of a Young Girl, Anne Frank

To escape the Nazi death camps, Anne Frank and her family hid for years in an attic. Her journal tells a story of love, fear, and courage.

Gifted Hands, Ben Carson

Dr. Carson is now a world-famous neurosurgeon at one of the best hospitals in the world; his book tells how he got to where he is today.

A Hope in the Unseen, Ron Suskind

A determined young man travels from deep in the inner city to the Ivy League.

I Know Why the Caged Bird Sings, Maya Angelou

The author writes with love, humor, and honesty about growing up black and female in the South.

Man's Search for Meaning, Viktor Frankl

How do people go on when they have been stripped of everything, including human dignity? Frankl movingly describes life in a concentration camp and what he learned there about survival.

Fiction

Bud, Not Buddy, Christopher Paul Curtis

A motherless boy goes on a heartwarming and unforgettable journey to find his missing father.

Charlotte's Web, E. B. White

This best-loved story for children and adults is about a pig named Wilbur and his best friend, a spider named Charlotte, who must come up with a plan to save him from being killed and eaten.

A Day No Pigs Would Die, Robert Peck

A very moving human story for people of all ages about the daily struggles of a poor family living on a farm.

Flowers for Algernon, Daniel Keyes

A scientific experiment turns a retarded man into a genius—with joyous and tragic results.

Lord of the Flies, William Golding

Could a group of children survive alone on a tropical island in the midst of World War Three? Golding shows us that the real danger is not the war outside but "the beast" within each of us.

To Kill a Mockingbird, Harper Lee

A controversial trial is the centerpiece of this story about adolescence, bigotry, and justice.

Watchers, Dean Koontz

An incredibly suspenseful story about two dogs that undergo lab experiments. One dog becomes a monster programmed to kill, and it seeks to track down the couple that knows its secret.

---

4   Speaking about the Benefits of Reading

Imagine that you have been asked to give a speech on the benefits of regular reading to a class of students who will be entering college in the fall. Prepare a talk full of practical advice that really communicates with them. Imagine that the students have been told beforehand that you will be as stiff and dry as a board and that your talk will have little relevance or value. You have two goals, then: 1) to use language and images that really connect with students, and 2) to pack your talk with lots of truly helpful information. Your speech should be five to ten minutes long.

4 / Managing Your Time

HOW ORGANIZED ARE YOU?

Do you consider yourself an organized or a disorganized person? Check the description below that applies to you:

___ *I'm organized.* I get to places on time, I keep up with school work, I'm always ready for tests, and I allow plenty of time for planning and working on papers.

___ *I'm somewhere in the middle* between being organized and being disorganized.

___ *I'm disorganized.* I'm often late for appointments, or I forget them; I miss classes; I work on papers and cram for tests at the last minute.

If you have not checked the first item above, you need to learn more about how to control your time. The skillful use of time will help you enormously in school and, indeed, in all phases of your life. This chapter describes five steps to help you organize your life and control your time.

FOUR STEPS TO TIME CONTROL

Step 1: Use Your Course Outline

At the beginning of a school semester, each of your instructors will probably pass out a course outline, or *syllabus*. If you do *not* want to take a giant step toward controlling your time, throw away this syllabus or put it in the back of a notebook and never look at it.

The syllabus is your instructor's plan for the course. Chances are it will explain the instructor's grading system and on what factors your grade will be based. Chances are it will give you the dates of exams and will tell you when papers or reports are due. Chances are it will outline what topics will be covered in each week of class, and it may list the chapters in the textbook that you may be expected to read.

In other words, the syllabus will put you inside your instructor's head and help you learn exactly *what you must do* to succeed in the course. The syllabus is often the key to doing well in a course.

Believe it or not, many students ignore the syllabus. Don't make this mistake! Instead, use the syllabus to help organize your work for the course: move the exam dates and the paper due dates to a large monthly calendar. Refer to the syllabus on a regular basis to make sure you are doing just what your instructor expects you to do.

Step 2: Keep a Large Monthly Calendar

You should buy or make a large monthly calendar. Be sure your calendar has a good-sized block of white space for each date. Then use the course outlines that your instructors give you to write on the calendar when each test will be given and when each paper is due.

Hang the calendar in a place where you will see it every day, perhaps above your desk or on a bedroom wall. Such a calendar is an excellent step toward organizing and controlling your time. It allows you, in one quick glance, to get a clear picture of what you need to do during the semester.

- Where is the best place for you to hang a monthly calendar? _____

Look at the example of a student's calendar that appears below and answer the following questions.

- What quizzes or tests will the student have? On which dates? _____

- What papers does the student have to write? When are they due? _____

- When is an oral report scheduled? _____

November						
Sun	Mon	Tues	Wed	Thurs	Fri	Sat
			1	2	3	4
5	6 English paper	7	8 Math quiz	9	10	11
12	13	14	15 Psy. test	16	17	18
19	20	21	22 Math quiz	23 No school	24 No school	25
26	27 English paper	28	29 Bus. oral report	30		

Helen Rowe is a student at the University of Pennsylvania.

On Using a Syllabus:

Helen: *"Never throw a syllabus away. I see other students glance at a syllabus on day one and never look at it again. But it's often the key to doing well in a course."*

Kenyon: *"The syllabus is a blueprint for what you have to do in a course. It often tells you what the instructor expects you to do to pass the course."*

Michelle: *"Don't just stuff a course outline in a notebook and never look at it again! It provides the most specific information about the class that you're ever going to find in one place."*

Kenyon Whittington

Michelle Miller

On Using a Calendar:

Kenyon: *"I have a large calendar in my room. I take my syllabus the first day of class, and I pick out all the important dates of tests and papers due and textbook chapters that have to be read, and I put them on the calendar."*

Lamel: *"I have a large monthly calendar on which I write only essential things: exams, papers due, meetings. That calendar shows me everything I have to do. In another place I keep a list of things I want to do—fun stuff, social stuff, everyday stuff like getting my hair done. If anything I want to do interferes with my big calendar, I do it another time."*

Lamel Jackson is a student at Haverford College.

Step 3: Make Up a Daily "To Do" List

A *"to do" list* is a written list—on paper—of things that need to get done. It is a very powerful tool for organizing one's life and making the best use of one's time. Corporate CEOs, school administrators, company managers, and successful people in all walks of life use the "to do" list. With a pen and a piece of paper, you can have exactly the same tool to organize and manage your life.

Important Notes about the "To Do" List"

Point 1: Carry the list with you throughout the day. A small notebook can be kept in a purse, and a four- by six-inch slip of paper can be put in a pocket or wallet.

- What do you think is the best way for you to carry a daily "to do" list? _____

  _____

Point 2: Decide on priorities. Label items A, B, and C in importance. Making the best use of your time means focusing on top-priority items rather than spending hours on low-priority activities. When in doubt about what to do at any time in the day, ask yourself, "What are the most important items to get done?" and choose one of them.

- Do you think the idea of listing "to do's" and then focusing on the most important

  ones will be helpful for you?   _____

Point 3: Cross out items as you finish them. What is left can be moved to the next day's list.

Tina's "To Do" List

- Look over Tina's "to do" list for one day, as shown below. Label each of the items *A, B,* or *C* depending on what seems to be its level of importance.

To Do — Wednesday

1. *Daily journal entry for English class.*
2. *Get milk and cat food!*
3. *Study for math quiz tomorrow.*
4. *Return CDs to Stephanie.*
5. *Read Ch. 6 of business text.*
6. *Go on Internet to find article for business class.*
7. *Balance checkbook.*
8. *Call Nadia to get psychology notes from class you missed.*
9. *Do laundry.*
10. *Answer Roger's e-mail.*
11. *Exercise if time.*
12. *Give Mom a call.*

➤ **Activity: Your "To Do" List**

Use this space to make up your own "to do" list for tomorrow. If you cannot think of at least seven items, add things that you want to do over the rest of the week. Then label each item as *A, B,* or *C* in priority.

To Do

Dr. Ben Carson

Jennifer McCaul is a student at
Alvernia College.

On Using a "To Do" List:

Dr. Carson: *"In college I wrote down everything that I had to do on a piece of paper. And I would usually post it in some prominent place. It would have been a fatal mistake to just tuck that paper away somewhere. That piece of paper was my time organizer, and it's a strategy I use even today."*

Jennifer: *"At first I would write everything down on a list. I'd put down schoolwork, laundry day, whatever. But then I wouldn't really look at it. After I started having real trouble with time in college, I went back to the 'to do' list. I'd mark off the most important items and focus on them, and I would keep the list with me as I went through the day. It actually made my day easier. I knew what I had to do, and everything was ordered in such a way that I was making the best use of my time."*

Step 4: Use a Daily Planner

A *daily planner* (also called a *datebook* or *time organizer*) is an inexpensive purchase at any bookstore or office supply store. It combines a calendar with space for a daily "to do" list. If you actively use the planner—carrying it with you every day and consulting it and adding or crossing out items on a regular basis—it will definitely help you organize your time.

Ginger Jackson

> **On Using a Daily Planner:**
>
> **Ginger:** "I use a daily planner, which I carry with me constantly. I write everything in it: my classes, meetings, rugby practice, even meals if the day is really crazy. Having everything written down in one place makes me feel in control."
>
> **Marcos:** "I used a time organizer my first year in school, and it didn't do me any good. I'd write something down and then put the organizer away. Now the organizer is front and center. It's always with me and always open on my desk. For example, I'll write 'Read Chs. 3–4 of economics book' and list whatever else I have to do today."
>
> **Helen:** "With my job and classes, I'm very busy. I carry a daily planner everywhere. I write down all my commitments, including class assignments, meetings, and exams. It really helps me manage my time."

Marcos Maestre is a student at Millersville University.

Helen Rowe

A Final Thought

You now have several practical and powerful steps for gaining control of your time. Pay close attention to your course syllabus; record test and paper dates on a monthly calendar; carry around a "to do" list; use a daily planner.

Time can seem as abundant as the sand on a beach. But if you are not careful, all that time can slip through your fingers. To become a success, you need to learn to organize your life and control your time. Don't forget that the ability to control time is the mark of almost all successful people!

The question that only you can answer is: **Will you take control of your time?** If you do, you can take command of your life and get more work done than ever before.

- Do you think you will take the steps needed to gain control of your time? Honestly rate your chances:

____ 100%   ____ 90%   ____ 80%   ____ 70%   ____ 60%

____ 50%   ____ 40%   ____ 30%   ____ 20%   ____ I truly don't know.

Aaron Benson is a student at West Chester University.

Aaron: "I realized in my first semester in college that putting things off made everything very, very impractical. It was almost impossible for me to do things in the time that I had left. As the semester progressed, a lot of things were coming up, papers were coming due, and I felt I was being overwhelmed. What I learned to do was control my time. I'd get out a piece of paper and write down what I needed to do each day. And then I would cross items off at the end of the day. I learned to manage things as opposed to having everything whirl around in my head and not getting anything done."

May: "Like almost everyone, I had trouble figuring out how to manage my time. I didn't take classes seriously enough. In high school, I didn't need to study, really. College is very, very different. I kept thinking, 'I can remember that—I don't have to write it down.' That was OK for assignments that were due in the next class. But in college there are assignments due two weeks from now, or a month from now. That sounded so far away, I'd put off doing them and forget them until the last minute. I learned the hard way that I needed to organize my time."

May Lam

FINAL ACTIVITIES

1   Check Your Understanding

Answer the following questions to check your understanding of the chapter.

1. Which of the following is a time control technique *not* discussed in this chapter?
   a. Transferring important tasks to a large monthly calendar
   b. Wearing a wristwatch at all times
   c. Carefully examining your course outline
   d. Using a daily planner

2. An instructor's plan for a course is called a
   a. daily planner.
   b. "to do" list.
   c. calendar.
   d. syllabus.

3. Why did the use of a daily planner *not* benefit Marcos Maestre at first?
   a. He put the planner away where he wouldn't look at it.
   b. He had too many activities to keep track of.
   c. He could not read his own handwriting.
   d. He lost the planner.

4. As Lamel Jackson writes down an item to do, how does she decide whether to put it on her large calendar or on a smaller list?
   a. The large calendar is for things she has to do, while the list is for things she'd like to do.
   b. The large calendar is for special projects, while the list is for daily assignments.
   c. The large calendar is for social engagements, and the list is for assignments.
   d. The large calendar is for work or family commitments; the list is for school assignments.

5. According to Kenyon Whittington, what does a class syllabus tell you?
   a. The instructor's name, address, telephone number, and e-mail address.
   b. When papers are due and exams are scheduled.
   c. What the instructor expects you to do in order to pass the course.
   d. What chapters to read in the textbook each week.

2   Questions for Writing or Discussion

You may find it helpful to think about and write out your answers to the following questions. Or your instructor may put you in a small group or pair you with another student and have you discuss the questions with each other.

1. How did you rate yourself according to the descriptions that open the chapter—organized, partly organized, or disorganized? Which portions of your life do you find easy to keep organized? Why? Which are harder to manage? Why?

2. Currently, how do you keep track of upcoming tests, papers due, and other school commitments? Can you think of more effective techniques for doing so?

3. Get together with one or more partners. Each of you make a list of at least seven things that you want or need to get done over the next several days. Prioritize those items by

marking each one A, B, or C. Show your list to your partners and explain why you have given a higher priority to some items than others. Ask your partners if they think a "to do" list will work for them and why or why not.

4. Use a check (✓) to show your attitude about each of the following time-control tools:

A large monthly calendar on which you write test dates, paper due dates, etc.

__I already do it.   __I'll do it.   __I might do it.   __I probably won't do it.   __I won't do it.

A daily "to do" list

__I already do it.   __I'll do it.   __I might do it.   __I probably won't do it.   __I won't do it.

A daily planner (datebook, organizer)

__I already do it.   __I'll do it.   __I might do it.   __I probably won't do it.   __I won't do it.

Get together in a group with two or three students and explain why you have checked the statement you have for each item.

3   Writing about Time Control

Write a paragraph in which you evaluate how well you organize and control your time. Of the four steps to time control described in this chapter, which do you practice? Which do you not practice? Begin your paragraph with one of the **points** below.

> **Point:** I successfully manage my time; I practice some of the steps described in this chapter.
>
> **Point:** I have not been a good time manager; I practice none of the steps described in this chapter.
>
> **Point:** My time management skills are mixed; I organize my time in some ways but not others.

After you have chosen your point, provide **supporting details or examples** to back up your point. For instance, to support the third point above, you might say in part:

> I do use a big wall calendar on which I write down test dates and due dates for papers and projects. But I don't do a good job of managing my time on a daily basis. Instead of keeping a daily "to do" list and getting important items out of the way first, I spend a lot of time on activities like hanging out with friends or going to the mall. Then I realize sometime around bedtime that I still have to read two chapters for biology or write a paper for Spanish class.

When writing your paragraph, use examples and details based on your actual experience.

4   Speaking about Time Control

Imagine that you have been asked to give a speech on time management to a class of students who will be entering college in the fall. Prepare a talk full of practical advice that really communicates with them. Imagine that the students have been told beforehand that you will be as stiff and dry as a board and that your talk will have little relevance or value. You have two goals, then: 1) to use language and images that really connect with students, and 2) to pack your talk with lots of truly helpful information. Your speech should be five to ten minutes long.

5   Evaluating Your Daily Use of Time

To gain better control of your time, first write down your typical daily schedule. What you learn from doing this can help you prepare a weekly study schedule. Before developing your own daily schedule, look at Tina's schedule, below.

How Tina Actually Spends Her Time

6:30–7:30	Get up, shower, breakfast
7:30–8:00	Travel to school
8:00–9:00	Class (English)
9:00–10:00	Coffee in student center
10:00–11:00	Class (math)
11:00–1:00	Lunch and hanging out in cafeteria
1:00–2:00	Class (business)
2:00–2:30	Read magazines in library
2:30–3:00	Drive to work
3:00–6:00	Work at Wal-Mart
6:00–7:30	Travel home, eat dinner, watch news
7:30-9:30	Nap, telephone, and homework
9:30-11:00	TV
11:00	Bed

- Tina has three classes. Assuming that every hour of class time may need at least one hour of study time, how could Tina revise her schedule so that she would have at least three full study hours in addition to time for rest and relaxation? Make your suggested changes by crossing out items and adding study time to her schedule.

How You Actually Spend Your Time

- Now make up a schedule of a typical day in your life. Use the form on the next page to record just how you spend your time. Include the time you need for all of the following:

getting up and having breakfast	each of your classes
traveling to school	lunch
hanging out	television

working   nap

dinner   whatever else you spend time on

Be honest when you do this! If you are not honest, the exercise will be worthless. You want to see clearly just what you are doing so that you will be able to plan ways to use your time more effectively.

- Write in the number of hours you *actually* used for study in your typical day: _____ hours. Next, go back to your chart and block off time in the day that you *could* have used for study. (Remember to still allow for rest and relaxation time, which you also need.) Write in the number of hours you could have used for study in the day: _____ hours.

6 Preparing a Weekly Study Schedule

Now that you have a sense of how you spend your time each day, you are ready to prepare a weekly study schedule. Take a look first at the master weekly schedule, shown on the next page, that Tina prepared to gain control of her time. (Note that "R&R" refers to rest, relaxation, socializing, games, parties, and the like.)

How Tina Could Spend Her Time

Time	Monday	Tuesday	Wednesday	Thursday	Friday	Saturday	Sunday
6–7 am							
7–8 am	Breakfast and travel		Breakfast and travel		Breakfast and travel		
8–9 am	English	Breakfast and travel	English	Breakfast and travel	English	Breakfast	
9–10 am	STUDY	STUDY	STUDY	STUDY	STUDY	Travel	Breakfast
10–11 am	Math	Psychology	Math	Psychology	Math	Job	R&R
11 am–12 noon	STUDY	STUDY	STUDY	Psychology	STUDY	Job	R&R
12–1 pm	Lunch		Lunch	STUDY	Lunch	Job	R&R
1–2 pm	Business	Lunch	Business	Lunch	Business	Job	Lunch
2–3 pm	Travel	R&R	Travel	R&R	Travel	Job	STUDY
3–4 pm	Job	R&R	Job	R&R	Job	Job	STUDY
4–5 pm	Job	STUDY	Job	STUDY	Job	Travel	STUDY
5–6 pm	Job	STUDY	Job	STUDY	Job	R&R	R&R
6–7 pm	Travel	R&R	Travel	R&R	Travel	Dinner	Dinner
7–8 pm	Dinner	Dinner	Dinner	Dinner	Dinner	R&R	STUDY
8–9 pm	STUDY	STUDY	STUDY	STUDY	R&R	R&R	STUDY
9–10 pm	STUDY	STUDY	STUDY	STUDY	R&R	R&R	STUDY
10–11 pm	R&R	R&R	R&R	R&R	R&R	R&R	R&R
11 pm–12 mid	Bed	Bed	Bed	Bed	R&R	R&R	Bed
12–1 am							
1–2 am							
Study hours	4	7	4	6	2	0	6

- How many separate blocks of study time has Tina built into her schedule? _____

- What is the total number of study hours that Tina has scheduled? _____

How You Could Spend Your Time

Use the form below to make up your own realistic weekly study schedule. Write in the names and times of your classes first, then your travel times, then your hours for meals, then your rest and relaxation times, then your study times. (Should your schedule change or should you wish to make additional copies, another blank form appears on the next page.)

Carry your weekly study schedule with you, or hang it next to your monthly calendar. If you use it regularly, you will have taken another powerful step toward organizing your time.

Time	Monday	Tuesday	Wednesday	Thursday	Friday	Saturday	Sunday
6–7 am							
7–8 am							
8–9 am							
9–10 am							
10–11 am							
11 am–12 noon							
12–1 pm							
1–2 pm							
2–3 pm							
3–4 pm							
4–5 pm							
5–6 pm							
6–7 pm							
7–8 pm							
8–9 pm							
9–10 pm							
10–11 pm							
11 pm–12 mid							
12–1 am							
1–2 am							
Study hours							

Time	Monday	Tuesday	Wednesday	Thursday	Friday	Saturday	Sunday
6–7 am							
7–8 am							
8–9 am							
9–10 am							
10–11 am							
11 am–12 noon							
12–1 pm							
1–2 pm							
2–3 pm							
3–4 pm							
4–5 pm							
5–6 pm							
6–7 pm							
7–8 pm							
8–9 pm							
9–10 pm							
10–11 pm							
11 pm–12 mid							
12–1 am							
1–2 am							
Study hours							

5 / Taking Notes in Class

WHAT YOU REALLY NEED TO KNOW

Here more than almost anything else is what you must do to succeed in school:

1 Go to class.

2 Take good notes.

Why You Must Attend Class

The instructor will use class time to present the key ideas of the course. If you are not in class to hear and write down these ideas, you are not going to learn anything. In addition, you will greatly increase your chances of failing the course!

There are only two alternatives to class attendance. You can read and study the textbook and hope to learn the key ideas of the course from it. But textbook study will take you many hours, and you still won't know which ideas the teacher feels are most important. Those ideas are sure to be the ones that appear on exams.

You can also use the notes of another student, but those notes cannot make up for the experience of actually being in class and hearing the instructor talk about key ideas. At best, the notes of another student can help you fill out missing information in your own notes.

Why You Must Take Notes

You must write down the material presented in class *because forgetting begins almost immediately!* Studies have shown that within two weeks you will probably forget a good deal of what you have heard in class. In fact, how much class material do you think most people *do* forget in just two weeks?

____ 20 percent is forgotten within two weeks

____ 40 percent is forgotten within two weeks

____ 60 percent is forgotten within two weeks

____ 80 percent is forgotten within two weeks

Studies have shown that within two weeks most people forget 80% of what they have heard!

Now see if you can guess how much class material people typically forget within four weeks:

____ 85 percent is forgotten within four weeks

____ 90 percent is forgotten within four weeks

____ 95 percent is forgotten within four weeks

The fact is that within four weeks people typically forget 95% of the information they have heard in class! So the reality of the matter is that, no matter how carefully you listen to a classroom lecture, you forget very quickly—and you forget a great deal. To guard against forgetting, you should write down much of the information presented in class. If you just listen and don't write, you're heading for trouble. The point bears repeating: **you should get a written record of what an instructor presents in class.**

How many notes should you take? If you pay attention in class, you will soon develop an instinct for what is meaningful and what is not. If you are unsure whether certain terms, facts, and ideas are significant, here is a good rule to follow:

When in doubt, write it down.

This doesn't mean you should (or could) get down every word, but you should be prepared to do a good deal of writing in class.

Taking Notes versus Listening

Some students will read the advice above and say, "But I can't really understand the material if I have to concentrate on writing it down. I'm better off just listening carefully." If you choose to listen carefully and not take many notes in class, then you should be sure to find time after class to expand your notes. Write down as complete an understanding as you have of the material while it is still fresh in your memory. You know that your clear understanding is likely to fade as other information enters your mind and the reality of forgetting sets in.

I remember trying this technique when I was in college: listening during class and taking more notes right afterward. The trouble was that some instructors covered so much information in class that I simply could not remember it all. Also, sometimes I didn't have time right after class to write down ideas I had not recorded during the lecture. When I began to take more notes in class, my grades on tests improved to B's and A's.

I did find that when I concentrated on writing more, I often understood less. But because I took such complete notes, I had no trouble understanding the material when I began to study my notes later.

Some students will say, "The instructor wants me to sit and listen and understand and ask questions and not worry so much about taking notes." It's true that if you are actively listening and questioning, the class is more interesting for the instructor. But the truth is that the instructor is not going to have to take a test on the material. The truth is that he or she is going to test *you* on the material covered in class. You had better write that material down so that you do not forget it and so that you can study it for tests.

Andy Cao is a student at
Drexel University.

Krystal Buhr

Jhoselyn Martinez is a graduate of
Chestnut Hill College.

Andy: *"The most important thing you can do is be in class. You learn how to read the teacher and to know what he or she is going to want on tests. You could read an entire textbook, but that wouldn't be as good as being in class and writing down a teacher's understanding of ideas."*

Floyd: *"You've got to go to all your classes. College teachers aren't going to push you about attendance. I got off to a bad start my first year in college. But when I started going to every class and taking lots of notes, my grades started uphill."*

Floyd Allen

Krystal: *"I got off to a shaky start because I didn't take enough notes in class. Then I began to take a lot of notes during a lecture. That really made the difference in my becoming a good student."*

Ryan Klootwyk

Ryan: *"Attendance is very important—as important as studying itself. Taking notes is also very important. I take notes even in classes where they say you don't have to take notes. It's very easy to forget material otherwise."*

Jhoselyn: *"You definitely have to take a lot of notes. When the teacher is talking and you're just listening, everything is very clear. But you're just not going to remember it all. You have to get it down on paper."*

➤ **Activity: Telling Your Student Fortune**

Take a minute here to find out what will happen to you in school.

Check the item that applies to you:	Here's what is likely to happen:
___ I am going to class and taking notes regularly.	You'll earn A's and B's.
___ I am going to class at times and taking notes at times.	You may earn C's and D's at best.
___ I am not going to class much or taking notes.	You'll flunk out. (It might be better to leave school for a while. Return to school when you're more ready to do the work.)

SIX STEPS TO GOOD NOTE-TAKING

The following six steps will help you take effective classroom notes.

Step 1: Sit at the Front

Sit where the teacher will see you and where you can see the board clearly and easily. Your position near or at the front will help you stay tuned in to what the instructor does in class. If you sit in the back or are hidden in a corner, there may be a reason for your behavior. Maybe you are worried that you'll be noticed and called on (a common anxiety), or maybe you don't really want to be in the classroom at all (something worth thinking about).

Analyze your attitude. If you're hiding, know that you're hiding and try to understand why. It is all right not to want to be in a class; teachers can be boring and subjects uninteresting. However, the danger in such cases is that you may slide into a passive state where you won't listen or take notes. Don't fool yourself. If a class is deadly, there is all the more reason to make yourself take good notes—that way you will pass the course and get out of the class once and for all.

Step 2: Write Your Notes in a Systematic Way

a Use full-size 8½-by-11-inch paper. Do *not* use a small note tablet. As explained below, you will need the margin space provided by full-sized paper. Also, on a single page of full-sized paper, you can see relationships among ideas more clearly.

b Use a ballpoint pen. You will often need to write quickly—something that you cannot do as well with a pencil or a felt-tip pen. (Don't worry about making mistakes that you can't erase. Just cross them out, and move on!)

c Date each day's notes.

d Leave space at the top of the page and at the left-hand margin. (You might use notebook paper that has a light red line down the left side.)

Leaving margins gives you space to add to your notes if you want to. You may, for example, write in ideas taken from your textbook or other sources. Also, the margins can be used to prepare study notes (see pages 98–99) that will help you learn the material.

e   Write as legibly *and* as fast as you can. When you prepare for a test, you want to spend your time studying—not deciphering your handwriting.

f   To save time, abbreviate recurring terms. Put a key to abbreviated words in the top margin of your notes. For example, in a biology class *ant* could stand for *antibody;* in a psychology class *stm* could stand for *short-term memory.* (When a lecture is over, you may want to go back and fill in the words you have abbreviated.)

Kenyon Whittington

On Sitting in the Front:

Kenyon: "I think you declare yourself as a student or non-student as soon as you walk into the classroom. If you walk to the back, you might as well walk out of the room and leave campus and go home. If you sit in the front, you don't have to strain like you do if you sit in the back. And sitting in the front will help you get on the good side of the teacher."

Marcos: "I now sit in the very front. It really gets me more involved with the class, and the professor regards me in a positive way."

Marcos Maestre

On Taking Systematic Notes:

Terry: "I use full-size sheets of paper, and I abbreviate a lot. For example, if a professor is lecturing about operant conditioning, I'll write 'oc = operant conditioning' at the top or in the margin of my notes. Then all through my notes I just have to write 'oc.' I also abbreviate numbers. Abbreviating really saves time and allows me to take more notes."

Kenyon: "When I take notes, I use single sheets, writing on one side only. I don't like having to look at one side and then flip to the other side and go back and forth. It's easier to organize and study notes if you use only one side of a page."

Terry Oakman

Step 3: Watch for Signals of Importance

a   Write down whatever your teacher puts on the board. Ideally, PRINT such material in capital letters. If you don't have time to print, write as you usually do and put the letters OB in the margin to indicate that the material was written on the board. Later, when you review your notes, you will know which ideas the teacher emphasized. The chances are good that they will come up on exams.

b   Always write down definitions and lists. Most people write down definitions— explanations of key terms in the subject they are learning. But they may ignore lists, which are often equally important.

    Teachers use lists to show the relationship among a group of ideas. Lists are signaled in such ways as "The four steps in the process are . . ."; "There were three reasons for . . ."; "Five characteristics of . . ."; "The two effects were . . ."; and so on. When you write a list, always mark the items with 1, 2, 3, or other appropriate symbols. Also, always be sure to include a clear heading that explains what a list is about. For example, if you list and number six kinds of defense mechanisms, make sure you write at the top of the list the heading "Kinds of Defense Mechanisms."

c   Your instructor may say outright that an idea is important: "This is an important reason . . ."; or "A point to really remember is that . . ."; or "The chief cause was . . ."; or "The basic idea here is . . ."; or "Don't forget that . . ."; or "Pay special attention to . . ."; and so on. Needless to say, be sure to write down ideas that the instructor openly states are worth remembering. Then write IMP in the margin to show their importance.

d   A teacher's voice may slow down, become louder, or otherwise signal that you are expected to write down exactly what is being said, word for word. Of course you should do so! And if your instructor repeats a point, that also is a clear signal that an idea should be written down.

- Which two signals of importance do you think will be most helpful for you to remember?

_____

_____

Step 4: Write Down Examples and Connecting Information

Write down any examples the teacher provides and mark them with *ex.* The examples help you understand complex and abstract points. They help bring ideas down to earth and make them clear.

    Also be sure to write down the details that connect or explain main points. Too many students copy only the major points the teacher puts on the board. They do not realize that as time passes, they may forget the connections between key ideas. Be sure, then, to record the connecting details which the instructor provides. That way you will better remember the relationships among the major points in your notes.

Ginger Jackson

Jhoselyn Martinez

On Signals of Importance:

Ginger: *"Slowly I got better at knowing what was essential to write down. I listen for key phrases like 'You really ought to know . . . ,' or 'The first point is . . . .' I also notice when the instructor begins a lecture with a question like 'Why did so-and-so happen?' I know that question and its answer are things I need to write down and understand."*

Jhoselyn: *"One of the biggest signals is when teachers repeat something and signal it in that way. It's like they're saying, 'This is important.' Or their tone of voice will tell you it's important."*

Terry Oakman

On Examples:

Terry: *"I always write down the exact words a professor will give for a definition, but I also write down more. As a term is explained with examples, I continue to take notes. This way I get a full understanding. If I didn't write down the examples, I might not remember them."*

Michelle: *"Always write down any examples a teacher provides. They get you right down to the nitty-gritty of a lecture's main ideas."*

Michelle Miller

Step 5: Read Your Textbook in Advance of Class

Read material in your textbook before your instructor presents that material in class. If you go into class with a general sense of a subject, you'll understand more and be able to take better notes. If your course syllabus doesn't say what chapter you should read, then simply ask the instructor, "Is there a chapter in the textbook that it will help me to read before the next class? I'd like to get a head start on the material." Your instructor will be favorably impressed.

Step 6: Review Your Notes Soon after Class

Go over your notes soon after class. A day later may be too late because forgetting sets in almost at once.

As you review your notes, do all of the following:

• Make sure that your punctuation is clear and that all words are readable and correctly spelled. You may also want to write out completely words that you abbreviated during the lecture.

• Wherever appropriate, add connecting statements and other comments to complete any unfinished ideas and to clarify the material.

• Make sure that important items—material on the board, definitions, lists, and so on—are clearly marked.

• Improve the organization, if necessary, so that you can see at a glance the differences between main points and supporting material as well as any relationships among the main points.

This review does more than make your notes clear: It is also a vital step in the process of mastering the material. During class, you have almost certainly been too busy taking notes to absorb all the ideas. Now, as you review the notes, you can roll up your sleeves and wrestle with the ideas presented and think about the relationships among them. You can, in short, do the work needed to reach the point where you can smile and say, "Yes, I understand—and everything I understand is written down clearly in my notes."

Floyd Allen

On Reading the Textbook in Advance:

Floyd: *"I started to read the textbook before going to class. The chapter gave me a head start on taking notes and on participating in class. It really helped me get into the class."*

Aaron: *"I use my course syllabus to know what chapter is going to be covered in class each day. Then I read the chapter in advance. That initial reading helps me participate in class and also take better notes."*

Michelle: *"I read textbook material before class. If you do this in advance, the class will make a lot more sense. Always read your assignments ahead of time like your teachers tell you to. You may think, 'Oh, I'll just get it all in the lecture,' but that's not going to happen. If you go in cold with your assignment unread, you're not going to get nearly as much out of the lecture as you could."*

Aaron Benson

Michelle Wimberly is a graduate of Wesleyan University.

On Reviewing Notes after Class:

Kenyon: *"Go over notes right after class. The sooner the better. Get your brain to process the information as soon as possible. I go back to my room after a class, organize the notes, and make them clear. And if I feel I have energy to study right then, I go with it."*

Michelle: *"I review class notes right after the class is over or later in the day while the material is fresh in my mind. If I waited until a week later, they would look like gibberish to me. And reviewing the past notes every day with the present ones helps out tremendously as a refresher."*

Kenyon Whittington

METHODS FOR STUDYING CLASS NOTES

Study Method 1: Recall Words

Here is one effective way to study your notes:

1   Use the margin space at the side (or top) of each page. Jot down in the margin a series of key words or phrases from your notes. These key words or phrases, known as *recall words,* will help you pull together and remember the important ideas on the page.

On the facing page are notes from a communications course. (You'll see that the student, Gail, carefully labeled and dated her notes at the top. She also wrote down certain abbreviations she used to save time while taking notes.) As you look over Gail's notes, you'll notice in the side margin the recall words that she used for studying her notes.

2   To test yourself on the material, turn the recall words in the margin into questions. For instance, Gail asked herself, "What are the five ways to deal with conflict?" After she could recite the answer without looking at it, she asked herself, "What is the definition and an example of withdrawal?" Gail then went back and retested herself on the first question. When she could recite the answer to both the first and the second question, she went on to the third one, and so on.

This study method—jotting down key words, turning them into questions, and reciting them—is an excellent way to study. The next chapter, "Improving Your Memory and Study Power," will explain self-testing in more detail.

Lamel Jackson

Lamel: "*I'll write down little words in the margins of my notes. Then I use the words to test myself on remembering the material. I'll go over and over the material until I can recite it all to myself.*"

Aaron: "*I'll put key words in the margin of my notes and use them to test myself, to see how much of my notes I can recite.*"

Aaron Benson

Gail's Classroom Notes

	Communication 101 *11-17-01*
5 WAYS TO	*w = withdrawal sur = surrender agg = aggression per = persuasion*
DEAL WITH	
CONFLICT:	*Conflict in relationships: In any relationship there will be conflict and disagreement.*
	5 ways of dealing with conflict:
Withdrawal	*1. Withdrawal—removing oneself from the situation.*
	* Can be physical w. (ex.—leave room where someone is smoking) or psycho-*
	logical w. (ex.—try to ignore the smoke and focus on watching TV instead).
	* Often a negative way to deal with conflict except when the conflict is between*
	people who seldom see each other. Ex.—if you don't like someone smoking but see
	her only for a few minutes a month, it might be better to ignore it.
Surrender	*2. Surrender—giving in immediately to avoid conflict.*
	* Ex.—Husband doesn't want to go to a party but his wife does so he agrees.*
	* Habitual sur. is a negative way to deal with conflict. Can cause a lot of hidden*
	anger.
Aggression	*3. Aggression—the use of physical or psychological force to get one's way.*
	* Ex.—Person wins an argument because he is bigger and louder and more*
	threatening.
	* Agg. is always negative, increasing conflict and not resolving it.*
Persuasion	*4. Persuasion—the attempt to change the attitude or behavior of another person by*
	argument and reasoning.
	* Ex.—Husband persuades wife they should get a larger car rather than a mid-*
	size one so they'll have more room for family luggage on trips.
	* Pers. can be a positive way to resolve conflict except if it turns into manipulation.*
Discussion	*5. Discussion—verbally considering the pros and cons of the issues in a conflict.*
	* Ex.—Husband and wife work together and try to come up with all the pluses*
	and minuses of buying a certain kind of car.
	* The best way to deal with a conflict because it preserves equality. It's often hard*
	to do unless people are ready to cooperate and do their honest, objective best.

Study Method 2: Study Sheets

Some students prefer to write out on separate sheets of paper the material they want to learn. They prepare study sheets that often use a question-and-answer format. The very act of writing out study notes is itself a step toward remembering the material. Shown below is a study sheet that Gail could have prepared.

Sample Study Sheet

	What are the five ways to deal with conflict?
	1) withdrawal 2) surrender 3) aggression 4) persuasion 5) discussion
	What is withdrawal and an example?
	W. means removing oneself from a situation. Physical w. (leave a room where
	someone smoking) or psychological w. (ignore smoke and focus on TV instead)
	What is surrender and an example?
	Sur. is giving in immediately to avoid conflict. Husband doesn't want to go to a
	party but his wife does so he agrees.
	What is aggression and an example?
	Agg. is the use of physical or psychological force to get one's way. Person wins an
	argument because he is bigger and louder and more threatening.
	What is persuasion and an example?
	Pers. is the attempt to change the attitude or behavior of another person by
	argument and reasoning. Husband persuades wife to get a larger car so more
	room for luggage.
	What is discussion and an example?
	Discussion is verbally considering the pros and cons of the issues in a conflict.
	Couple works together to look at all the pluses and minuses of buying a certain
	car.

Study Method 3: Note Cards

Many students use note cards as a handy way to study material. They can easily carry the cards around and study them at different times during the day. Each card has a question on one side and the answer on the other side.

Sample Note Card

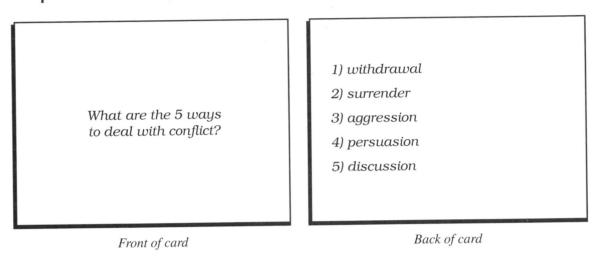

*What are the 5 ways
to deal with conflict?*

1) withdrawal

2) surrender

3) aggression

4) persuasion

5) discussion

Front of card   *Back of card*

Two Final Thoughts

1 If you are serious about succeeding in school, you must go to class and take good notes. If you are not doing these things, try to take an honest look inside yourself to figure out just why.

2 You should go right on from this chapter to the next one. In "Improving Your Memory and Study Power," you will get a detailed explanation of just how to master your classroom notes in preparation for exams.

FINAL ACTIVITIES

1   Check Your Understanding

Answer the following questions to check your understanding of the chapter.

1. How much material do most people forget after they've heard it in class?
    a. 20 percent in two weeks and 60 percent in four weeks.
    b. 40 percent in two weeks and 80 percent in four weeks.
    c. 80 percent in two weeks and 95 percent in four weeks.
    d. 60 percent in two weeks and 100 percent in four weeks.

2. Which of the following is *not* one of the six steps in good note-taking?
    a. Write your notes in a systematic way.
    b. Write down examples.
    c. Review your notes once every week.
    d. Sit in the front of the classroom.

3. When the author tried the technique of listening during class and writing down notes afterward, what happened?
    a. His grades improved.
    b. He remembered everything he heard.
    c. He failed the class.
    d. He could not remember much of what the instructor said.

4. If you are bored by a class, you should
    a. drop it and take it another semester.
    b. explain to the instructor that you find the class boring.
    c. skip it frequently and take few notes.
    d. make yourself do well in it so you get it over with.

5. You should always write down
    a. anything the instructor puts on the board.
    b. definitions.
    c. lists.
    d. all of the above.

2   Questions for Writing or Discussion

You may find it helpful to think about and write out your answers to the following questions. Or your instructor may put you in a small group or pair you with another student and have you discuss the questions with each other.

1. Where do you typically choose to sit in a classroom? Why? What effect does sitting in that location have on your performance in class? How might sitting in another location affect your performance?

2. On the question of what to write down in class, the text says that "you will soon develop an instinct for what is meaningful and what is not." What are some of *your* personal guidelines that help you decide what to write down during a lecture? What clues do you look for that something is important?

3. Do you take notes in a systematic way—that is, do you have a system that you follow regarding what paper and pens you use, how much of the page you use, and what abbreviations or symbols you use? If you have a system, describe it. If not, explain why you think a system would or would not be beneficial to you.

4. Get together with a partner and look at the following notes from a college criminal justice class:

Police action on a federal level is carried out by more than 60 agencies. The five largest of those agencies are

1. *Federal Bureau of Investigation (FBI). Founded in 1908. Now largest federal police agency with 28,000 employees. In World War II era FBI focused on national security—investigating Nazi and Communist activity in U.S. Today FBI is primarily concerned today with organized crime, street gangs, and drug activity.*

2. *Drug Enforcement Administration (DEA). Founded 1973. Enforces federal laws concerning use, sale, and distribution of narcotics in U.S. Also helps foreign governments reduce availability of illegal drugs.*

3. *Bureau of Alcohol, Tobacco, and Firearms (ATF). Created in 1919 to enforce Prohibition laws banning alcohol. Focus now on reducing illegal use of firearms.*

4. *Immigration and Naturalization Service (INS). Established 1924. Oversees the admission, naturalization, and deportation of aliens. The Border Patrol (BP) is division of INS. BP patrols 8,000 miles of U.S. international borders to prevent illegal entry of aliens.*

5. *U.S. Secret Service (SS). Established in 1865 to investigate counterfeiting. Became responsible for protecting president after assassination of Pres. McKinley in 1901. Protects the president, vice president, presidential candidates, visiting heads of state, and executive buildings.*

One of you try out *Study Method 1: Recall Words* as a method of studying these notes. In the margin of this page, jot down key words or phrases that will help you remember the important ideas presented. On a separate piece of paper, turn the recall words into questions that you could use to test yourself on the material

Meanwhile, the other partner should use *Study Method 2: Study Sheets.* On a separate piece of paper, write out questions and answers that would help you remember the ideas presented in these notes.

When you are both finished, show your partner what you have done. Discuss how effective you think the method you used would be in helping you remember the material presented.

3 Writing about Classroom Note-taking

Write a paragraph in which you evaluate your classroom note-taking skills. Which of the steps in good note-taking described in this chapter do you practice? Which do you not practice? Begin your paragraph with one of the **points** on the next page.

Point: I am a good classroom note-taker; I practice many of the tips described in the chapter.

Point: I have not been a good classroom note-taker; I practice few if any of the tips described in the chapter.

Point: My classroom note-taking skills are mixed; I follow some helpful tips but ignore others.

After you have chosen your point, provide **supporting details or examples** to back it up. For instance, if you have decided to support the second point above, you might say in part:

In class I often doodle rather than take notes. I go into a kind of doodling trance and when the lecture is over, I have two pages of doodles and a couple of words the instructor put on the board. Since I wasn't paying attention, the words make make no sense whatsoever.

When writing your paragraph, use examples and details that are based on your actual experience.

4   Speaking about Class Note-taking

Imagine that you have been asked to give a speech on good note-taking to a class of students who will be entering college in the fall. Prepare a talk full of practical advice that really communicates with them. Imagine that the students have been told beforehand that you will be as stiff and dry as a board and that your talk will have little relevance or value. You have two goals, then: 1) to use language and images that really connect with students, and 2) to pack your talk with lots of truly helpful information. Your speech should be five to ten minutes long.

6 / Improving Your Memory and Study Power

WHY AND HOW TO MEMORIZE

To do well in school, you must know how to learn material in an effective way. Much learning involves memorizing the most important ideas that you hear in class and read in textbooks. The word "memorize" may turn you off—but it should not. Effective memorizing will not only help you *remember* ideas; it will also help you more fully *understand* those ideas. The following pages show you three key steps for developing a powerful memory. Some other study hints are then provided as well.

Step 1: Organize the Material to Be Learned

Let's say you're in a social science class and the instructor is talking about the different kinds of personal space in everyday life. The instructor explains that there are four personal zones or spaces.

- The first zone is *intimate distance*, from body contact to one foot away. This space is reserved for just a few people—lovers, parents and children, health professionals such as doctors or dentists.

- The second zone is *personal distance*, from one to four feet away. This zone is for personal conversations with close friends. On a crowded elevator, where people may get very close to us, we often avoid eye contact as a way of protecting our personal space.

- The third zone is *social distance*, from four to ten feet. This zone is used for social conversations and business transactions.

- The final zone is *public distance*, which is ten feet and beyond. Communication in a large lecture hall or a performance on a stage are examples.

The instructor takes time to explain all this information about personal space. She writes the four kinds of personal space on the board and defines and gives examples of each kind of space. If you're being a good student, you realize that the instructor regards this information as important, so you write it down. You are now ready to study it and remember it. Here's how to proceed.

Your first step is to **organize the material to be learned.** How do you do this?

One of the best ways to organize material is to create a numbered list using the numbers 1, 2, 3, and so on. In the above case, here is the list you could create:

Study Notes

Four Kinds of Personal Space

1. *Intimate distance (body contact to one foot away; ex. is parent holding a child)*
2. *Personal distance (one to four feet; ex. is conversation with a friend)*
3. *Social distance (four to ten feet; ex. is social conversation)*
4. *Public distance (ten feet and beyond; ex. is lecture)*

Now that you have organized the material, you are ready to memorize it. The next step explains how to do so.

Step 2: Test Yourself Repeatedly on the Material to Be Learned

Memorizing is done through repeated self-testing. Look at the first item in your notes, and then look away and try to repeat it to yourself. When you can repeat the first item, look at the next item; then look away and try to repeat it. When you can repeat the second item, go back without looking at your notes and test yourself again on the first and second items. After you can recall the first and second items without referring to your notes, go on to the third item. In short, follow this procedure: *After you learn each new item, go back and test yourself on all the previous items.* This constant review is at the heart of self-testing and is the key to effective memorization.

See if you can complete each of the following statements.

- If you were memorizing a list of five definitions, what would you do after you mastered the second definition? _____

  _____

- What would you do after you mastered the third definition? _____

  _____

- What would you do after you mastered the fifth definition? _____

  _____

- Memorize the four kinds of personal space. Take five to ten minutes to do so. Then, on a blank sheet of paper, see if you can write down from memory the four kinds of space, including the definition and an example for each one.

Teron Ivery is a student at Millersville University.

Teron: "*I always start by organizing things; that's the key first step. I often do this by preparing flashcards based on class and textbook notes. After I get all my material together, then I go to study it in a quiet spot.*

"*The object is for me to be able to answer the questions on the flashcards without looking at the answers. I try to say the material to myself. When I can say an answer without looking at it, I go on to the next flashcard. After I'm done with a flashcard, I go back and review the old flashcards. I just keep going over the material again and again like this until it's all in my head.*"

Michelle: "*I start by organizing all my notes. Once you have everything on sheets of paper in front of you, you can start to memorize it. You know you have it memorized when you can say it without looking at it. And you just have to keep reviewing as you go.*"

Michelle Wimberly

May Lam

May: " *I work my way backward through my notes. First I go over what I've just learned until I can say it to myself. Then I work my way back, reviewing everything else. You have to be able to say everything to yourself.*"

Terry: "*The first step in memorizing is to get everything organized. I get my notes as clear as I can and add in anything from the textbook that makes sense. Then I'll write key words in the margins of my notes. I'll convert them to little questions and see if I can say the answers to myself. You have to do that and just keep reviewing to get it in your head.*"

Terry Oakman

Step 3: Use Key Words and First-Letter Words

Key words can be used as "hooks" to help you remember ideas. A *key word* stands for an entire idea. It is so central to the idea that if you remember the key word, you are almost guaranteed to remember the entire concept that goes with the word.

In the example above, the key words are *intimate, personal, social,* and *public.* If you can memorize and remember these words, they will help you remember the information that goes with each word.

Now you can just memorize these words "cold," if you like, but it is much easier to use a first-letter word. A *first-letter word* is a word made up of the first letters of key words. (Sometimes first-letter words are called *acronyms* or *made-up words* or *catchwords.*) Look again at the four key words that help you remember the four kinds of personal spaces:

Intimate
Personal
Social
Public

Here are the first letters of these key words: IPSP. Take a moment and see if you can rearrange these letters to form an easily recalled first-letter word. (The word does not have to be a real word; it can be a made-up word. What counts is that if you make up the word, you will be likely to remember it.)

- *My first-letter word is* _____

One first-letter word that might help you remember the letters IPSP is SIPP.

After you create a first-letter word, test yourself until you are sure each letter stands for a key word in your mind. Here is how you might use SIPP to pull into memory the four kinds of personal space:

SIPP

S = social
I = intimate
P = personal
P = public

To study with the help of a first-letter word, cover the key words with a sheet of paper, leaving only the first letter exposed. Look at the letter *S* and test yourself until you can recall the key word *social* and the information that goes with it (four to ten feet; for example, a social conversation). Next, look at the letter *I* and test yourself until you can remember the key word *intimate.* Then do the same with the letter *P*, making sure it helps you call into memory the key words *personal* and *public.* In each case, the first letter serves as a hook to pull into memory a key word, and the key word is also a hook that helps you remember an entire idea.

Now when you go into an exam, you can write down your made-up word, SIPP, as soon as you get the test. If there is a question about the four kinds of personal space, you'll be all set. Each of those letters can help you call into memory a key word, and each of those key words can help you remember an entire idea.

➤ **Activity: First-Letter Words**

1. An instructor gives a lecture on reasons for drug use. Three reasons that he cites are 1) escape, 2) rebellion, and 3) despair. See if you can make up a first-letter word that helps you remember the first letters of these three words: E, R, and D. Write your word here: _____

2. A science instructor talks about the three ways that America deals with its waste disposal problem: 1) incineration, 2) landfills, and 3) recycling. Make up a first-letter word that helps you remember the three methods of waste disposal. Write your word here: _____

3. A health instructor spends a class talking about three kinds of fatigue: 1) physical, 2) emotional, and 3) pathological. She also talks about four ways to offset fatigue: 1) diet, 2) exercise, 3) sleep, and 4) breaks. Make up two first-letter words to help you remember this material. Write your words here: _____ _____

4. A business instructor presents in class four methods of relating to employees:

    a. Show a genuine interest in what employees have to say.
    b. Call employees by their first names.
    c. Look workers in the eye when speaking to them.
    d. Admit mistakes.

    Pick out a key word for each method—a word that will help you remember the method. Write your key words here: _____ _____

    _____ _____

    Among your best choices for the four key words would be *interest, first, eye,* and *mistakes.*

    Now see if you can make up a four-letter word that will help you remember the four key words. (The key words will, in turn, help you remember the four methods of relating to employees.) Write your word here: _____

5. A psychology instructor writes on the board several built-in problems of every marriage:

    a. Freedom is limited.
    b. Arguments about money often arise.
    c. The couple is often an isolated unit, living apart from relatives.
    d. The romance of falling in love is replaced by the hard work of everyday living.

    Pick out a key word within each problem—a word that will help you remember the problem. Write your key words here: _____ _____

    _____ _____

    Among your best choices for the four key words would be *freedom, money, isolated,* and *romance.*

    Now see if you can make up a four-letter word that will help you remember the four key words. (The key words will, in turn, help you remember the four built-in problems of every marriage.) Write your word here: _____

An Important Note about First-Letter Sentences

Another way to remember key words is to form an easily recalled *first-letter sentence*. Each word in a first-letter sentence begins with the first letter of a different key word. For example, it would be helpful to remember the four kinds of personal space in sequence, from the closest to the farthest away:

Four Kinds of Personal Space

1. Intimate distance (body contact to one foot away; ex. is parent holding a child)
2. Personal distance (one to four feet; ex. is conversation with a friend)
3. Social distance (four to ten feet; ex. is social conversation)
4. Public distance (ten feet and beyond; ex. is lecture)

To remember the kinds of space in order, you could write a four-word sentence with the first word beginning with *I*, the second word with *P*, the third word with *S*, and the final word with *P*. Here is a first-letter sentence you might create:

I **P**atted **S**ome **P**igs.

Note that your first-letter sentence (it can also be a phrase) does not have to be perfect grammatically, and it does not have to make perfect sense. It simply needs to be a line that you create and will stick in your memory. Sometimes the more crazy and colorful the line, the more likely it is you will remember it!

➤ Activity: First-Letter Sentences

1. Suppose a psychology instructor wants you to learn the three stages of very young children's play.

   Three stages in young children's play:

   1. Solitary (individual play rather than play with others)
   2. Parallel (children take part in similar activities, such as digging in the sand; they are often near one another, but they hardly interact at all)
   3. Cooperative (children began to interact with each other, perhaps building something in the sand together)

   Make up a first-letter phrase or sentence that will help you remember *in sequence* the three stages of children's play. Write the phrase or sentence here:

   _____

2. Suppose a business instructor wants you to remember the four ways of transporting products, from the least expensive to the most expensive.

   Four ways to transport products:

   1. Boat (least expensive)   3. Railroad
   2. Truck   4. Airplane (most expensive)

   Make up a first-letter phrase or sentence that will help you remember *in sequence* the methods of transportation. Write your phrase or sentence here:

   _____

3. Suppose a sociology instructor wants you to learn the following five influences on a child's personality, which are listed in order of importance.

Influences on Children:

1. Parents
2. Siblings (brothers and sisters)
3. Friends
4. Relatives
5. Teachers

Make up a first-letter sentence that will help you remember *in order* the five influences on children. Write the sentence here:

_____

David Killingsworth is a student at West Chester University.

David: "I use made-up words and even made-up sentences to help me remember things. For example, to remember the four reasons why people join groups (security, community, achievement, power), I made up the word SCAP. The 'S' in SCAP helps me remember 'security,' the 'C' helps me remember 'community,' and so on."

Michelle: "To remember something in sequence, I would make up funny sentences that were easy to remember. If I made up the sentence, I would remember it. The funny sentences—you call them first-letter sentences—were a great help. For example, if a professor wanted me to know Abraham Maslow's five basic human needs in their order of importance (biological, safety, companionship, esteem, and self-actualization), I'd use the made-up sentence, 'Billy's sister can't e-mail Shakira.'"

Michelle Wimberly

SOME OTHER STUDY TIPS

1 Intend to Remember

An important aid to memory is that you *decide* to remember. This bit of advice appears so obvious that many people overlook its value. But if you have made the decision to remember something and you then work at mastering it, you *will* remember. No one is born with a naturally poor memory; if you work at it, you can have a memory like a bear trap.

- Do you ever have trouble, as many people do, in remembering the names of persons you are introduced to? _____ Yes _____ No

- If you do, the reason is probably that you did not consciously decide to remember their names. Suppose you were introduced to a person who was going to borrow money from you. Is it safe to say you would make it a point to remember (and so would remember) the person's name? _____ Yes _____ No

The lesson here is that *your attitude is crucial in effective memorization.* You must begin by saying, "I am going to master this." If you *decide* to remember, you *will* remember.

2 Spread Out Memory Work and Give Yourself Rewards

If you try to do a great deal of studying at any one time, you may have trouble absorbing the material. Always try to spread out your memory work. For instance, three one-hour sessions will be more effective than one three-hour session.

Spacing memory work over several time periods gives you a chance to review and lock in material you have studied in an earlier session but have begun to forget. Research shows that we begin to forget a good deal of information right after studying it. However, review within a day reduces much of this memory loss. So try to review new material within twenty-four hours after you first study it. Then, if possible, review again several days later to make a third impression or "imprint" of the material in your memory. If you work consistently to retain ideas and details, they are not likely to escape you when you need them during an exam.

- Do you typically try to study the material for a test all at once, or do you spread out your study over several sessions?

  _____

- How might you spread out ten hours of memory work that you need to do for a biology exam?

  _____

  _____

After you have put in a solid period of study, give yourself a reward. For example, after forty-five minutes of study, take a fifteen-minute break. Call a friend, watch TV, listen to a song, chat for a few minutes, get a snack.

Tynara Chappelle

Andy Cao

Jasmin Santana

Tynara: *"Cramming was the only way I studied for a while, and my grades went downhill. Then I started putting everything on note cards, and I'd carry those with me wherever I'd go. With the cards I'd be able to take quick study breaks at work and any other time I had to study. I spread out study rather than jamming it all into one crazy cram session."*

Jennifer: *"I came up with this reward system. For example, I'd tell myself that if I read three chapters, afterward I would watch my favorite television show. The rewards really motivated me."*

Andy: *"I study whenever I can: at lunch, between classes, early in the morning. You have to take advantage of time you have. You can't do it all at once."*

Michelle: *"I built in rewards as I study. If I concentrated well for 90 minutes, I let myself step out to get a soda or make a phone call. A 10–15 minute break would refresh me so I could get back to work."*

Jasmin: *"Instead of stuffing my brain with new material before an exam, I study whenever and wherever I can all through the term. If I get a break at work, I study. At lunch, I study. I grab little bits and pieces of time all day to study. And once I'm home, it's pretty much studying from after dinner until bedtime, with some short reward breaks along the way."*

Jennifer McCaul

Michelle Wimberly

3   Get Your Body Involved in the Study Process

Do not try to study in a completely relaxed position. If you stretch out on a bed or slouch in an easy chair, you're telling your body to relax, not to focus. Slight muscular tension promotes the concentration needed for study. So sit on an upright chair or sit in a cross-legged position on your bed with a pillow behind you. Keep in mind, also, that you do not have to study while sitting down. Many students stay alert and focused by walking back and forth across the room as they test themselves on material they must learn.

- What is your usual position when you study? _____

- Are your muscles slightly tense in this position, or are they completely relaxed?

  _____

4   Study before Going to Bed

Study material you need to learn right up until the time you go to sleep. Don't watch a late movie or allow other activities to interfere with your new learning. Chances are your mind will work through and absorb much of this material during the night. Set your clock a half hour earlier than usual so that you will have time to go over the material as soon as you get up. The morning review will help fix the material solidly in your memory.

- Have you ever used this technique and found it to be helpful? _____

5   Focus on the Future

Few students have a deep interest in every one of their courses. Chances are that at least some of the studying you have to do involves uninteresting material. In such cases, you must simply decide that you will make yourself study, because someday the course will be forgotten, but your education and degree will be benefiting your life.

- What are the most unpleasant study tasks you will have this semester? _____

  _____

- Is graduation important enough for you to do these unpleasant tasks? _____

Dr. Ben Carson

Dr. Carson: "*I had this problem in school. I would fall asleep when I began studying my assignments. I soon discovered an effective solution: I would stand up—or actually walk around the room—while I read. The standing and walking kept me awake.*"

Terry: "*I never try to study by sitting or lying on the bed; I'll go to sleep. If I'm home, I'll walk around and actually recite the material out loud to myself. I'll get my body into it because I can focus and concentrate more.*"

Terry Oakman

Lamel Jackson

Lamel: "*You've got to know your learning style. Me, I remember things when they're connected with something physical, like using my hands. As I'm studying I talk aloud to myself, explain something to myself, and I'll gesture with my hands in a certain way.*"

Kenyon: "*When I study material, I say it out loud. I may be walking on campus, or sitting or walking around in my room. Also, I normally go over material right before I go to sleep. Then I get up a little early to review it. It works for me.*"

Kenyon Whittington

FINAL ACTIVITIES

1   Check Your Understanding

Answer the following questions to check your understanding of the chapter.

1. Effective memorizing helps you
   a. create ideas.
   b. remember ideas.
   c. understand ideas.
   d. remember and understand ideas.

2. Before you try to memorize material, you need to
   a. test yourself on it.
   b. organize it.
   c. use key words.
   d. give yourself a reward.

3. Which of the following does the author call "the heart of self-testing"?
   a. Constant review of the material you are memorizing.
   b. Creating numbered lists.
   c. Making flashcards.
   d. Intending to remember.

4. As defined in this chapter, a "key word" is
   a. a word, real or nonsense, made up of the first letters of the words you are memorizing.
   b. an acronym.
   c. a word that is central to the idea you are memorizing.
   d. the first word in the idea you are memorizing.

5. Which of the following is *not* recommended by the author?
   a. Spread memory work over several sessions.
   b. Build in rewards after solid periods of study.
   c. After an evening study session, relax by watching a movie.
   d. Study in a position that makes your body slightly tense.

2   Questions for Writing or Discussion

You may find it helpful to think about and write out your answers to the following questions. Or your instructor may put you in a small group or pair you with another student and have you discuss the questions with each other.

1. What is your typical internal response when you face the need to memorize material?

   ____ "No problem—I know how to do this."

   ____ "Memorize! I can't memorize!"

   ____ Something in between.

   Why do you feel the way you do?

2. You have learned in this chapter that the key to memorization is to organize the material first. Do you typically organize material in some way before you memorize it? How do you organize the material?

3. What is a class you have taken that required a good deal of memorization? How successful (or unsuccessful) at memorizing the material were you? How much effort (honestly now!) did you put into trying to memorize the material?

4. Suppose in a sociology class you are told to memorize three factors that help to determine a person's social status. Those three factors are **wealth**, **education**, and **occupation**. What first-letter word could you use to help you remember those three factors? _____

5. Imagine that for your psychology class, you need to memorize a list of four stimulants. Those stimulants are **caffeine**, **nicotine**, **amphetamines**, and **cocaine**. Invent a first-letter sentence that would help you remember those four items.

_____

6. A psychology instructor spends a class talking about four reasons why people daydream: 1) to **escape** a boring class or job, 2) to let go of **anger**, 3) to **compensate** for some missing need, and 4) to plan for the **future**. Make up a first-letter word (a real word or a nonsense word) to help you remember the four boldfaced words. _____

7. Suppose you have taken the following notes in a speech class:

    Methods for a speaker to get an audience's attention:

    1. *Surprise your audience. Begin a speech on nutrition by saying, "Americans are shortening their lives with dinner."*
    2. *Ask questions. Could ask questions like, "What did you have for dinner this evening? Will it add to your health?"*
    3. *Tell a story. It can be a true story or even a tall tale that makes your point.*
    4. *Use a quotation.*

    You know you'll need to remember for a test all four methods of getting an audience's attention. Your first step should be to pick out a key word that will help you remember each method. Write your four key words here:

    _____   _____   _____   _____

    Among your best choices for the four key words would be *surprise, ask, story*, and *quotation*. What is a first-letter sentence that will help you remember these key words?

    _____

8. Suppose a history instructor expects you to remember certain material from a textbook chapter. Here is one passage from that chapter and your outline of the passage:

    In colonial America, medical science was so dangerous that it was often safer to remain sick than it was to be treated for illness. One of the most popular treatments for illness was bloodletting. This involved cutting a patient's skin and allowing him or her to bleed in order to remove the cause of a disease. Sometimes so much blood was lost that patients would grow weak and die. Another example of a harmful treatment used in colonial America was "sweating." A patient would be forced to stay in a small, hot room covered in the heaviest clothing and blankets available. Often the heat would worsen the patient's condition. The result was extreme weakness, heat exhaustion, and sometimes death. A final treatment that hurt patients more than it helped them was purging. This treatment was based on the idea that a poison was in the body and could be removed by vomiting. Patients would be forced to take a syrup-like mixture that would make them uncontrollably sick to the stomach. With all these treatments, the "cure" was usually worse than the disease.

Study outline

Dangerous medical treatments in colonial America:

1. Bloodletting—cutting skin and letting patient bleed
2. Sweating—forcing a patient to stay in a small hot room, heavily covered
3. Purging—forcing patients to take a liquid that would make them vomit.

What is a first-letter phrase or sentence that will help you remember the three dangerous treatments? _____

9. Suppose a sociology instructor wants you to remember the five stages of the dying process identified by Elisabeth Kübler-Ross, from the first stage to the final one.

   1. Denial   4. Depression
   2. Anger   5. Acceptance
   3. Bargaining

What is a first-letter phrase or sentence that will help you remember in sequence the five stages in the process? _____

3 Writing about Memory and Study Skills

Write a paragraph in which you evaluate your memory and study skills. Which steps or tips described in the chapter do you practice? Which do you not practice? Begin your paragraph with one of the **points** below.

Point: I am good at memory and study skills; I practice the tips in this chapter.

Point: I have not been good at memory and study skills; I practice few if any of the tips described in this chapter.

Point: My memory and study skills are mixed; I use some helpful tips and ignore others.

After you have chosen your point, provide **supporting details or examples** to back up your point. For instance, to support the second point above, you might say in part:

> When it comes to studying and memorizing material, I've never seriously tried any special techniques. I just read the material and hope I remember it. I often catch myself just reading words without thinking about what the words mean. For example, I'll just keep reading over and over the definition of sublimation without thinking about what it really means. As a result, I often don't remember terms when I take a test.

When writing your paragraph, use examples and details based on your actual experience.

4 Speaking about Memory and Study Skills

Imagine that you have been asked to give a speech on memory and study skills to a class of students who will be entering college in the fall. Prepare a talk full of practical advice that really communicates with them. Imagine that the students have been told beforehand that you will be as stiff and dry as a board and that your talk will have little relevance or value. You have two goals, then: 1) to use language and images that really connect with students, and 2) to pack your talk with lots of truly helpful information. Your speech should be five to ten minutes long.

7 / Reading Textbooks and Taking Notes

A CAUTION ABOUT RELYING ON THE TEXTBOOK ALONE

Before you begin this chapter, consider the following: *You may not even need to read your textbook if you take good classroom notes!* The truth is that, in many courses, good class notes will be enough to earn you a decent grade! Your textbook may be needed only once in a while to fill out or add to important ideas presented in class.

And here's another truth: *Not all textbooks are well written.* You're in a heap of trouble if you have to depend for your knowledge of a subject on a textbook that may not present its ideas in a clear, organized way. Your best source of information on your subject is what your instructor presents in class, *so be there and take good notes.*

A PROVEN TEXTBOOK STUDY METHOD

Your idea of studying a textbook assignment may be simply to read it once or twice. If that's all you do, chances are you'll have little to show for it. To succeed, you need a *systematic* way to read and study. The PRWR system described below is an excellent way to boost your study power. By using PRWR, you'll become a better reader, you'll remember much more of what you read, and you'll be able to study effectively.

PRWR stands for the system's four steps:

1 **P**review the reading.
2 **R**ead the material and mark important parts.
3 **W**rite notes to help you study the material.
4 **R**ecite the ideas in your notes.

You can put this system to work immediately. Each step is explained in detail on the pages that follow, and a textbook selection is included for you to practice on.

Step 1: Preview the Reading

When you go to a party, you might look the scene over to locate the food, check out the music, and see who's there. After getting an overview of what's happening, you'll feel more at ease and ready to get down to the business of serious partying. In like manner, a several-minute preview of a reading gives you a general overview of the selection before you begin to read closely. By "breaking the ice" and providing a quick sense of the new material, the preview will help you get into the reading more easily. There are four parts to a good preview:

- **Consider the title.** The title is often a tiny summary of the selection. Use it to help you focus on the central idea of the material. For instance, a selection titled "Theories of Personality" will tell you to expect a list of differing theories of personality.

- **Read over the first and last paragraphs of the selection.** The first paragraph or so of a reading is often an introduction. It may give you a quick sense of the main ideas in the selection. The last paragraphs may be a summary of the reading and give you another general view of the main ideas.

- **Notice headings and relationships between headings.** Main headings tell you what sections are about. They are generally printed in darker or larger type; they may be printed in capital letters or in a different color. The main headings under the title "Theories of Personality," for example, would probably tell you which theories are being covered.

     Subheadings fall under main headings and help identify and organize the material under main heads. Subheads are printed in a way that makes them more prominent than the text but less prominent than the main headings. A selection may even contain sub-subheadings to label and organize material under the subheads. Here is how a series of heads might look:

MAIN HEAD (at the margin in larger type)
Subhead (indented and in slightly smaller type)
Sub-subhead (further indented and in even smaller type)

Together, the headings may form a general outline of a selection. Notice, for instance, the main heading and subheads in the textbook selection on the next three pages.

- **Sample the text here and there.** Read some of the items that are set off in **boldface** or *italic* type. Get a sense of how many definitions and examples there are. Look at some of the visuals (pictures, diagrams, and graphs).

Does all this sound like a waste of time to you? Wouldn't it be better just to get on with reading the assignment? Not at all! The simple fact is that previewing *works*. The few minutes spent on previewing will help you to better understand a selection once you do read it.

➤ Activity: Previewing

To see how previewing works, take about three minutes to preview the following textbook selection, taken from a widely used college textbook: *Communicate!* Sixth Edition, by Rudolph F. Verderber (Wadsworth).

DISCLOSING FEELINGS

An extremely important aspect of self-disclosure is the sharing of feelings. We all experience feelings such as happiness at receiving an unexpected gift, sadness about the breakup of a relationship, or anger when we believe we have been taken advantage of. The question is whether to disclose such feelings, and if so, how. Self-disclosure of feelings usually will be most successful not when feelings are withheld or displayed but when they are described. Let's consider each of these forms of dealing with feelings.

Withholding Feelings

Withholding feelings—that is, keeping them inside and not giving any verbal or nonverbal cues to their existence—is generally an inappropriate means of dealing with feelings. Withholding feelings is best exemplified by the good poker player who develops a "poker face," a neutral look that is impossible to decipher. The look is the same whether the player's cards are good or bad. Unfortunately, many people use poker faces in their relationships, so that no one knows whether they hurt inside, are extremely excited, and so on. For instance, Doris feels very nervous when Candy stands over her while Doris is working on her report. And when Candy says, "That first paragraph isn't very well written," Doris begins to seethe, yet she says nothing—she withholds her feelings.

Psychologists believe that when people withhold feelings, they can develop physical problems such as ulcers, high blood pressure, and heart disease, as well as psychological problems such as stress-related neuroses and psychoses. Moreover, people who withhold feelings are often perceived as cold, undemonstrative, and not much fun to be around.

Is withholding ever appropriate? When a situation is inconsequential, you may well choose to withhold your feelings. For instance, a stranger's inconsiderate behavior at a party may bother you, but because you can move to another part of the room, withholding may not be detrimental. In the example of Doris's seething at Candy's behavior, however, withholding could be costly to Doris.

Displaying Feelings

Displaying feelings means expressing those feelings through a facial reaction, body response, and/or paralinguistic reaction. Cheering over a great play at a sporting event, booing the umpire at a perceived bad call, patting a person on the back when the person does something well, and saying, "What are you doing?" in a nasty tone of voice are all displays of feelings.

Displays are especially appropriate when the feelings you are experiencing are positive. For instance, when Gloria does something nice for you, and you experience a feeling of joy, giving her a big hug is appropriate; when Don gives you something you've wanted, and you experience a feeling of appreciation, a big smile or an "Oh, thank you, Don" is appropriate. In fact, many people need to be even more demonstrative of good feelings. You've probably seen the bumper sticker "Have you hugged your kid today?" It reinforces the point that you need to display love and affection constantly to show another person that you really care.

Displays become detrimental to communication when the feelings you are experiencing are negative—especially when the display of a negative feeling appears to be an overreaction. For instance, when Candy stands over Doris while she is working on her report and says, "That first paragraph isn't very well written," Doris may well experience resentment. If Doris lashes out at Candy by screaming, "Who the hell asked you for your opinion?" Doris's display no doubt will hurt Candy's feelings and short-circuit their communication. Although displays of negative feelings may be good for you psychologically, they are likely to be bad for you interpersonally.

Describing Feelings

Describing feelings—putting your feelings into words in a calm, nonjudgmental way—tends to be the best method of disclosing feelings. Describing feelings not only increases chances for positive communication and decreases chances for short-circuiting lines of communication, it also teaches people how to treat you. When you describe your feelings, people are made aware of the effect of their behavior. This knowledge gives them the information needed to determine whether they should continue or repeat that behavior. If you tell Paul that you really feel flattered when he visits you, such a statement should encourage Paul to visit you again; likewise, when you tell Cliff that you feel very angry when he borrows your jacket without asking, he is more likely to ask the next time he borrows a jacket. Describing your feelings allows you to exercise a measure of control over others' behavior toward you.

Describing and displaying feelings are not the same. Many times people think they are describing when in fact they are displaying feelings or evaluating.

If describing feelings is so important to effective communication, why don't more people do it regularly? There seem to be at least four reasons why many people don't describe feelings.

1. *Many people have a poor vocabulary of words for describing the various feelings they are experiencing.* People can sense that they are angry; however, they may not know whether what they are feeling might best be described as annoyed, betrayed, cheated, crushed, disturbed, furious, outraged, or shocked. Each of these words describes a slightly different aspect of what many people lump together as anger.

2. *Many people believe that describing their true feelings reveals too much about themselves.* If you tell people when their behavior hurts you, you risk their using the information against you when they want to hurt you on purpose. Even so, the potential benefits of describing your feelings far outweigh the risks. For instance, if Pete has a nickname for you that you don't like and you tell Pete that calling you by that nickname really makes you nervous and tense, Pete may use the nickname when he wants to hurt you, but he is more likely to stop calling you by that name. If, on the other hand, you don't describe your feelings to Pete, he is probably going to call you by that name all the time because he doesn't know any better. When you say nothing, you reinforce his behavior. The level of risk varies with each situation, but you will more often improve a relationship than be hurt by describing feelings.

3. *Many people believe that if they describe feelings, others will make them feel guilty about having such feelings.* At a very tender age we all learned about "tactful" behavior. Under the premise that "the truth sometimes hurts" we learned to avoid the truth by not saying anything or by telling "little" lies. Perhaps when you were young your mother said, "Don't forget to give Grandma a great big kiss." At that time you may have blurted out, "Ugh—it makes me feel yucky to kiss Grandma. She's got a mustache." If your mother responded, "That's terrible—your grandma loves you. Now you give her a kiss and never let me hear you talk like that again!" then you probably felt guilty for having this "wrong" feeling. But the point is that the thought of kissing your grandma made you feel "yucky" whether it should have or not. In this case what was at issue was the way you talked about the feelings—not your having the feelings.

4. *Many people believe that describing feelings causes harm to others or to a*

relationship. If it really bothers Max when his girlfriend, Dora, bites her fingernails, Max may believe that describing his feelings to Dora will hurt her so much that the knowledge will drive a wedge into their relationship. So it's better for Max to say nothing, right? Wrong! If Max says nothing, he's still going to be bothered by Dora's behavior. In fact, as time goes on, Max will probably lash out at Dora for other things because he can't bring himself to talk about the behavior that really bothers him. The net result is that not only will Dora be hurt by Max's behavior, but she won't understand the true source of his feelings. By not describing his feelings, Max may well drive a wedge into their relationship anyway.

If Max does describe his feelings to Dora, she might quit or at least try to quit biting her nails; they might get into a discussion in which he finds out that she doesn't want to bite them but just can't seem to stop, and he can help her in her efforts to stop; or they might discuss the problem and Max may see that it is a small thing really and not let it bother him as much. The point is that in describing feelings the chances of a successful outcome are greater than they are in not describing them.

To describe your feelings, first put the emotion you are feeling into words. Be specific. Second, state what triggered the feeling. Finally, make sure you indicate that the feeling is yours. For example, suppose your roommate borrows your jacket without asking. When he returns, you describe your feelings by saying, "Cliff, I [indication that the feeling is yours] get really angry [the feeling] when you borrow my jacket without asking [trigger]." Or suppose that Carl has just reminded you of the very first time he brought you a rose. You describe your feelings by saying, "Carl, I [indication that the feeling is yours] get really tickled [the feeling] when you remind me about that first time you brought me a rose [trigger]."

You may find it easiest to begin by describing positive feelings: "I really feel elated knowing that you were the one who nominated me for the position" or "I'm delighted that you offered to help me with the housework." As you gain success with positive descriptions, you can try negative feelings attributable to environmental factors: "It's so cloudy; I feel gloomy" or "When the wind howls through the cracks, I really get jumpy." Finally, you can move to negative descriptions resulting from what people have said or done: "Your stepping in front of me like that really annoys me" or "The tone of your voice confuses me."

If you have previewed the above selection carefully, you already know a bit about it—without even having really read much. To confirm this for yourself, answer the following questions by just glancing back at the text:

- What is the selection about?   _____

- What are three ways of dealing with our feelings?

_____

_____

_____

- What are four reasons why many people don't describe feelings?

_____

_____

_____

_____

Thanks to the preview, you have picked out the important ideas in the selection—*even before you have fully read the selection.* Previewing can be a valuable first step to understanding and remembering textbook material.

Jasmin Santana

> ***Jasmin:*** *"When I start a new textbook chapter, I flip right away to the end of the chapter. There's often a little summary there that gives you an idea what important themes and ideas are covered in the chapter. Reading that first gives me a good preview of what I should be looking for as I study the whole chapter."*

> ***Helen:*** *"Before I begin a textbook, I spend a while previewing it. I read the index. I flip through the whole thing, noticing what's in bold type or set off in boxes. I look at pictures and read the captions. I also like to read the introduction. After that, I have a framework for the book as a whole and have a better idea what to expect of it."*

Helen Rowe

Step 2: Read the Material and Mark Important Parts

After previewing a selection, take the time to read it through from start to finish. Keep reading even if you run into some parts you don't understand. You can always come back to those parts. By reading straight through, you'll be in a better position to understand the difficult parts later.

As you read, mark points you feel are important. Marking will make it easy for you to find them later when you take study notes. The most important ideas of a selection include:

- Definitions
- Helpful examples
- Major lists of items
- Points that receive the most space, development, and attention

Because you noted some of these ideas during the preview, identifying them as you read will be easier.

Ways to Mark

Here are some ways to mark off important ideas:

- Underline definitions and identify them by writing *DEF* in the margin.
- Identify helpful examples by writing *EX* in the margin.
- Number 1, 2, 3, etc. the items in lists.
- Underline obviously important ideas. You can further set off important points by writing *IMP* in the margin. If important material is several lines long, do not underline it all, or you will end up with a page crowded with lines. Instead, draw a vertical line alongside the material, and perhaps underline a sentence or a few key words. If you're not yet sure if material merits marking, simply put a check by it; you can make a final decision later.

As you mark a selection, remember to be selective. Your markings should help you highlight the most significant parts of the reading; if everything is marked, you won't have separated out the most important ideas. Usually you won't know what the most important ideas in a paragraph or a section are until you've read all of it. So it's good to develop the habit of reading a bit and then going back to do the marking.

> *Joe:* "*I'll go through the text and highlight definitions and examples. I'll write numbers in front of each item in a list. I'll also put lines in the margin next to items that feel like they might be important.*"

Joe Davis

Step 3: Write Study Notes

After reading and marking a selection, you are ready to take study notes. Note-taking is a key to successful learning. In the very act of deciding what is important enough to write down, and then writing it down, you begin to learn and master the material.

Here are some guidelines to use in writing study notes:

1. After you have previewed, read, and marked the selection, reread it. Then write out the important information on 8½- by 11-inch sheets of paper. *Write on only one side of each page.* (You don't want to have to keep flipping back and forth when studying your notes.)

2. Write clearly. Then you won't waste valuable study time trying to decipher your handwriting.

3. Use a combination of the author's words and your own words. Using your own words at times forces you to think about the material and work at understanding it.

4. Organize your notes into a rough outline that will show relationships between ideas. Do this as follows:

   a. Write the title of the selection at the top of the first sheet of notes.

   b. Write main headings at the margin of your notes. Indent subheads about half an inch away from the margin. Indent sub-subheads even more.

   c. Number items in a list, just as you did when marking important items in a list in the text. Be sure each list has a heading in your notes.

Try preparing a sheet of study notes for the material on feelings. Here is a start for such a sheet of study notes:

Three Ways of Dealing with Feelings

A. *Withholding feelings—keeping them inside and not giving any verbal or nonverbal clues to their existence.*
   Ex.—poker player with a "poker face."

The activity of taking notes will help you see how useful it is to write out the important information in a selection.

Step 4: Recite the Ideas in Your Notes

After writing your study notes, go through them and write key words in the margin of your notes. The words will help you study the material. For example, here are the key words you might write in the margin of notes taken on the material about disclosing feelings.

3 ways of dealing with feelings	Describing feelings: def and ex
Withholding feelings: def and ex	4 reasons many people don't describe feelings
Displaying feelings: def and ex	3 steps to describing feelings

To study the material, turn the words in the margin into questions. First ask yourself, "What does 'describing feelings' mean?" Then recite the answer until you can say it without looking at your notes. Then ask yourself, "What are the four reasons many people don't describe their feelings?" Then recite that answer until you can say it without looking at your notes.

Then—and this is a key point—go back and review your answer to the first question. Test yourself—see if you can say the answer without looking at it. Then test yourself on the second answer. As you learn each new bit of information, go back and test yourself on the previous information. *Such repeated self-testing is the secret of effective learning.*

A Final Thought

Let's summarize: The PRWR study system will help you learn textbook material that you need to know. On a regular basis, you should preview your reading assignments, read them, write study notes on them, and recite your notes. By doing so, and by reciting and learning your classroom notes as well, you'll be well prepared to deal with exams.

Joe: "*After I'm done highlighting, I'll read through the material again. I decide what's most important and copy it onto 3-by-5 cards. Later, I'll read those cards out loud to myself. The combination of writing down new material and speaking it aloud really works for me. I go over and over those cards until they're locked in my memory.*"

Joe Davis

Terry Oakman

Terry: "*I primarily do a skim reading of a textbook, focusing on things I know are important. I'll look at boldfaced terms and examples. I'll look at heads and subheads and especially the relationship between them. I'll look at study aids in the front and back of the chapter. Then I'll take notes on the important material. I'll have those notes along with my class notes and then study everything. I'll actually recite material out loud to myself. As I master each new item, I'll go back and review the previous items.*"

FINAL ACTIVITIES

1   Check Your Understanding

Answer the following questions to check your understanding of the chapter.

1. According to the author, how important is your textbook compared with your class notes?
   a. It is far more important—in fact, if you read your textbook thoroughly, you don't need to take class notes.
   b. They are equal in importance.
   c. Your textbook is slightly less important than your class notes.
   d. Your class notes are often far more important than your textbook.

2. A good systematic way to study a textbook includes four steps in which order?
   a. Preview. Read. Recite. Write.
   b. Read. Write. Preview. Recite.
   c. Preview. Read. Write. Recite.
   d. Preview. Recite. Write. Read.

3. Previewing a chapter includes
   a. writing down key words and phrases that you come across.
   b. reading the entire chapter carefully.
   c. asking yourself questions based on the material you've read.
   d. briefly noticing the title, heads and subheads, photos, and diagrams.

4. In the textbook excerpt provided here, how many reasons are provided for people's failure to describe their feelings?
   a. One.
   b. Two.
   c. Three.
   d. Four.

5. The final paragraphs of a chapter
   a. usually introduce new ideas to be covered in the next chapter.
   b. often summarize the main ideas that were covered in that chapter.
   c. are usually not important enough to read.
   d. often tell you how the main headings relate to the subheads.

2   Questions for Writing or Discussion

You may find it helpful to think about and write out your answers to the following questions. Or your instructor may put you in a small group or pair you with another student and have you discuss the questions with each other.

1. Do you currently use a method anything like the PRWR system of studying a textbook? How is your approach to textbook study similar to or different from the one described in this chapter? Do you think that the four-step PRWR system could benefit you?

2. The author describes previewing a chapter as being like what most people do when they first arrive at a party. Can you come up with another example in real life in which you "preview" a situation before you plunge into it?

3. In your experience, is it true that taking lecture notes is more important than reading the textbook? What can you get out of the classroom experience that you cannot get from reading the textbook?

4. Work together with another student to look over a chapter in a textbook from one of your courses. Do the following :

    a. Look at the first few paragraphs. Do they provide a preview of what the chapter is about?

    b. Look at the final paragraph or paragraphs. Do they restate some of the main ideas that were introduced in the chapter?

    c. Identify the main headings in the chapter. Under those, do you find smaller subheads, and maybe even sub-subheads?

    d. Are any items set off in italic or boldface type?

    e. Find at least one definition and at least one example.

5. One student, Ryan Klootwyk, provided a detailed account of how he learned to study a textbook. Read his account and then do the activity that follows.

When Ryan got his first look at college textbooks, he was "floored." "They were wordy and highfalutin, and they seemed to convey a message that was over my head. I consider myself an intelligent person, but they were just plain frustrating." Fortunately, Ryan got through this initial discouragement. He began to seek help—help from tutors, help from his instructors. "I got into the habit of taking my books to them and saying, 'What is this?'"

Gradually, thanks to help from those outside sources and his own drive to succeed, Ryan worked out effective methods of dealing with those intimidating texts. He begins the process as soon as he gets a new book.

"First, I find a quiet time and place to look through the whole thing," he says. "I don't try to plow in and read it. I get the big picture first. I leaf through it, look at the illustrations, the captions, the headings, the titles, and try to get a sense of the book as a whole."

After he's gotten acquainted with the textbook, Ryan begins studying with highlighter in hand, marking key words and phrases—but the important word here is "key." "I highlight very restrictively," he says emphatically. "Before I touch the highlighter to the page, I search out the absolutely most essential ideas. Textbooks tend to overload you with tiny details, and if you treat them all as equally important, you'll drive yourself crazy." When Ryan buys used textbooks, he is amazed to see how much of the text the previous user has highlighted. "Sometimes there is more material highlighted than not," he says. "Highlighting like that would be of absolutely no help to me."

Another of Ryan's habits is to make notes in the margins of his textbooks as he studies. "I jot down main ideas, key words, paraphrases of the most important themes," he said. "In a pinch, if I'm running short of time to study for an exam, I can just read the highlighted material and my margin notes and be in decent shape."

A final trick of Ryan's is to keep his textbook open during class lectures. As his instructor presents ideas that are related to textbook material, Ryan jots down notes right there on the textbook page. "That way, I don't forget the relationship between the lecture and the book, the way I might if I just wrote the notes in my notebook."

Each of Ryan's textbook-study techniques is designed with the same goal in mind: to help him thoroughly understand main concepts, rather than mindlessly memorize less important details. "I don't want to overload my brain," Ryan says with a laugh. "I'd rather know five things well than sort of know ten."

- What is your reaction to Ryan's textbook note-taking? Discuss which of his comments you agree with and that you think will work for you.

3 Studying a Textbook Selection

Use the method described in this chapter to study the following excerpt from a psychology textbook.

Step 1: Preview the Reading

Preview the selection below for thirty seconds. Think about the title and subtitles and the relationship between them.

Kinds of Conflicts

One researcher, Kurt Lewin, has specified three types of goal conflict that people experience. Each of these three types of conflicts leads to a feeling of frustration.

Approach-Approach Conflicts. Of the three types of conflicts, these are the least frustrating. An *approach-approach* conflict is one that results from having to choose between two desirable goals. You cannot possibly reach both goals at the same time. Maybe there are two good parties in different parts of town at exactly the same time on the same night. You must miss one, but which one? Or assume a rich aunt hands you $50,000 to buy yourself a new car. Both a Mercedes and a BMW look appealing. You must make a choice, but indeed it is a pleasant problem. In an approach-approach conflict, you always win, even if you must lose another appealing alternative. As a result, approach-approach conflicts are only mildly frustrating.

Avoidance-Avoidance Conflicts. These are the most frustrating of the three types of conflicts. Here the conflict results from being forced to choose between two undesirable goals. Did your mother ever tell you to clean your messy closet or go to bed? Assuming you disliked cleaning closets and were not tired, you experienced an *avoidance-avoidance* conflict. The thought of wasting hours cleaning a cluttered closet was dreadful, but the notion of suffering hours of boredom was also unappealing. The usual reaction to an avoidance-avoidance conflict is to attempt to escape. Perhaps you threatened to run away from home. When no escape is possible, facing the conflict is inevitable. The result is being forced to make an unpleasant choice. The choice is accompanied by intense frustration and anger.

Approach-Avoidance Conflicts. These are the most common of the three types of conflicts. The conflict results from weighing the positive and negative aspects of a single goal. Eating a piece of chocolate fudge will provide a delicious taste. But it will also cause tooth decay and, perhaps, unwanted pounds. Studying for an exam will result in a better grade, but it will require an evening away from friends.

Step 2: Read the Material and Mark Important Parts

Read the passage straight through. As you do, underline the definitions you find. Mark with an *Ex* in the margin an example that makes the definitions clear for you. Also, number the items in the list you'll find. And put a check next to what seem to be important details.

Step 3: Write Notes to Help You Study the Material

On a separate sheet of paper, number and list the three kinds of conflicts. Also write their definitions and an example of each.

Step 4: Recite the Ideas in Your Notes

Perhaps you'll write in the margin simply "3 kinds of conflict." Then study the material until you can recite all three kinds of conflict, along with definitions and examples, without looking at your notes.

4   Writing about Textbook Reading and Taking Notes

Write a paragraph in which you evaluate your textbook reading and note-taking skills. Which steps described in the chapter do you practice? Which do you not practice? Begin your paragraph with one of the **points** below.

Point: I am good at textbook reading and note-taking. I practice most of the steps described in the chapter.

Point: I am not good at textbook reading and note-taking. I practice few if any of the steps described in the chapter.

Point: My textbook reading and note-taking skills are mixed. I follow one or two of the steps but not the others.

After you have chosen your point, provide **supporting details or examples** to back up your point. For instance, to support the first point above, you might say in part:

I couldn't take decent notes in class if I didn't read my textbook ahead of time. I'll already have a general idea of a subject because I read a chapter in advance. For instance, if an economics teacher is talking about the different kinds of economic resources, I know where she's going because I read the book before her lecture. It's easier for me to take notes, and I'll often mark in my textbook the areas where she spends most of her time.

When writing your paragraph, use examples and details that are based on your actual experience.

132 TEN SKILLS YOU REALLY NEED TO SUCCEED IN SCHOOL

5 Speaking about Textbook Reading and Taking Notes

Imagine that you have been asked to give a speech on textbook reading and note-taking to a class of students who will be entering college in the fall. Prepare a talk full of practical advice that really communicates with them. Imagine that the students have been told beforehand that you will be as stiff and dry as a board and that your talk will have little relevance or value. You have two goals, then: 1) to use language and images that really connect with students, and 2) to pack your talk with lots of truly helpful information. Your speech should be five to ten minutes long.

8 / Taking Tests

THE KEY TO DOING WELL ON TESTS

A familiar complaint of students is, "I'm always afraid I'll panic during an exam. I'll know a lot of the material, but when I sit down and start looking at the questions, I forget things that I know. I'll never get good grades as long as this happens. How can I avoid it?" The answer is that if you are *well prepared*, you are not likely to block or panic on exams.

"How, then," you might ask, "should a person go about preparing for exams?" There is only one answer that makes sense: You must go to class consistently, take notes, and study those notes. If necessary, you must also read and take notes on your textbook and study those notes. In short, you must start preparing for exams on the first day of the semester. The pages that follow offer suggestions on how to use your study time efficiently.

Note: This chapter assumes that you know how to take effective classroom and textbook notes and that you know how to memorize such notes. If you have not developed these essential skills, refer to pages 89–104 and 105–132.

• *Complete the following sentence*: You are unlikely to forget material during exams if you

   are _____.

WHAT TO STUDY

To prepare for either an objective or an essay exam, you should, throughout a course, study the following.

Key Terms

Always write down key terms and their definitions. It's also important to write down examples that help make the definitions clear. For study purposes, you might want to write a term on one side of an index card and a definition and an example of the term on the other side of the card.

Here is a sample study card for a key term:

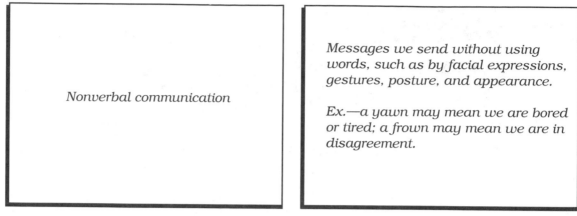

Front of card   *Back of card*

Enumerations

Look for enumerations (lists of items) in your class and textbook notes.

Items in a list often have a heading with a word that ends in *s*. Here are some examples:

Causes of the First World War	*Types* of marriage
Reasons why people join groups	*Stages* of the water cycle
Schools of psychology	*Results* of the Industrial Revolution
Methods of waste disposal	*Steps* in the writing process
Kinds of defense mechanisms	*Ways* to deal with conflict

Be sure to include the heading that describes a list as well as the numbered items in the list. For study purposes, you might want to write the heading on one side of an index card (for example, the stages of the water cycle) and the numbered list of items (the different stages of the water cycle) on the other side of the card.

Here is a sample study card for an enumeration:

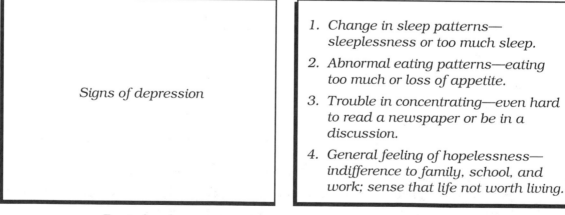

Front of card   *Back of card*

Points Emphasized

Look for points that are emphasized in class or in the text. Often phrases such as *the most significant, of special importance,* and *the chief reason* are used to call attention to important points in a book or a lecture.

Also, as you go through your class notes, concentrate on areas where the instructor spent a good deal of time. For example, if the instructor spent a week talking about present-day changes in the traditional family structure, you can expect to get an exam question on that topic. Likewise, if many pages in your textbook deal with one area—say, the reasons for divorce—you might expect a question about these reasons on an exam.

Finally, pay attention to areas your instructors have advised you to study. Some instructors conduct in-class reviews during which they tell students what material to focus on when they study. Always write down these pointers; your instructors have often made up the test or are making it up at the time of the review and are likely to give valuable hints about what is actually on the exam. Other instructors may help by passing out reviews or study guides.

- One study-skills instructor has said, "I sometimes sit in on classes, and time and again I have heard teachers tell students point-blank that something is to be on an exam. Some students quickly jot down this information; others sit there in a fog."

  Which group of students do you belong to? _____

- What are some specific study aids instructors have given to help you prepare for tests? _____

Jhoselyn Martinez

Jennifer McCaul

Jhoselyn: "*I did reach a point where I could figure out what a teacher was going to put on a test. Each teacher has his or her own style, and by talking to teachers and listening to them every day in class, you get a sense of what it is you should study.*"

Jennifer: "*You can tell a lot about what is going to be on a test from what the instructor has emphasized in class. If an instructor spends a lot of time on an area, that's important. Anything on the board is important. Handouts are important.*"

RIGHT BEFORE THE EXAM

The following hints can help you make the most of your time right before a test. Read the hints and also note how many of the hints you already follow.

1   Spend the night before an exam making a final review of your notes. Then go right to bed without watching television or otherwise interfering with the material you have learned. Your mind will tend to work through and absorb the material during the night. To further lock in your learning, get up a half hour or an hour earlier than usual the next morning and review your notes.

   • Do you already review material on the morning of an exam? _____

   • If so, have you found this review to be helpful? _____

2   Make sure you take with you any materials (pen, paper, eraser, dictionary, and other aids allowed) you will need during the exam.

   • Do you already follow this hint?   ___ Yes   ___ Sometimes   ___ No

3   Be on time for the exam. Arriving late sets you up to do poorly.

   • Do you already follow this hint?   ___ Yes   ___ Sometimes   ___ No

4   Sit in a quiet spot. Some people are very talkative and noisy before an exam. Since you don't want anything to interfere with your learning, you are better off not talking with other people during the few minutes before the exam starts. You might want to use those minutes to review your notes one more time.

   • Do you already follow this hint?   ___ Yes   ___ Sometimes   ___ No

   • How do you typically spend the minutes in class right before an exam?   _____

   _____

5   Read over carefully all the directions on the exam before you begin. Also listen carefully to any spoken directions or hints the instructor may give.

   • Do you already follow this hint?   ___ Yes   ___ Sometimes   ___ No

6   Budget your time. Take a few seconds to figure out roughly how much time you can spend on each section of the test. You don't want to end up with ten minutes left and a fifty-point essay still to write or thirty multiple-choice questions to answer.

   • Do you already follow this hint?   ___ Yes   ___ Sometimes   ___ No

DEALING WITH OBJECTIVE EXAMS

Objective exams include multiple-choice, true-false, fill-in, and matching questions. The following hints will help you take objective exams. As you read them, you should also note which hints you already practice.

1 Answer all the easier questions first. Don't linger over hard questions. You may end up running out of time and not even getting a chance to answer the questions you can do easily. Instead, put a light check mark (✓) beside difficult questions and continue working through the entire test, answering all the items you can do right away.

   • Do you already follow this hint?   ___ Yes   ___ Sometimes   ___ No

2 Go back and spend the time remaining on the difficult questions. Sometimes information in other questions on the test will help you answer these harder questions.

   • Do you already follow this hint?   ___ Yes   ___ Sometimes   ___ No

3 Answer *all* questions. Guess when you have to; guessing can help you pick up at least a few points!

   • Do you already follow this hint?   ___ Yes   ___ Sometimes   ___ No

4 Put yourself in the instructor's shoes when you try to figure out the meaning of a confusing item. In light of what was covered in the course, which answer do you think the instructor would say is correct?

   • Do you already follow this hint?   ___ Yes   ___ Sometimes   ___ No

5 Circle or underline the key words in difficult questions. This strategy can sometimes help you untangle complicated questions.

   • Do you already follow this hint?   ___ Yes   ___ Sometimes   ___ No

6 Take advantage of the full time given. If you finish before time is up, go over the exam carefully for possible mistakes. Change an answer if you decide there is a good reason for doing so.

   • Do you already follow this hint?   ___ Yes   ___ Sometimes   ___ No

➤ Activity 1: Choosing Helpful Hints

Write here what you think are the three most important of the preceding hints for you to remember in taking objective exams.

   1. _____

   2. _____

   3. _____

Specific Hints for Answering Multiple-Choice Questions

1 Remember that a perfect answer to every question may not be provided in multiple-choice exams. You must choose the best *available* answer.

2 Cross out answers you know are incorrect. Eliminating answers is helpful because it focuses your attention on the most reasonable options.

3 With difficult items, read the question and then the first possible answer. Next, read the question again and the second possible answer, and so on until you have read the question with each separate answer. Taking the items one at a time may help you identify the best answer to the question.

4 Use the following clues, which may signal correct answers, *only* when you have no idea of the answer and must guess.

   a The longest answer is often correct.

- *Use this clue to answer the following question:* The key reason students who are well prepared still don't do well on exams is that they (a) are late to the test, (b) don't have all their materials, (c) forget to jot down first-letter words, (d) haven't studied enough, (e) don't read all the directions before they begin the test.

    The correct answer is *e*, the longest answer.

   b The most complete and inclusive answer is often correct.

- *Use this clue to answer the following question:* If you have to cram for a test, which of these items should receive most of your attention? (a) The instructor's tests from other years, (b) important ideas in the class and text notes, including such things as key terms, their definitions, and clarifying examples, (c) the textbook, (d) class notes, (e) textbook notes.

    The correct answer is *b*, the most complete and inclusive choice. Note that the most complete answer is often also the longest.

   c An answer in the middle, especially if it is longest, is often correct.

- *Use this clue to answer the following question:* Many students have trouble with objective tests because they (a) guess when they're not sure, (b) run out of time, (c) think objective exams are easier than essay tests and so do not study enough, (d) forget to double-check their answers, (e) leave difficult questions to the end.

    The correct answer is *c*, which is in the middle and is longest.

   d If two answers have opposite meanings, one of them is probably correct.

- *Use this clue to answer the following question:* Before an exam starts, you should (a) sit in a quiet spot, (b) join a group of friends and talk about the test, (c) review the textbook one last time, (d) read a book and relax, (e) study any notes you didn't have time for previously.

    The correct answer is *a*. Note that *a* and *b* are roughly opposite.

   e Answers with qualifiers, such as *generally, probably, most, often, some, sometimes,* and *usually,* are frequently correct. Answers with absolute words such as *all, always, never, none,* and *only* are usually incorrect.

- *Use this clue to answer the following question:* In multiple-choice questions, the answer in the middle with the most words is (a) always correct, (b) always incorrect, (c) often correct, (d) never wrong, (e) never right.

The correct answer is *c*; all the other answers use absolute words and are incorrect.

➤ Activity 2: Choosing Helpful Clues

Write here what you think are the three most helpful clues for you to remember when you are guessing the answer to a multiple-choice question.

1. _____

2. _____

3. _____

Ed Hamler is a student at Philadelphia University.

Ed: "In an exam I always answer the easier questions first. The worst thing to do is to get stuck on the hard questions right away, because it takes away time. I mark off the hard questions and come back to them after I complete the rest of the test.

"When I come upon a confusing item, I try to put myself in the mind of the instructor. If you know the instructor's style, that can help you figure out what answer is wanted."

Teron: "When I take a test, I do the easiest section of a test first. I knock that out and then move on to the harder sections. I generally do the essay last. But it helps to pile up some points first. I do budget my test time, and I do read directions carefully."

Teron Ivery

DEALING WITH ESSAY EXAMS

Essay exams include one or more questions to which you must respond in detail, writing your answers in a clear, well-organized essay of one or more paragraphs. To do well with essay exams, follow these five steps:

1 Figure out probable questions.

2 Prepare and memorize an informal outline answer for each question.

3 Look at the exam carefully and plan your approach.

4 Prepare a brief, informal outline before answering an essay question.

5 Write a clear, well-organized essay.

Each step is explained on the pages that follow.

Step 1: Figure Out Probable Questions

Because exam time is limited, the instructor can give you only a few questions to answer. He or she is likely to ask questions dealing with the most important areas of the subject. You can probably guess most of them. To help you do so, go through your class notes and mark those areas where your instructor has spent a good deal of time.

Pay special attention to definitions and examples and to basic lists of items (enumerations). Enumerations in particular are often a key to essay questions. For instance, if your instructor spoke at length about the causes of the Great Depression, or about the long-range effects of water pollution, or about the advantages of capitalism, you should probably expect a question such as "What were the causes of the Great Depression?" or "What are the wide-range effects of water pollution?" or "What are the advantages of capitalism?"

If your instructor has given you study guides, look for probable essay questions there. (Some teachers choose their essay questions from among those listed in a study guide.) And consider very carefully any review that the instructor provides. Essay questions are likely to come from areas the instructor emphasizes.

- *Fill in the missing words:* Very often you can predict essay questions, for they usually concern the most _____ areas of the subject.

Step 2: Prepare and Memorize an Informal Outline Answer for Each Question

Write out each question you have made up and, under it, list main points to be discussed. Put important supporting information in parentheses after each main point. You now have an informal outline that you can go on to memorize.

If you have spelling problems—and many students do—make up a list of words you might have to spell in writing your answers. For example, if you are having a psychology test on the principles of learning, you will want to write down and study such terms as *conditioning, reinforcement, Pavlov, reflex, stimulus,* and so on.

An Example of Step 2

Here is an outline that a student named Curtis prepared while studying for a psychology exam. The instructor had spent several days talking about the defense mechanisms that people use to avoid unpleasant truths. Curtis expected, then, that one essay question would be on the different kinds of defense mechanisms. So Curtis wrote:

Name and describe the kinds of defense mechanisms:

1. *Denial—refusing to admit a painful reality (ex.—people who learn they are dying often deny it at first)*
2. *Repression—forgetting an unacceptable thought (ex.—woman who is angry at and afraid of her husband "forgets" her anger)*
3. *Regression—reverting to childlike behavior (ex.—adult throws temper tantrum)*
4. *Rationalization—making up an excuse for not doing something (ex.—student does poorly in a class and puts all the blame on the teacher)*
5. *Fantasizing—escaping into a make-believe world (ex.—too much daydreaming)*

DRRRF (Dirty rats run really fast)

• Complete this explanation of what Curtis did to prepare for the essay question.

First, Curtis wrote down one likely essay question and then listed the five answers under it. Next, he wrote brief definitions of the five kinds of defense mechanisms. Also, he added a clear _____ in parentheses of each definition. Then he wrote down the first letter of each key word and a first-letter sentence that he could easily remember. Finally, he _____ himself over and over until he could recall all five of the words that the first letters stood for. He also made sure that each word he remembered truly stood for an _____ in his mind and that he recalled much of the supporting material that went with each idea.

Dr. Ben Carson

Dr. Carson: *"You can reach a point where you can go into an essay test and pretty much know what the questions are going to be. I often had outlines in my mind with answers to the questions I expected. Then, at the start of the exam, I would jot down my little outlines."*

Rod: *"As you take a course, keep asking yourself, 'What are the major ideas this instructor wants us to take away from this class?' Chances are those ideas will be the focus of the essay questions."*

Rod Sutton

Step 3: Look at the Exam Carefully and Plan Your Approach

- Get an overview of the exam by reading all the questions on the test.

- Budget your time. Write in the margin the number of minutes you should spend on each essay. For example, if you have three essays worth an equal number of points and a one-hour time limit, allow twenty minutes for each one. Make sure you are not left with only a couple of minutes to do a major essay.

- Start with the easiest question. Getting a good answer down on paper will help build up your confidence and momentum. Number your answers plainly so that your instructor will know which question you answered first.

An Example of Step 3

After Curtis received the exam, he looked it over and budgeted thirty minutes for each of two essay questions. He started with the question he had expected, which was "Discuss the different kinds of defense mechanisms."

Step 4: Jot Down a Brief, Informal Outline before Answering an Essay Question

Use the margin of the exam to jot down quickly, as they occur to you, the main points you want to discuss in each answer. Then decide in what order you want to present these points. Put *1* in front of the first item, *2* beside the second item, and so on. You now have an informal outline to guide you as you answer your essay question.

Ideally, the questions on the exam will be ones that you guessed and studied for in advance. If so, take a minute to write down the outline that you memorized.

An Example of Step 4

Curtis jotted down his brief outline:

Dirty rats run really fast.

> *D—Denial—as of death*
> *R—Repression—forgetting bad thought*
> *R—Regression—childlike tantrum*
> *R—Rationalization—excuse such as blaming teacher*
> *F—Fantasizing—escape as in daydreams*

Step 5: Write a Clear, Well-Organized Essay

Write carefully, doing the following:

First, start your essay with a sentence that clearly states what it will be about. Then make sure that everything in your essay relates to your opening statement.

Second, provide as much support as possible for your points.

Third, use transitions to guide your reader through your answer. Words such as *first, second, also, next,* and *finally* make it easy for the reader to follow your train of thought.

Last, leave time to proofread your essay for sentence-skills mistakes you have made while you concentrated on writing your answer. Look for words that are omitted, miswritten, or misspelled (if permitted, bring a dictionary with you); for incorrect punctuation; and for whatever else makes your writing unclear.

An Example of Step 5

Curtis wrote the following essay:

> There are five kinds of defense mechanisms that people use to avoid ~~truths~~ unpleasant truths. One mechanism is denial, which is not owning up to something painful. An example is that a person who is dying will often refuse to admit it at first. Another defense mechanism is repression, which is forgetting ~~a thought~~ an unacceptable thought. An example would be a woman who is angry at her husband but is also afraid of him. Her fear of him makes her forget her anger. A third defense mechanism is regression, when a person shows ^childlike behavior. An adult who throws a temper tantrum is using regression. Also a defense mechanism is ~~rationilation~~ rationalization. People often make up excuses for not doing something. For instance, a student who does poorly on a test and blames the teacher is rationalizing. A final defense mechanism is fantasizing, or escaping into a make-believe world. A person who daydreams a great deal of the time is using fantasy.

- The following sentences comment on Curtis's essay. Fill in the missing word or words in each case.

    1. Curtis begins with a sentence that expresses the _____ of his essay. Always begin an essay answer in this way.

    2. The transition words that Curtis used to guide his reader, and himself, through the five points of his answer include

       _____   _____   _____

       _____   _____

    3. In the time remaining, Curtis used a dictionary to correct a misspelled word ("_____"). He used an insertion sign (caret) to add a missing word ("_____"). Also, in writing his answer, Curtis used crossouts rather than losing time by trying to erase miswritten words ("truths" is replaced with "_____"; "a thought" is replaced with "_____").

FINAL ACTIVITIES

1   Check Your Understanding

Answer the following questions to check your understanding of the chapter.

1. People are not likely to panic during an exam if they are
   a. brave.
   b. well-rested.
   c. prepared.
   d. absent.

2. Which of the following is *not* a recommended technique for preparing for an exam?
   a. Go to bed directly after studying, without watching television.
   b. Once you arrive in the exam room, relax by chatting with friends.
   c. Get up earlier than usual to review your notes the morning of the exam.
   d. Read all the test instructions before beginning to write.

3. Which of the following is *not* a valid hint for choosing the best answer to a multiple-choice item?
   a. The most complete answer is often correct.
   b. Answers including absolute words such as *all, always, never*, and *none* are usually correct.
   c. The answer in the middle is often correct, especially if it is longest.
   d. If two answers have opposite meanings, one of them is often correct.

4. The best way to proceed through a test is to
   a. answer the hardest questions first.
   b. alternate between essay questions and objective questions.
   c. start in the middle.
   d. answer the easiest questions first.

5. Which of the following is *not* a good way to figure out probable essay questions?
   a. Pay attention to any enumerations.
   b. Pay attention to definitions and examples.
   c. Pay attention to areas that your instructor has spent a lot of time discussing.
   d. Pay attention to textbook passages that your teacher has mentioned only briefly.

2   Questions for Writing or Discussion

You may find it helpful to think about and write out your answers to the following questions. Or your instructor may put you in a small group or pair you with another student and have you discuss the questions with each other.

1. Which of the following statements describes you best?

   a. I am generally well-prepared for tests, so they don't make me feel very anxious.
   b. I try to prepare for tests, but there's no way to know if I've studied the right material.
   c. Tests always make me feel panicky.

Discuss which item you've chosen and why. If you've chosen *b* or *c,* what steps could you take in order to feel more confident about taking tests?

2. When you sit down to take an exam, do you usually plunge right in, start with the first question, and continue to the end? Or do you follow some other sequence?

3. The author writes, "This chapter assumes that you know how to take effective classroom and textbook notes and that you know how to memorize such notes." Why does he bring up these other skills in a chapter about taking tests?

4. Return to the textbook excerpt on pages 121–123. Following the suggestions given in this chapter, see if you can identify one likely essay question that might appear on an exam covering that excerpt. Write out that question, and then prepare an informal outline of its answer.

3 Writing about Test Taking

Write a paragraph in which you evaluate your test-taking skills. Which of the suggestions for taking tests described in this chapter do you practice? Which do you not practice? Begin your paragraph with one of the **points** below:

Point: I am good at preparing for and taking tests. I practice many of the suggestions described in this chapter.

Point: I am not good at preparing for and taking tests. I practice few if any of the suggestions described in the chapter.

Point: My skills in preparing for and taking tests are mixed. I follow some helpful suggestions but ignore others.

After you have chosen your point, provide **supporting details or examples** to back up your point. For instance, to support the third point, you might say in part:

I am usually pretty well prepared for my exams. I think I know how to pick out important points that are likely to appear on the exams. What I don't do well is budget my time when I'm actually taking the test. I spend too much time on multiple-choice and true-false items. Then I have to rush to finish the essay questions and don't get full credit for them.

When writing your paragraph, use examples and details that are based on your actual experience.

4 Speaking about Test Taking

Imagine that you have been asked to give a speech on test taking to a class of students who will be entering college in the fall. Prepare a talk full of practical advice that really communicates with them. Imagine that the students have been told beforehand that you will be as stiff and dry as a board and that your talk will have little relevance or value. You have two goals, then: 1) to use language and images that really connect with students, and 2) to pack your talk with lots of truly helpful information. Your speech should be five to ten minutes long.

9 / Achieving Basic Goals in Writing

THE TWO BASIC GOALS IN WRITING

Here in a nutshell is what you need to write effectively. You need to know how to:

1 Make a point.

2 Support the point.

The heart of any effective paper, whether it is a paragraph, a several-paragraph essay, or a longer paper, is that you **make a point** and **support that point**.

Now look for a moment at the following cartoon:

PEANUTS reprinted by permission of United Feature Syndicate, Inc.

See if you can answer the following questions:

- What is Snoopy's point in his paper?

  Your answer: His point is that _____

- What is his support for his point?

  Your answer: _____

Explanation

Snoopy's point, of course, is that dogs are superior to cats. But he offers no support whatsoever to back up his point! There are two jokes here. First, he is a dog and so is naturally going to believe that dogs are superior. The other joke is that his evidence ("They just are, and that's all there is to it!") is a lot of empty words. His somewhat guilty look in the last panel suggests that he knows he has not proved his point. To write effectively, you must provide *real* support for your points and opinions.

EFFECTIVE PARAGRAPHS

A *paragraph* is a series of sentences about one main idea, or point. A paragraph typically starts with a point (also called the *topic sentence*), and the rest of the paragraph provides specific details to support and develop that point.

Example 1

Look at the following paragraph written by a student named Cheryl.

A Terrible Roommate

Choosing Dawn as a roommate was a mistake. For one thing, Dawn was a truly noisy person. She talked loudly, she ate loudly, and she snored loudly. She never just watched TV or listened to a CD. Instead, she did both at once. I'd walk into the apartment with my hands clapped over my ears and turn off the first noisemaking machine I reached. Then I would hear her cry out, "I was listening to that." Secondly, Dawn had no sense of privacy. She would come into my bedroom even while I was dressing. She'd sit down on my bed for a chat while I was taking a nap. Once she even came in into the bathroom while I was taking a bath. Last of all, Dawn had too many visitors. I would return to the apartment after an evening out and trip over one or more of Dawn's sisters, cousins, or friends asleep on our living room floor. Dawn's visitors would stay for days, eating our groceries and tying up the bathroom and telephone. After one month I told Dawn to find another place to live.

The above paragraph, like many effective paragraphs, starts by stating a main idea, or point. In this case, the point is that choosing Dawn as a roommate was a bad idea.

In our everyday lives, we constantly make points about all kinds of matters. We express such opinions as "That was a stupid movie" or "My English instructor is the best teacher I have ever had" or "My brother is a generous person" or "Eating at that restaurant is a mistake" or "Our team should win the playoff game" or "Waitressing is a very hard job." In talking to people, we don't always give the reasons for our opinions. **In writing, however, we must provide specific evidence to support an idea.** Only by supplying solid evidence for any point that we make can we communicate effectively with readers.

An effective paragraph, then, not only must *make* a point but also must *support* it with specific evidence—reasons, examples, and other details. Such specifics help prove to readers that the point is a reasonable one. Even if readers do not agree with the writer, at least they have in front of them the writer's evidence. Readers are like juries: they want to see the evidence for themselves so that they can make their own judgments.

Take a minute now to look at the evidence that Cheryl has provided to back up her point about Dawn as a roommate. Complete the following outline of Cheryl's paragraph by summarizing in a few words the reasons and details that she gives to support her point. The first reason and its supporting details are summarized for you as an example.

Point: Choosing Dawn as a roommate was a mistake.

Reason 1: Noisy person

Details that develop reason 1: Talked, ate, snored, and played things loudly.

Reason 2: _____

Details that develop reason 2: _____

_____

Reason 3: _____

Details that develop reason 3: _____

_____

As the outline makes clear, Cheryl really backs up her point. She gives us three specific reasons to support her idea that rooming with Dawn was a mistake. (Dawn was a noisy person, she had no sense of privacy, and she had too many visitors.) Cheryl also provides vivid details to back up each of her reasons. With the evidence Cheryl has given us, we can see for ourselves why she feels as she does about Dawn. Cheryl has written an effective paragraph, making a point and fully supporting that point.

To write an effective paragraph, then, aim to do what Cheryl has done: begin by making a point, and then go on to back up that point with strong specific evidence.

Terry Oakman

Terry: "*What's really helped my writing is that I learned early on that I have to begin with a clear point of some kind. If my point is clear, that keeps me from going out in left field. Then I can proceed with getting down my support for that point.*"

Example 2

Here is another example of an effective paragraph. Read it and see if you can explain why it is effective.

A Vote for Uniforms

High schools should require all students to wear uniforms. First of all, uniforms would save money for parents and children. Families could simply buy two or three inexpensive uniforms. They would not have to constantly put out money for designer jeans, fancy sneakers, and other high-priced clothing. Also an advantage of uniforms is that students would not have to spend time worrying about clothes. They could get up every day knowing what they were wearing to school. Their attention, then, could be focused on schoolwork and learning and not on making a fashion statement. Finally, uniforms would help all students get along better. Well-off students would not be able to act superior by wearing expensive clothes, and students from modest backgrounds would not have to feel inferior because of lower-cost wardrobes.

Complete the following statement: The above paragraph is effectively written because

_____

_____

Explanation

You should have answered that the paragraph is effective for two reasons: it makes a clear point ("High schools should require all students to wear uniforms"), and it provides effective support to back up that point. Complete the following outline of the paragraph:

Main idea: High schools should require all students to wear uniforms.

1. _____

   a. Families could just buy two or three inexpensive uniforms.

   b. _____

   _____

2. _____

   a. Students would know what they were going to wear every day.

   b. _____

   _____

3. _____

   a. Well-off students would not be able to act superior.

   b. _____

   _____

Kenyon Whittington

Kenyon: *"To write an effective paper, you need to know what your purpose will be. You need to make a thesis that tells in one sentence what the paper is to be about. You probably want to have an introduction which will contain the thesis. Then go on to use evidence to develop your paper."*

Jhoselyn: *"What I learned about writing effectively is that first of all you want to present an idea. Then you need to develop your idea with a lot of supporting information. You need to be careful that all your information is backing up your idea. Once I understood that framework, it was a matter of practice—getting comfortable with how to proceed."*

Jhoselyn Martinez

Teron Ivery

Teron: *"I write effectively by making sure I have a definite thesis. Then I do an outline with supporting points for that thesis. My goal is to back up my thesis with enough support."*

Krystal: *"My English professor tore my paper up as I watched. I was stunned. . . . It was the first paper of my freshman year. What I basically needed to learn was how to organize my writing—to begin with an idea and then to have a series of supporting points for that idea. Before I started using that logical structure, my writing was all over the place."*

Krystal Buhr

UNDERSTANDING MORE ABOUT POINTS AND SUPPORTING DETAILS

Chapter 2 has already introduced you to the difference between point and support. You might find it helpful to review that chapter. In particular, look at the point on page 24 that Dr. Ben Carson makes about his mother ("My mother is one tough lady") and look again at the specific supporting evidence that Dr. Carson uses to support his point convincingly.

Here are three activities that will sharpen your understanding of points and the specific details that are needed to support points.

1   Recognizing the Difference between Point and Support

Each group of sentences below could be written as a short paragraph. Circle the letter of the point (often called the topic sentence) in each case. To find the topic sentence, ask yourself, "Which is a general statement supported by the specific details in the other three statements?"

Begin by trying the example item below. First circle the letter of the sentence you think expresses the main idea. Then read the explanation.

Example   a. The brakes are badly worn.
　　　　　　　b. My old car is ready for the junk pile.
　　　　　　　c. The car floor has rusted through, and water splashes on my feet when the road is wet.
　　　　　　　d. My mechanic says its engine is too old to be repaired, and the car isn't worth the cost of a new engine.

Explanation

Sentence *a* explains one problem with the car. Sentences *c* and *d* also detail specific problems with the car. Sentence *b*, on the other hand, presents the general idea that the car is ready for the junk pile. The other sentences support that idea by providing examples. Sentence *b*, then, is the topic sentence; it expresses the author's main idea.

➤ Activity: Point and Support

Circle the letter of the item that expresses a point supported by the other three items.

1. a. "I couldn't study because I forgot to bring my book home."
　　b. "I couldn't take the final because my grandmother died."
　　c. Students use some common excuses with instructors.
　　d. "I couldn't come to class because I had a migraine headache."

2. a. TV can promote violent behavior.
　　b. TV may weaken a child's imagination.
　　c. TV has powerful effects on young children.
　　d. TV can make a child think that school should be fast-paced and entertaining.

3. a. The last time I ate at the diner, I got food poisoning and was sick for two days.
    b. The city inspector found roaches and mice in the diner's kitchen.
    c. Our local diner is a health hazard and ought to be closed down.
    d. The toilets in the diner often back up, and the sinks have only a trickle of water.

4. a. Tobacco is one of the most addictive of all drugs.
    b. Selling cigarettes ought to be against the law.
    c. Nonsmokers are put in danger by breathing the smoke from others' cigarettes.
    d. Cigarette smoking kills many more people than all illegal drugs combined.

5. a. Parents should turn off the TV at times and just sit and read.
    b. A TV set should not be put in a child's bedroom.
    c. Reading should be associated with times of family togetherness and fun.
    d. Parents can do several things to discourage TV watching and encourage reading.

2 Getting a Better Understanding of Specific Details

A major step in becoming an effective writer is to truly understand the nature and purpose of specific details. *Specific details* are examples, reasons, particulars, and facts. Such details are needed to support and explain a topic sentence effectively. They provide the evidence needed for us to understand, as well as to feel and experience, a writer's point.

Here is a topic sentence followed by two sets of supporting sentences. Which set provides sharp, specific details?

Topic sentence: Some poor people must struggle to make meals for themselves.

a. They gather up whatever free food items they can find in fast-food restaurants and take them home to use however they can. Instead of planning well-balanced meals, they base their diet on anything they can buy that is cheap and filling.

b. Some add hot water to the free packets of ketchup they get at McDonald's to make tomato soup. Others live on peanut butter and jelly sandwiches and discount loaves of white bread.

Explanation

The second set provides specific details: instead of a general statement about "free food items they find in fast-food restaurants and take . . . home to use however they can," we get a vivid detail we can see and picture clearly: "free packets of ketchup they get at McDonald's to make tomato soup."

Instead of a general statement about how the poor will "base their diet on anything they can buy that is cheap and filling," we get exact details: "Others live on peanut butter and jelly sandwiches and discount loaves of white bread."

Specific details are often like the information we find in a movie script. They provide us with such clear pictures that we could make a film of them if we wanted to.

You would know just how to film the information given in the second cluster. You would show a poor person breaking open a McDonald's packet of ketchup and mixing it with water to make a kind of tomato soup. You would show someone opening a large tub of peanut butter and a large jar of jelly and making sandwiches.

In contrast, the writer of the first cluster fails to provide the specific information needed. If you were asked to make a film based on the first cluster, you would have to figure out for yourself just what particulars you were going to show.

When you are working to provide specific supporting information in a paper, it might help to ask yourself, "Could someone easily film this information?" If the answer is "yes," you probably have effective details.

➤ Activity 1: Recognizing Specific Details

Each topic sentence below is followed by two sets of supporting details. Write S (for *specific*) in the space next to the set that provides specific support for the point. Write G (for *general*) next to the set that offers only vague, general support.

1. **Topic sentence: My sister is very aggressive.**

   _____ a. Her aggressiveness is apparent in her personal life in the way she acts around guys. She is never shy in social situations. And in her job she does not hesitate to be aggressive if she thinks that doing so will help her succeed.

   _____ b. When she meets a guy she likes, she is quick to say, "Let's go out sometime." In her job as a furniture salesperson, she will follow potential customers out onto the sidewalk as she tries to convince them to buy.

2. **Topic sentence: Our new kitten causes us lots of trouble.**

   _____ a. He has shredded the curtains in my bedroom with his claws. He nearly drowned when he crawled into the washing machine. And my hands look like raw hamburger from his playful bites and scratches.

   _____ b. It seems he destroys everything he touches. He's always getting into places where he doesn't belong. Sometimes he plays too roughly, and that can be painful.

3. **Topic sentence: My landlord is a softhearted person.**

   _____ a. Even though he wrote them himself, he sometimes ignores the official apartment rules in order to make his tenants happy.

   _____ b. Although the lease agreement states, "No pets," he brought my daughter a puppy after she told him how much she missed having one.

4. **Topic sentence: The library is a distracting place to try to study.**

   _____ a. It's hard to concentrate when a noisy eight-person poker game is going on on the floor beside you. It's also distracting to be passed notes like, "Hey, baby, what's your mother's address? I want to thank her for having such a beautiful daughter."

_____ b. Many students meet in the library to do group activities and socialize with one another. Others go there to flirt. It's easy to get more interested in all that activity than in paying attention to your studies.

5. **Topic sentence: Some children expect their parents to do all the household chores.**

_____ a. They expect hot meals to appear on the table as if by magic. After eating, they go off to work or play, never thinking about who's going to do the dishes. They drop their dirty laundry in their room, assuming that Mom will attend to it and return clean, folded clothes.

_____ b. They don't give any thought to what must be done so that they will not go hungry. They don't take any responsibility for the work that's needed to keep the household organized, and they act as if their parents are servants hired to clean up after them and take care of their needs.

➤ Activity 2: Recognizing Specific Details in a Paragraph

At several points in the following student paragraph, you are given a choice of two sets of supporting details. Write S (for *specific*) in the space next to the item that provides specific support for the point. Write G (for *general*) next to the item that offers only vague, general support. (*Hint:* In each case, which item contains information that could go into a movie script?)

A Good-for-Nothing Young Man

My daughter's boyfriend is a good-for-nothing young man. After knowing him for just three months, everyone in our family is opposed to the relationship.

For one thing, Russell is lazy.

___ a. His attitude about his job is a poor one. To hear him tell it, he deserves special treatment. He thinks he's gone out of his way if he just shows up on time. And Russell never pitches in and helps with chores around our house, even when he's asked directly to do so.

___ b. He didn't report to work one day last week because it was his *birthday*—as if that was a good excuse for taking a day off. And when my husband asked Russell to help put storm windows on the house this Saturday, Russell answered that he uses his weekends to catch up on sleep.

Another quality of Russell's which no one likes is that he is cheap.

___ c. When my daughter's birthday came around, Russell said he wanted to buy her a really nice pair of earrings. But the earrings that he gave her were obviously cheap ones. Street vendors in the neighborhood sell earrings like that for less than five dollars.

___ d. He makes big promises about all the nice things he's going to get for my daughter, but he never comes through. His words are cheap, and so is he. He's all talk and no action. If you listen to him, he wants to spend money on my daughter, but he spends as little as possible.

Worst of all, Russell is mean.

_____ e. Russell seems to get special pleasure from hurting people when he has a chance to make a joke. I have heard him make remarks that to him were just funny but that were really very insensitive. You've got to wonder about someone who needs to be ugly to other people just for the sake of showing off. Sometimes I want to let him know how I feel. All of us are hoping that my daughter realizes what's going on.

_____ f. When my husband was out of work, Russell said to him, "Well, you've got it made now, living off your wife." After my husband glared at him, he said, "Why're you getting sore? I'm just kidding." Sometimes he snaps at my daughter, saying things like "Don't make me wait—there are plenty of other babes who would like to take your place." At such times I want to blow off his head with a cannon. Everyone in the family is hoping for the day when my daughter opens her eyes to the real Russell.

TWO OTHER IMPORTANT GOALS IN WRITING

You now have a good sense of the two basic goals in effective writing:

1 **Make a point.** As a guide for yourself and for the reader, it is often best to state that point in the first sentence of your paper. In all three paragraphs you've looked at, the point has been in the first sentence:

- Choosing Dawn as a roommate was a mistake.

- High school students should be required to wear uniforms.

- My daughter's boyfriend is a good-for-nothing young man.

2 **Support the point.** To do so, you need to provide specific reasons, examples, and other details that explain and develop the point. Based on the specific evidence you provide, the reader can decide whether or not to agree with your opening point.

It is time now to look at two other important goals in effective writing:

3 **Organize the support.** There are two common ways to organize the support in a paragraph. You can use either a listing order or a time order. At the same time, you should use signal words, known as *transitions*, to move your reader clearly from one supporting idea to the next. More information about organization appears in the rest of this chapter.

4 **Check for word and sentence mistakes.** But don't worry about such mistakes while you're working on your paper! Your focus should be on making a clear point, supporting the point, and organizing the support. Only when you're almost finished with the paper should you make sure that you've spelled words correctly and that you've followed grammar, punctuation, and usage rules. To do so, you should have nearby a good dictionary and a helpful grammar handbook.

More about Organization

The most common ways to organize the supporting material in a paragraph (or a longer paper, for that matter) is to use a listing order or a time order, as explained below.

Listing Order

In a *listing order*, the writer organizes the supporting evidence in a paper by providing a list of three or more reasons, examples, or other details. Often the most important or interesting item is saved for last because the reader is most likely to remember the last thing read.

Transition words that show you a list is present are often called *addition words*. Addition words tell us that writers are *adding to* their thoughts; they are presenting items in a list. Addition words include the following:

Addition Words

for one thing	secondly	another	next	last of all
first of all	also	in addition	moreover	finally

Look again at the paragraph about Dawn, which uses a listing order.

A Terrible Roommate

Choosing Dawn as a roommate was a mistake. For one thing, Dawn was a truly noisy person. She talked loudly, she ate loudly, and she snored loudly. She never just watched TV or listened to a CD. Instead, she did both at once. I'd walk into the apartment with my hands clapped over my ears and turn off the first noisemaking machine I reached. Then I would hear her cry out, "I was listening to that." Secondly, Dawn had no sense of privacy. She would come into my bedroom even while I was dressing. She'd sit down on my bed for a chat while I was taking a nap. Once she even came in into the bathroom while I was taking a bath. Last of all, Dawn had too many visitors. I would return to the apartment after an evening out and trip over one or more of Dawn's sisters, cousins, or friends asleep on our living room floor. Dawn's visitors would stay for days, eating our groceries and tying up the bathroom and telephone. After one month I told Dawn to find another place to live.

The paragraph lists three reasons why Dawn was a bad roommate, and each of those three reasons is introduced by one of the transitions in the box above. In the spaces below, write in the three transitions:

_____   _____   _____

Explanation

The first reason in the paragraph about Dawn is introduced with *for one thing*; the second reason by *secondly*; and the third reason by *last of all*.

Now turn back to the paragraph about high school uniforms (page 150), which also uses a listing order. It lists three reasons why students should wear uniforms, and each of the reasons is introduced by one of the addition words in the box. In the spaces below, write in the three addition words:

_____   _____   _____

Explanation

The first reason is introduced with *first of all*; the second reason with *also*; and the third reason with *finally*.

Time Order

In addition to a listing order, time order can be used to organize a paragraph. In *time order*, supporting details are presented in the order in which they occurred. *First* this happened; *next* this; *after* that, this; *then* this; and so on. Many paragraphs, especially ones that tell stories or give a series of directions, are organized in a time order.

Transition words that show time relationships include the following:

Time Words

first	before	after	when	then
next	during	now	while	as

Read the paragraph below, which is organized in a time order. Choose appropriate time transitions from the box and write them in the spaces provided.

An Upsetting Incident

An incident happened yesterday that made me very angry. I got off the bus and started walking the four blocks to my friend's house. _____ I walked along, I noticed a group of boys gathered on the sidewalk about a block ahead of me. _____ they saw me, they stopped talking. A bit nervous, I thought about crossing the street to avoid them. But as I came nearer and they began to whistle, a different feeling came over me. Instead of being afraid, I was suddenly angry. Why should I have to worry about being hassled just because I was a woman? I stared straight at the boys and continued walking. _____ one of them said, "Oooh, baby. Looking fine today."_____ I knew what I was doing, I turned on him. "Do you have a mother? Or any sisters?" I demanded. He looked astonished and didn't answer me. I went on. "Is it OK with you if men speak to them like that? Shouldn't they be able to walk down the street without some creeps bothering them?" _____ I spoke, he and the other boys looked guilty and backed away. I held my head up high and walked by them. An hour later, I was still angry.

The writer makes the main point of the paragraph in her first sentence: "An incident happened yesterday that made me very angry." She then supports her point with a specific account of just what happened. Time words that could be used to help connect together her details include the following: "*As* (or *While*) I walked along"; "*When* they saw me"; "*Then* one of them said"; "*Before* I knew"; "*After* I spoke."

Michelle Wimberly

Michelle: "I love transitions! Words like although, however, *and* in addition *are lifesavers that help you provide smooth transitions between sentences and new paragraphs. The creation of a new paragraph with a different idea can be extremely awkward without the help of transitional words."*

Jennifer McCaul

Jennifer: "In the first writing course I took in college, the instructor really drummed into us how transitions make a paper flow more smoothly. I realized she was right. In fact, recently I had to write a paper that had headings for each section instead of transitions between sections, and I found it really hard to write. It seemed so choppy to jump from one subject to the other without using words like 'Another' or 'Also.'"

Krystal: "I find that transitions are a terrific way to organize my thoughts on paper, similar to an outline. Personally, I tend to worry a lot about whether my paper flows smoothly. Transitions help my paper to read well. Also, they can add to the effectiveness of the point that you are trying to make."

Krystal Buhr

Caren: "When I read material that doesn't contain good transitions, it feels choppy to me. I enjoy reading material that flows naturally. That's what transitions are for."

Caren Blackmore

➤ Activity 1: Organizing Details in Short Paragraphs

A. Use a *listing order* to arrange the scrambled list of sentences below. Number each supporting sentence 1, 2, 3, . . . so that you go from the least to the most important item.

Note that addition words will help make the relationships between sentences clear.

Topic sentence: My after-school job has provided me with important benefits.

_____ Since the job is in the morning, it usually keeps me from staying up too late.

_____ Without the money I've earned, I would not have been able to pay my tuition.

_____ A second value of the job is that it's helped me make new friends.

_____ For one thing, it's helped me manage my time.

_____ One of my coworkers loves baseball as much as I do, and we've become sports buddies.

_____ The biggest advantage of the job is that it's allowed me to stay in school.

B. Use *time order* to arrange the scrambled sentences below. Number the supporting sentences in the order in which they occur in time (1, 2, 3 . . .).

Note that time transitions will help make the relationships between sentences clear.

Topic sentence: There are several steps you can take to find an apartment.

_____ Check the classified ads and two or three real estate offices for apartments within your price range and desired location.

_____ When you have chosen your apartment, have a lawyer or a person who knows about leases examine your lease before you sign it.

_____ Then make up a list of the most promising places.

_____ As you inspect each apartment, make sure that faucets, toilets, stove, and electrical outlets are working properly.

_____ After you have a solid list, visit at least five of the most promising apartments.

➤ Activity 2: Adding Transitions to a Paragraph

A. The following paragraph uses a listing order. Fill in the blanks with appropriate addition words from the box above the paragraph. Use every transition once.

Next	One	Another

There are several reasons people daydream. _____ cause of daydreaming is boring jobs that are bearable only when workers imagine themselves doing something else. Some production line workers, for instance, might dream about running the company. _____ reason for daydreaming is lacking something. A starving person will dream about food, or a poor person will dream about owning a house or car. _____, people may daydream to deal with angry feelings. For example, an angry student might dream about dropping his instructor out of a classroom window.

B. The following paragraph uses a time order. Fill in the blanks with appropriate transitions from the box above the paragraph. Use every transition once.

Then	While	After	When

To relieve the stress I feel after a day of work and school, I take the following steps. To start with, I get off the bus a mile from my apartment. I find that a brisk walk helps me shake off the dragged-out feeling I often have at the day's end. _____ I get home, I make myself a cup of tea and lie down on the couch with my feet up. _____ I lie there, I often look through a catalog and imagine having the money to buy all the nice things I see. _____, if I've had an especially hard day, I run a deep bath with plenty of nice-smelling bath oil in it. _____ a good long soak in the hot water, I find the cares of the day have drifted away.

Final Thoughts

1 When you are asked to write a paper, here is what to aim for:

- Decide what point you will make in your paper.
- Develop enough supporting details for that point. If you can't come up with enough details, choose another topic.
- Use a method of organization such as a listing order or time order to organize your supporting information. Also use transitions.
- Check for word and sentence mistakes.

2 One question still remains: how *do* you go about actually writing the paper? Just *how* do you decide on your point? *How* do you develop good details? *How* do you find a good method of organization? All these matters are explained in the next chapter, which deals with the writing process.

FINAL ACTIVITIES

1 Check Your Understanding

1. The Snoopy cartoon is provided as an example of a writer who
   a. doesn't make a point.
   b. makes a point but doesn't support it.
   c. offers support, but doesn't make a point.
   d. makes a point and supports that point.

2. If you provide effective support for your points, your readers will
   a. always agree with you.
   b. be confused by you.
   c. understand why you believe your point is true.
   d. disagree with you.

3. To judge whether you have provided clear, specific details, the author suggests that you ask yourself,
   a. "Do I have enough details?"
   b. "Could I make a film of these details?"
   c. "Have I provided good transitions?"
   d. "Have I made spelling or grammar mistakes?"

4. Addition words, such as *for one thing, in addition,* and *another,* indicate that a paper is organized in
   a. alphabetical order.
   b. time order.
   c. order of importance.
   d. listing order.

5. If you can't come up with enough details to support the point of your paper, you should
   a. choose another topic.
   b. repeat the same details, putting them in slightly different words.
   c. invent more details, even if they aren't very relevant to your point.
   d. make do with the few supporting details you have.

2 Questions for Writing or Discussion

You may find it helpful to think about and write out your answers to the following questions. Or your instructor may put you in a small group or pair you with another student and have you discuss the questions with each other.

1. The author points out that in everyday conversation, we constantly make points—that is, we state our opinions about all kinds of things. ("That was a stupid movie." "My English instructor is the best teacher I have ever had.") He also indicates that in conversation, we may not always give reasons (support) for our opinions. Why, then, is it important to provide solid support for our points in writing? Why can you get away with making unsupported points more easily in casual conversation than in formal writing?

2. Two common ways of organizing the support in a paragraph are listing order and time order. When you use listing order, you provide a list of supporting reasons, examples, or other details, often saving the most important or interesting for last. When you use time order, you present supporting details in the order in which they occurred. Consider each of the following main points. In each case, do you think it would be more logical to use listing order or time order to organize the supporting details? Explain why you made the choice you did.

> I had an awful day from the moment I woke up until the moment I went to bed.
>
> ___ Listing order   ___ Time order
>
> There are several easy ways you can save money on your grocery bill.
>
> ___ Listing order   ___ Time order
>
> You can keep your car in good condition longer if you follow these suggestions.
>
> ___ Listing order   ___ Time order
>
> A person who is diagnosed with a serious disease often goes through the following emotional stages.
>
> ___ Listing order   ___ Time order

3. The first paragraph that follows uses a listing order, and the second paragraph uses a time order. Fill in the blanks with appropriate transitions from the boxes above the paragraph. Use each transition once.

most of all	one	also

    Watching a football game or another sports event on television is better than going to the game itself. _____ advantage is that it's cheaper to watch a game at home. Going to a sports events might cost $25 for an admission ticket plus another $10 for a parking space and refreshments. _____, it's more comfortable at home. There is no bumper-to-bumper traffic to and from a sports arena or stadium. There are no noisy, pushy crowds of people to deal with while trying to get to one's seat, which is made out of hard plastic or wood. _____, watching a game on television is more informative. Camera coverage is so good that every play is seen close up, and many plays are shown on instant replay. At the same time, the game is explained in great detail by very informed commentators. The fan at home always enjoys an insider's view of what is happening in the game at every minute.

before	then	finally	when

If you are a smoker, the following steps should help you quit. After making a definite decision to stop smoking, select a specific "quit day." You should _____ write down your decision to quit and the date of your "quit day" on a card. Place the card in a location where you will see it every day. _____ your "quit day," have a medical checkup to make sure it will be OK for you to begin an exercise program. _____ your "quit day" arrives, stop smoking and start your exercise program. _____, remind yourself repeatedly how good you will feel when you can confidently tell yourself and others that you are a nonsmoker.

4. Each point below is followed by one item of support. See if you can add a second and third specific item in each case. Make sure your items truly support the point.

Point 1. I love to eat salty snacks.

a. After my first class in the morning, I'll munch a small bag of potato chips.

b. _____

c. _____

Point 2. My friend suffered several injuries in the car accident.

a. His forehead hit the windshield and required thirty stitches.

b. _____

c. _____

Point 3. Lunch at that cafeteria is terrible.

a. The french fries are always lukewarm and soggy.

b. _____

c. _____

Point 4. My brother's room was a mess.

a. Two of his shirts were lying on the floor, unbuttoned and inside out.

b. _____

c. _____

Point 5. I grew up in a very strict household.

a. I was allowed to watch TV for one hour a day, period.

b. _____

c. _____

Point 6. Insects have invaded the house.

a. Wasps have built a nest in the attic and have been finding a way into a bedroom.

b. _____

c. _____

Point 7. The library can be a distracting place to try to study.

a. Some students are just there to flirt and spend their time talking and laughing with each other.

b. _____

c. _____

Point 8. Charlene is a very generous person.

a. She sends her sister twenty dollars a week out of her paycheck, even though she has little money to spare.

b. _____

c. _____

Point 9. Our English teacher gives us a great deal of work.

a. Every two weeks we have to read and take a test on a short novel.

b. _____

c. _____

Point 10. I have a lot of everyday worries.

a. I worry about being called on in class and embarrassing myself with the wrong answer.

b. _____

c. _____

5. The following paragraph needs specific details to back up its three supporting points. In the spaces provided, write two or three sentences of convincing details for each supporting point.

An Unpleasant Eating Experience

My family and I will never eat again at the new neighborhood restaurant. First of all, the service was poor. _____

_____

_____

Second, the prices were very high. _____

_____

_____

Most of all, the food was not very good. _____

_____

_____

3   Writing about the Basic Goals of Writing

Write a paragraph in which you evaluate your basic writing skills. Which of the basic writing guidelines described in the chapter do you practice? Which do you not practice? Begin your paragraph with one of the following **points**.

Point: I already practice the basic principles of writing described in the chapter.

Point: I do not typically practice the basic principles of writing described in the chapter.

Point: I typically aim for one or two of the basic goals in writing but not the others.

After you have chosen your point, provide **supporting details or examples** to back up your point. For instance, to support the second point above, you might say in part:

My instructors often ask me, "What's the point of this paper?" I think that I have a point, but when they ask me to say it in one sentence, I realize that I can't. I usually do just one draft of whatever I hand in. One instructor told me that what I hand in sounds like the freewriting I should do before I even start writing my real paper. I guess I need to learn to revise more.

When writing your paragraph, use examples and details that are based on your actual experience.

4   Speaking about the Basic Goals of Writing

Imagine that you have been asked to give a speech on the basic goals of writing to a class of students who will be entering college in the fall. Prepare a talk full of practical advice that really communicates with them. Imagine that the students have been told beforehand that you will be as stiff and dry as a board and that your talk will have little relevance or value. You have two goals, then: 1) to use language and images that really connect with students, and 2) to pack your talk with lots of truly helpful information. Your speech should be five to ten minutes long.

10 / Understanding the Writing Process

Chapter 9 described four basic goals in writing:

1 Make a point.

2 Support the point.

3 Organize the support.

4 Check for word and sentence mistakes.

This chapter will explain the writing process that will help you reach those goals. First, however, take a few minutes to consider your attitude toward writing.

YOUR ATTITUDE TOWARD WRITING

Your attitude toward writing is an important part of your learning to write well. To get a sense of just how you regard writing, read the following statements. Put a check beside those statements with which you agree. This activity is not a test, so try to be as honest as possible.

_____ 1. A good writer should be able to sit down and write a paper straight through without stopping.

_____ 2. Writing is a skill that anyone can learn with practice.

_____ 3. I'll never be good at writing because I make too many spelling, grammar, and punctuation mistakes.

_____ 4. Because I dislike writing, I always start a paper at the last possible minute.

_____ 5. I've always done poorly in English, and I don't expect that to change.

Now read the following comments about the five statements. The comments will help you see if your attitude is hurting or helping your efforts to become a better writer.

1. **A good writer should be able to sit down and write a paper straight through without stopping.**

The statement is *not true*. Writing is, in fact, a process. It is done not in one easy step, but in a series of steps, and seldom at one sitting. If you cannot do a paper all at once, that simply means you are like most of the other people on the planet. Please don't carry around the false idea that writing should be an easy matter!

Jhoselyn Martinez

On "A good writer should be able to sit down and write a paper straight through without stopping":

Jhoselyn: "Part of what I had to learn was that writing is a process. A lot of people have the idea that you just sit down and the writing just comes out almost automatically. I had to learn that you just don't sit down and naturally write it out. You have to do a lot of rewriting."

Krystal Buhr

Krystal: "I think that writing is a process and is not often done in one sitting. Personally speaking, I like to make an outline and then a rough draft. On any particular paper I will revise a draft three or four times before submitting the final draft. I also like to discuss my papers with others and give them the chance to read my paper and make suggestions before I write a final draft."

2. **Writing is a skill that anyone can learn with practice.**

This statement is absolutely *true*. Writing is a skill, like driving or cooking or word processing, that you can master with hard work. If you want to learn to write, you can. It is as simple as that. If you believe this, you are ready to learn how to become a competent writer.

Some people hold the false belief that writing is a natural gift which some have and others do not. Because of this belief, they never make a truly honest effort to learn to write—and so they never learn.

Caren Blackmore

On "Writing is a skill that anyone can learn with practice":

Caren: "Everyone can learn to write well enough to please the professors. You can learn the guidelines for a class and measure up to them. Sure, there will always be someone who loves to write and makes you feel bad because he or she can make the words sound sweet. But you can do well enough to get a B or an A."

Michelle Wimberly

3. **I'll never be good at writing because I make too many spelling, grammar, and punctuation mistakes.**

The first concern in good writing should be *content*—what you have to say. Your ideas and feelings are what matter most. You should *not* worry about spelling, grammar, and punctuation rules while working on content.

Unfortunately, some people are so self-conscious about making mistakes that they do not focus on the heart of the matter: coming up with a clear point and good support for that point. They need to realize that a paper is best done in stages, and that grammar and so on should wait until a later stage in the writing process. Through review and practice, you will eventually learn how to follow the rules with confidence.

Michelle Miller

Ginger Jackson

On "I'll never be good at writing because I make too many spelling, grammar, and punctuation mistakes":

Ginger: *"I completely disagree with that statement. I make various grammar and punctuation mistakes. My chief focus is on the content and the purpose of the paper. I worry about grammar afterward. If I was concerned with grammar as I went along, I would lose my train of thought and how I truly feel. When I get a paper back, if there are marks regarding grammar, then I really try to learn where I went wrong in my grammar or punctuation."*

4. Because I dislike writing, I always start a paper at the last possible minute.

This is all-too-common behavior. You feel you are going to do poorly, and then behave in a way to ensure that you *will* do poorly! Your attitude is so negative that you defeat yourself—not even allowing enough time to really try.

Again, what you need to realize is that writing is a process. Because it is done in steps, you don't have to get it right all at once. If you allow yourself enough time, you'll find a way to make a paper come together.

Caren Blackmore

On "Because I dislike writing, I always start at the last possible minute":

Caren: *"That's the worst idea ever. OK, you start at the last possible minute. But you still have to do the paper. And you won't have time to do a good job, so you're bound to end up with something crappy."*

Krystal Buhr

Krystal: *"This is not a legitimate excuse. By starting your paper at the last minute, you are placing a lot of pressure on yourself to produce quality work in a limited amount of time. It's been my experience that when I write a paper and then go two or three days without looking at it, I have fresh ideas and I'm able to add more to the paper. I try to start a paper maybe a week or two ahead of time."*

5. I've always done poorly in English, and I don't expect that to change.

How you may have performed in the *past* does not control how you can perform in the *present*. Even if you have done poorly in English until now, it is in your power to make English one of your good subjects. If you believe writing can be learned and then work hard at it, you *will* become a better writer.

Caren Blackmore

On "I've always done poorly in English, and I don't expect that to change":

Caren: *"If you care enough to practice, you can change anything."*

Ginger: *"If you work hard enough at it and have a positive attitude about overcoming your writing difficulties, you can improve in English. I see real improvements in my writing since I started college. Even if you didn't do well in English in high school, for example, that doesn't mean you can't improve later on. The more work you put into it, the better you will get over time."*

Ginger Jackson

In conclusion, your attitude is crucial. If you believe that you are a poor writer and always will be, chances are you will *not* improve. If you realize that you can become a better writer, chances are you *will* improve. Depending on how you allow yourself to think, you can be your own best friend or your own worst enemy.

UNDERSTANDING THE WRITING PROCESS

Even professional writers do not sit down and write a paper in a single draft. Instead, they have to work on it one step at a time. Writing a paper is a process that can be divided into the following five steps:

Step 1: Getting Started through Prewriting

Step 2: Preparing a Scratch Outline

Step 3: Writing the First Draft

Step 4: Revising

Step 5: Editing

These steps are described on the following pages.

Step 1: Getting Started through Prewriting

What you need to learn, first, are strategies that you can use to start working on a paper. These techniques will help you do the thinking needed to figure out both the point you want to make and the support you need for that point. Here are four helpful prewriting strategies:

- Freewriting
- Questioning
- Clustering
- List making

Each technique is explained in turn on the pages that follow.

Freewriting

Freewriting is just sitting down and writing whatever comes into your mind about a topic. Do this for ten minutes or so. Write without stopping, and without worrying in the slightest about spelling, grammar, or the like. Simply get down on paper all the information that occurs to you about the topic.

Below is the freewriting done by Cheryl (see page 148) on problems with her roommate Dawn. Cheryl had been given the assignment, "Write about a problem with a friend, a family member, or someone you know." Cheryl felt right away that she could write about her former roommate. She began prewriting as a way to explore her topic and generate details about it.

Example of Freewriting

One thing I would like to write about is my roomate. What a charakter. I learned my lesson with her, I am going to think twice before taking on a roomate again. She folowed me everywhere. Once when I was taking a bath. She didnt like to be alone. I could be taking a nap and she would just walk right in, I'd wake up and there she would be. Talking away. I had to lock doors all the time. To my bedroom and to my bathroom. Then I hurt her feelings. She did pay her rent on time. I'll say that for her. And she was a good cook. But other things were too much. She was on the phone a lot. She had more relatives and friends than anyone I ever knew. It seemed like they were living their. I got sick and tired of all the people around. She even had keys made up for them and gave them the keys! I really blowed up with her when that happen. There were always dishes in the sink. I would do mine, she not hers. She was a messy person. Cloths all over her bedroom. Stuff was always turned on. She liked things noisee. The TV was always blaring when I walked in. Give me a break, woman. I got back from a crazy day at school wanting some peace and quite. But what do I get? I needed to get her out of my life.

Notice that there are lots of problems with spelling, grammar, and punctuation in Cheryl's freewriting. Cheryl is not worried about such matters, *nor should she be at this stage*. She is just concentrating on getting ideas and details down on paper. She knows that it is best to focus on one thing at a time. At this stage, she just wants to write out thoughts as they come to her, to do some thinking on paper.

You should take the same approach when freewriting: explore your topic without worrying at all about writing "correctly." Figuring out what you want to say should have all your attention in this early stage of the writing process.

➤ **Activity: Freewriting**

On a sheet of paper, freewrite for at least ten minutes on the best or worst job or chore you ever had. Don't worry about grammar, punctuation, or spelling. Try to write—without stopping—about whatever comes into your head concerning your best or worst job or chore.

Terry Oakman

Terry: "*I'll start by freewriting and every so often maybe draw a line through something I know is going off the point. I just try to write everything out, and I get into my topic as I write about it. I'm really thinking as I'm writing. I don't worry at all about grammar and mistakes. I want to get the content and my ideas down on the page, and I can then shape it from there.*"

Questioning

Questioning means that you generate details about your topic by writing down a series of questions and answers about it. Your questions can start with words like *what, when, where, why,* and *how.*

Here are some questions that Cheryl might have asked while developing her paper:

Example of Questioning

- **Why** did I have a problem with Dawn? She was hard to live with.
- **How** was she hard to live with? She followed me around everywhere; I had no privacy. Also, she was noisy.
- **When** did I have no privacy? When I got back from school and wanted to be quiet and alone; when her relatives came.
- **Where** did I have no privacy? In my bedroom while I was napping; when her relatives were covering the floor when I walked in.
- **When** was she noisy? When I got back from school and when I'd try to study at night.
- **Where** was she noisy? The noise could be heard anywhere in the apartment.

➤ **Activity: Questioning**

On a sheet of paper, answer the following questions about your best or worst job or chore.

- When did you have the job (or chore)?
- Where did you work?
- What did you do?
- Whom did you work for?
- Why did you like or dislike the job? (Give one reason and some details that support that reason.)
- What is another reason you liked or disliked the job? What are some details that support the second reason?
- Can you think of a third reason you liked or did not like the job? What are some details that support the third reason?

Floyd: "*At first I tried to do a paper all at once. But I learned that the way to write is to freewrite or question first. Just write down everything that comes to you, or write out all the questions and answers you can think of about your topic. Then look for a meaning in what you are writing—try to come up with a point you can make.*"

Floyd Allen

Clustering

Clustering (also known as *diagramming* or *mapping*) is another strategy that can be used to generate material for a paper. It is helpful for people who like to do their thinking in a visual way.

In clustering, you begin by writing your subject in a few words in the center of a blank sheet of paper. Then as ideas come to you, put them in ovals, boxes, or circles around the subject and draw lines to connect them to the subject. Put minor ideas or details in smaller boxes or circles, and use connecting lines to show how they relate as well.

Keep in mind that there is no right or wrong way of clustering. It is a way to think on paper about how various ideas and details relate to one another. Here is an example of clustering that Cheryl could have done to develop her ideas.

Example of clustering

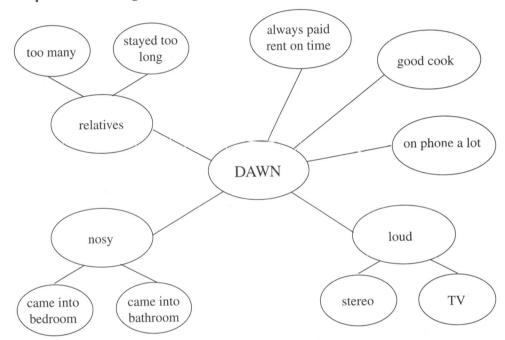

Notice that clustering, like freewriting, includes details that do not end up in the final paragraph. Cheryl decided later not to develop the idea that Dawn spent a lot of time on the phone. And she realized that the details about Dawn's paying the rent on time and being a good cook were not relevant to her point. It is natural for a number of such extra or unrelated details to appear as part of the prewriting process. The goal of prewriting is to get a lot of information down on paper. You can then shape, add to, and subtract from your raw material as you write a series of drafts.

➤ Activity: Clustering

In the center of a blank sheet of paper, write "best job (or chore)" or "worst job (or chore)" and circle it. Then, around the circle, add reasons and details about the job. Use boxes, circles, or other shapes, along with connecting lines, to set off the reasons and details. In other words, try to think about and explore your topic in a very visual way.

List Making

In *list making* (also known as *brainstorming*), you make a list of ideas and details that could go into your paper. Simply pile these items up, one after another, without worrying about putting them in any special order. Try to accumulate as many details as you can think of.

After Cheryl did her freewriting about her roommate, she made up the following list of details.

Example of list making

Dawn was always around
followed me into the bathroom
came into the bedroom when I was sleeping
walked in on me while I was dressing
I couldn't be alone when I wanted to
started locking doors behind me
talked a lot on the phone
talked when I was going out the door to school
had a lot of relatives
three sisters and they all visited
also cousins she was close to
I would come home and relatives would be there
sometimes they were there and Dawn wasn't
she had keys made for some of them
ate out sometimes because no room to cook in kitchen
lot of cooking smells in the house
a very good cook
never charged me for food she bought
also good about paying her rent on time
but hard to relax around
played TV all the time
played stereo at the same time
everything about Dawn was loud
even her clothes were loud

One detail led to another as Cheryl expanded her list. Slowly but surely, more supporting material emerged that she could use in developing her paper. By the time she had finished her list, she was ready to plan an outline of her paragraph and to write her first draft.

➤ Activity: List Making

On separate paper, make a list of details about the job (or chore). Don't worry about putting them in a certain order. Just get down as many details about the job as occur to you. The list can include specific reasons you liked or did not like the job and specific details supporting those reasons.

Important Notes about Prewriting Strategies

Some writers may use only one of the above prewriting strategies. Others may use bits and pieces of all four of them. Any one strategy can lead to another. Freewriting may lead to questioning or clustering, which may then lead to a list. Or a writer may start with a list and then use freewriting or questioning to develop items on the list or generate additional items. During this early stage of the writing process, as you do your thinking on paper, anything goes. You should not expect a straight-line progression from the beginning to the end of your paper. Instead, there probably will be a continual moving back and forth as you work to discover your point and just how you will develop it.

Keep in mind that prewriting can also help you choose among several topics. Cheryl might not have been so sure about which person to write about. Then she could have made a list of possible topics—names of people with whom she has had problems. After selecting two or three names from the list, she could have done some prewriting on each to see which seemed most promising. After finding a likely topic, Cheryl would have continued with her prewriting activities until she had a solid main point and plenty of support.

Finally, remember that you are not ready to begin writing a paper until you know your main point and many of the details that can be used to support it. Don't rush through prewriting. It's better to spend more time on this stage than to waste time writing a paragraph for which you have no solid point and too little interesting support.

Step 2: Preparing a Scratch Outline

A *scratch outline* is a brief plan for a paragraph. It shows at a glance the point of the paragraph and the support for that point. It is the logical framework on which the paper is built.

This rough outline often follows freewriting, questioning, clustering, list making, or all four. Or it may gradually emerge in the midst of these strategies. In fact, trying to outline is a good way to see if you need to do more prewriting. If a solid outline does not emerge, then you know you need to do more prewriting to clarify your main point or its support. And once you have a workable outline, you may realize, for instance, that you want to do more list making to develop one of the supporting details in the outline.

In Cheryl's case, as she was working on her list of details, she suddenly discovered what the plan of her paragraph could be. She went back to the list, crossed out items that she now realized did not fit, and added the comments shown below and on the next page.

Example of a list with added comments

I had a bad roommate—three reasons:

Dawn was always around
followed me into the bathroom
came into the bedroom when I was sleeping
walked in on me while I was dressing
I couldn't be alone when I wanted to
started locking doors behind me
~~talked a lot on the phone~~

Nosy

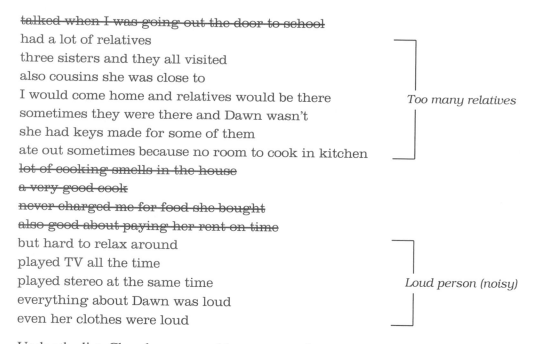

~~talked when I was going out the door to school~~
had a lot of relatives
three sisters and they all visited
also cousins she was close to
I would come home and relatives would be there   *Too many relatives*
sometimes they were there and Dawn wasn't
she had keys made for some of them
ate out sometimes because no room to cook in kitchen
~~lot of cooking smells in the house~~
~~a very good cook~~
~~never charged me for food she bought~~
~~also good about paying her rent on time~~
but hard to relax around
played TV all the time
played stereo at the same time   *Loud person (noisy)*
everything about Dawn was loud
even her clothes were loud

Under the list, Cheryl was now able to prepare her scratch outline:

Example of a scratch outline

I had a bad roommate.

1.   Too nosy (no sense of privacy)

2.   Too many relatives (put last—worst reason)

3.   Too noisy (put first)

After all her preliminary writing, Cheryl sat back pleased. She knew she had a promising paper—one with a clear point and solid support. Cheryl was now ready to write the first draft of her paper, using her outline as a guide.

➤ **Activity: Scratch Outline**

Using the list you have prepared, see if you can create a scratch outline made up of the three main reasons you liked or did not like the job.

_____ was the best (*or* worst) job (or chore) I ever had.

Reason 1:_____

Reason 2:_____

Reason 3:_____

Step 3: Writing the First Draft

When you do a first draft, be prepared to put in additional thoughts and details that didn't emerge in your prewriting. And don't worry if you hit a snag. Just leave a blank space or add a comment such as "Do later" and press on to finish the paper. Also, don't worry yet about grammar, punctuation, or spelling. You don't want to take time correcting words or sentences that you may decide to remove later. Instead, make it your goal to develop the content of your paper with plenty of specific details.

Here is Cheryl's first draft:

First Draft

Last fall, I decided that I needed to save money by sharing my apartment with someone. I put an ad in the paper and chose the first person who called which was Dawn. She was the loudest person I have ever known over the age of five. She talked loud, and she was a noisy eater. When you tried to sleep at night you sure knew what a loud snorer she was. The only other person who snored that loud was my father, and he would wake up everyone in the family. The TV was always on, it was loud. The same thing with the stereo. There was always noise when I walked into the apt. I would have to tell her to turn something off. Then she would complane I was too demandin. Dawn never gave me much privicy. She would come into the bedroom when I was naping. I'd be aware that someone was standing there. As soon as I woke she would start talking. ADD MORE DETAILS LATER. Her relatives seemed to come out of the woodwork. I'd walk in and they'd be covering the chairs and sofa and carpet. They were frendly people but too much. They'd be eating in the kitchen. Or watching TV. Or be in the bathroom when I wanted to go in. All this was too much.

After Cheryl finished the draft, she was able to put it aside until the next day. You will benefit as well if you can allow some time between finishing a draft and starting to revise.

➤ Activity: First Draft

Now write a first draft of your paper. Begin with your topic sentence stating that a certain job (or chore) was the best or worst one you ever had. Then state the first reason why it was the best or the worst, followed by specific details supporting that reason. Use a transition such as *First of all* to introduce the first reason. Next, state the second reason, followed by specific details supporting that reason. Use a transition such as *Secondly* to introduce the second reason. Last, state the third reason, followed with support. Use a transition such as *Finally* to introduce the last reason.

Don't worry about grammar, punctuation, or spelling. Just concentrate on getting down on paper the details about the job.

Step 4: Revising

Revising is as much a stage in the writing process as prewriting, outlining, and doing the first draft. *Revising* means that you rewrite a paper, building upon what has been done to make it stronger and better. One writer has said about revision, "It's like cleaning house—getting rid of all the junk and putting things in the right order." A typical revision means writing at least one or two more drafts.

Here is Cheryl's second draft.

Second Draft

Taking in Dawn as a roomate was a mistake. For one thing Dawn was noisy. She talked and ate loudly, and she snored loudly. She never just had on the TV or a CD in her stereo. She did both at once. Id walk into the apt. with my hands over my ears and turn off the first noisy machine I reached. I would hear her cry out I was listening to that. The second bad thing about Dawn was that she had no sense of privicy. She walked in on me when I was dressing. She sat down on my bed for a chat while I was naping. She even came into the bathroom once when I was taking a bath. The third thing about Dawn was that she had too many relatives. I counted over ten and they all came to the apartment. After a night out I would come in and trip over relatives asleep on the living room floor. Relatives would stay eating grocerys and tying up the bathroom and telephone. Dawn is gone now, and I've had to take a second job to handle the rent.

Notice that in redoing the draft, Cheryl started by clearly stating the point of her paragraph. Also, she inserted clear transitions to set off the three reasons why Dawn was a bad roommate. She omitted the detail about her father snoring, which was not relevant to a paragraph focusing on Dawn. She added more details, so that she would have enough support for each of her three reasons. She also began to correct some of her spelling mistakes and added a final sentence to round off the paragraph.

Cheryl then went on to revise the second draft. Since she was doing her paper on a computer, she was able to print it out quickly. She double-spaced the lines, allowing room for revisions, which she added in longhand as part of her third draft. (Note that if you are not using a computer, you may want to skip every other line when writing out each draft. Also, write on only one side of a page, so that you can see your entire paper at one time.)

Shown below are some of the changes that Cheryl made in longhand as she worked on her third draft. Notice that at this stage, her revision also includes some editing.

Part of Third Draft

Choosing ~~Taking in~~ Dawn as a *roommate* ~~roomate~~ was a mistake. For one thing, Dawn was *a truly noisy person.* ~~noisy~~.
She talked *loudly, she* ~~and~~ ate loudly, and she snored loudly. She never just ~~had on the~~ *watched* TV or a *listened to* CD ~~in her stereo~~. *Instead, s*~~S~~he did both at once. Id walk into the *apartment* ~~apt.~~ with my hands over
my ears and turn off the first *noisemaking* ~~noisy~~ machine I reached. *Then* I would hear her cry out "I
was listening to that." *Secondly,* ~~The second bad thing about~~ Dawn ~~was that she~~ had no sense
of *privacy* ~~privicy~~. . . .

You may be tired of working on the paper at this point, but you want to give the extra effort needed to make the paper as good as possible. The final work you do can mean the difference between a higher and a lower grade.

Tynara Chappelle

Michelle Nguyen

On Revising:

Tynara: *"At first, I never did a draft of any paper. I'd sit at the computer and just write down one draft. Later I learned to do an outline and do several rough drafts, making my paper better with each draft. Then I started getting good grades on papers."*

Michelle N.: *"After I do a draft of a paper, I take it to a tutor at the writing center and have her check it out. Then I revise, revise, revise. I still make mistakes, but with every draft I learn a little more about how to do it right."*

Jhoselyn: *"Writing a paper was hard for me because I wanted everything to be just right the first time. I'd just get all frustrated as I wrote because of the mistakes I knew I was making. Finally a friend told me, 'Don't try to make it perfect right away! Just get it down on paper and go from there.' That was good advice for me. Once it was written down, I could more calmly go back and revise and correct it."*

Michelle W.: *"Writing takes a while. You MUST write a paper ahead of time and give yourself time to read it over and revise it. Revision is part of the process. Your paper gets better if you allow time between drafts. If I work three days on a paper, it's a better paper than if I only work one day on it. A paper you do quickly just cannot be as good."*

Jhoselyn Martinez

Michelle Wimberly

After writing out all of her revisions, Cheryl typed them into her computer file and printed out the almost-final draft of her paper. She was now ready to do a final edit of her paper.

➤ **Activity: Revising the Draft**

Ideally, you will have a chance to put the paper aside for a while before doing later drafts. When you revise, try to do all of the following:

- Omit any details that do not truly support your topic sentence.

- Add more details as needed, making sure you have plenty of specific support for each of your three reasons.

- Be sure to include a final sentence that rounds off the paper, bringing it to a close.

Step 5: Editing

Editing, the final stage in the writing process, means checking a paper carefully for spelling, grammar, punctuation, and other errors. You are ready for this stage when you are satisfied that your point is clear, your supporting details are good, and your paper is well organized.

At this stage, *you should read your paper out loud.* Hearing how your writing sounds is an excellent way to pick up grammar and punctuation problems in your writing. Chances are that you will find sentence mistakes at every spot where your paper does not read smoothly and clearly. This point is so important that it bears repeating: *To find mistakes in your paper, read it out loud!*

At this point in her work, Cheryl read her latest draft out loud. She looked closely at all the spots where her writing did not read easily. She used a grammar handbook to deal with the problems at those spots in her paper, and she made the corrections needed so that all her sentences read smoothly. She also used her dictionary to check on the spelling of every word she was unsure about. She even took a blank sheet of paper and used it to uncover her paper one line at a time, looking for any other mistakes that might be there.

➤ **Activity: Editing**

When you have your almost-final draft of the paper, edit it in the following ways:

- Read the paper aloud, listening for awkward wordings and places where the meaning is unclear. Make the changes needed for the paper to read smoothly and clearly. In addition, see if you can get another person to read the draft aloud to you. The spots that this person has trouble reading are spots where you may have to do some revision and correct your grammar or punctuation mistakes.

- Using your dictionary (or the spell-check program on a computer), check any words that you think might be misspelled.

- Finally, take a sheet of paper and cover your paper, so that you can expose and carefully proofread one line at a time. Use your handbook to check any other spots where you think there might be grammar or punctuation mistakes in your writing.

Terry Oakman

Floyd Allen

Kenyon Whittington

On Editing:

Terry: "I'll read a paper out loud to myself to see that it makes sense and that it's flowing. If I have trouble reading something, I know I have to revise and edit it."

Floyd: "When I'd finish a paper, or I thought I had finished, I'd take it to the writing center. People there would ask me to read my paper out loud. They'd say, 'Read the paper to me. See what sounds right and what does not sound right.' Then I'd find out I wasn't done. Reading out loud would help me locate all the snags in my paper. Wherever it wasn't reading smoothly and clearly, there was a problem to address there. I learned you had to read aloud and then revise."

Kenyon: "Part of my writing technique is to read what I write out loud. If it doesn't read clearly, it has to be changed. You have to double-check yourself. The voice you have in your mind may not be clear to your readers. Reading out loud helps you pick up what's missing from the flow. The paper has to flow; when it does not flow, you know something is wrong. Look at a handbook when it's needed, especially when you're getting the final draft ready."

Final Thoughts

You have a paper to write. Here in a nutshell is what to do:

1 Write about what you know. If you don't know much about your topic, go onto the Internet (see pages 201–202 of this book), or go to the library to research the topic.

2 Use prewriting strategies to begin to write about your topic. Look for a point you can make, and make sure you have details to support it.

3 Write several drafts, aiming all the while for three goals in your writing: a clear point, strong support for that point, and well-organized support. Use transitions to help organize your support.

4 Then read your paper out loud. It should read smoothly and clearly. Look closely for grammar and punctuation problems at any rough spots. Check a grammar handbook or a dictionary as needed.

FINAL ACTIVITIES

1   Check Your Understanding

Answer the following questions to check your understanding of the chapter.

1. Which of the following statements about writing is *not* true?
   a. Writing is a process that is best accomplished in several sittings.
   b. People must be born with writing talent to become effective writers.
   c. A writer should not worry about grammar, punctuation, and spelling errors in the early stages of writing a paper.
   d. Like playing the piano or shooting baskets, writing is a skill that can be learned.

2. Preparing a scratch outline is a good idea after you have spent some time
   a. freewriting.
   b. questioning.
   c. clustering.
   d. doing any of the above.

3. Your attitude about irrelevant details that appear in your freewriting should be:
   a. "If I were a better writer, I wouldn't even have written those down."
   b. "I should stop and erase those before I freewrite any more."
   c. "I hate to waste anything, so I guess I'll use them in my final paper anyway."
   d. "The important thing is that I'm getting ideas down on paper—I can delete things later."

4. Your goal as you write the first draft of your paper should be to
   a. make few if any spelling or punctuation errors.
   b. develop a paper that contains plenty of specific details.
   c. make the first draft of your paper also the last.
   d. include very clear transitions between your supporting details.

5. What should you do in the editing of your paper that you have not been advised to do in an earlier stage?
   a. Add many more details.
   b. Read it out loud.
   c. Write a clear topic sentence.
   d. Take out supporting material that is not truly relevant.

2   Questions for Writing or Discussion

You may find it helpful to think about and write out your answers to the following questions. Or your instructor may put you in a small group or pair you with another student and have you discuss the questions with each other.

1. The beginning of this chapter describes several very common attitudes: "A good writer should be able to sit down and write a paper straight through without stopping"; "I'll never be good at writing because I make too many spelling, grammar, and punctuation mistakes"; and "I've always done poorly in English, and I don't expect that to change." Have you held any of these attitudes? What do you think has contributed to these attitudes? What do you think are good ways to change such attitudes?

2. The beginning of the chapter also describes a very common behavior. Because many students dislike writing, they often start a paper at the very last minute. Do you do this? How would you suggest changing this last-minute approach to writing?

3. Which of the prewriting techniques described in this chapter sounds like the one you would most enjoy trying? Why? Which are you least likely to try? Why?

4. Listed in the box below are five stages in the process of composing a paragraph titled "Living with Elderly Parents."

---

1. Prewriting (list)

2. Prewriting (freewriting, questioning, and scratch outline)

3. First draft

4. Revising (second draft)

5. Revising (final draft)

The five stages appear in scrambled order below and on the next page. Write the number 1 in the blank space in front of the first stage of development and number the remaining stages in sequence.

_____ It can be a good thing for adult children to have their elderly parents live with them. ~~When they need to call a babysitter~~ They rarely need to call a babysitter because they have live-in babysitters. ~~Children get extra attention.~~ Children benefit from the extra attention from their grandparents. Feeling useful is good for elderly people. Being involved with children is good for elderly people. Mrs. McMann is one older lady I know who seems much younger than she is because she watches her grandchildren. ~~They~~ The older people stay more active. More involved with family . . . keep more interested in life . . .

_____ Living with Elderly Parents

Adult children get live-in babysitter
Kids learn about past
Elderly people serve useful role in family
Elders help with household tasks
Kids get more attention
Elders stay active and interested in young people

_____   Living with Elderly Parents

There are advantages to everyone when elderly parents live with a family. First of all, the adult children can benefit. When they want to go out for an evening, they have a trusted babysitter right there in the home. Secondly, the children in the home profit from the arrangement. They get to know their older relatives and hear stories about the past. Children need attention from adults, so it's good for them to get the extra love and time from their grandparents. And finally, the arrangement is a good one for the elderly people. Too often older people feel cut off from their families. It's good for them to know they still play a useful role in the family. Being involved in the daily lives of younger people helps keep the older people active and involved in life. All in all, having elderly people live with their younger relatives is a good situation for everyone.

_____   When elderly parents live with their adult children, it can be a good situation for everyone. The adult children don't need to call a babysitter when they want to go out for an evening, because the grandparents can watch the children. Having their grandparents live with them is a great thing for young children, too. They like the extra attention that comes from the older adults. It's good too for children to learn about the past from the older generation. Most of all, older adults benefit from the arrangement. If they don't get along well with their children or grandchildren, of course, it's not such a great idea. But older people often enjoy feeling needed and useful in the family. By staying involved with younger people, they stay active and involved in life.

_____   Living with elderly parents can be a good idea. For example, giving elders useful role in family. Kids get more attention if grandparents are around. Live-in babysitter is useful too. Good for elderly people to stay active. Example Mrs. McMann—seems much younger than she is, involved with kids.

Whom does living with elderly parents benefit?
— Elderly parents
— Adult children
— Kids

When is living with elderly parents a good idea?
— When kids need babysitting
— When adults and elderly parents get along well

1. Live-in babysitter
2. Elderly people stay active
3. Kids like extra attention

3 Writing about Your Attitude

Write a paragraph in which you evaluate your attitude toward writing. Which of the five statements on page 167 apply to you? Which do not apply? Begin your paragraph with one of the following **points**.

Point: I have a positive attitude about writing.

Point: I've had a negative attitude about writing that until now has probably limited my chances to improve.

Point: My attitude about writing might be described as a mix of positive and negative feelings.

After you have chosen your point, provide **supporting details or examples** to back up your point. For instance, to support the second point above, you might say in part:

> I have never liked to write, and I don't expect that to change. I avoid classes that require a lot of writing. I don't like writing because when you write, you have to remember a lot of rules that don't make any sense to me. What difference does it make if you write fragments rather than complete sentences? People can still tell what you mean. If fragments aren't good in business writing, I'll be sure to have a secretary to fix my mistakes.

When writing your paragraph, use examples and details that are based on your actual experience.

4   Writing about the Writing Process

Write a paragraph in which you evaluate your understanding of the writing process. Which steps in prewriting and writing do you practice? Which do you not practice? Begin your paragraph with one of the following **points**.

> **Point:** I already understand and practice the steps in the writing process as described in this chapter.
>
> **Point:** I have not typically practiced the steps in the writing process as described in this chapter.
>
> **Point:** I practice some of the steps in the writing process but not the others.

After you have chosen your point, provide **supporting details or examples** to back up your point. For instance, to support the third point above, you might say in part:

> I have never done much of what the chapter calls prewriting. Although I think ahead of time about what I'm going to write, I don't usually write my ideas down on paper. But I do always make up a scratch outline for my paper. That saves me a lot of time. Otherwise, I just start writing and realize later that I've explained half of point A, then half of point B, and then eventually gotten back to finishing point A. Having an outline keeps my thoughts better organized. I do always write and re-write several drafts to make sure that I have made my papers as smooth and error-free as I can make them.

When writing your paragraph, use examples and details that are based on your actual experience.

5   Speaking about the Writing Process

Imagine that you have been asked to give a speech on the writing process to a class of students who will be entering college in the fall. Prepare a talk full of practical advice that really communicates with them. Imagine that the students have been told beforehand that you will be as stiff and dry as a board and that your talk will have little relevance or value. You have two goals, then: 1) to use language and images that really connect with students, and 2) to pack your talk with lots of truly helpful information. Your speech should be five to ten minutes long.

6   Writing Assignments

The best way to learn a skill is to practice that skill. Following, then, are a wide series of topics that you can use to practice writing. Here are guidelines to follow:

How to Proceed with Writing a Paper

1. Choose a topic in which you have an interest and—just as important—about which you have information. You will not be able to provide the support needed in a paper unless you have knowledge about the subject.

2. Think about the topic on paper. You may want to freewrite about it, write a series of questions and answers about it, create a cluster of possible details, or make up a list of details.

3. Continue thinking and prewriting until you know what the point of your paper could be and what your support could be for that point. Then prepare a scratch outline.

4. Use your scratch outline as a guide as you write your first and maybe second draft of the paper.

5. Ideally, put your paper aside for a while. When you reread it, chances are that you'll see ways to revise it and improve it. Your goals are to have a paper that *makes* a point, *supports* its point, and *organizes* its support (maybe with the help of transitions).

6. When you think the paper is done, read it out loud. Then edit and rework it until it reads smoothly and clearly.

1   **Best or Worst Childhood Experience.**   Some of our most vivid memories are of things that happened to us as children, and these memories don't ever seem to fade. In fact, many elderly people say that childhood memories are clearer to them than things that happened yesterday. Think back to one of the best or worst experiences you had as a child. Try to remember the details of the event—sights, sounds, smells, textures, tastes.

You might begin by freewriting for ten minutes or so about good or bad childhood experiences. That freewriting may suggest to you a topic you will want to develop.

After you have decided on a topic, try to write a clear sentence stating what the experience was and whether it was one of the best or worst of your childhood. For example, "The time I was beaten up coming home from my first day in fifth grade was one of my worst childhood moments."

You may then find it helpful to make a list in which you jot down as many details as you can remember about the experience. Stick with a single experience, and don't try to describe too much. If a week you spent at summer camp was an unpleasant experience, don't try to write about the entire week. Just describe one horrible moment or event.

When you write the paper, use a time order to organize details: first this happened, then this, next this, and so on.

As you write, imagine that someone is going to make a short film based on your paragraph. Try to provide vivid details, quotations, and pictures for the filmmaker to shoot.

2   A Special Photograph.   We tend to take photographs for granted, but they are magical things. They freeze moments forever, capturing small pieces of time within their borders. Find a photograph that has special meaning for you. Write a paper which describes the photograph and explains why it is special to you.

You might want to first describe the event, place, person, or persons that the photograph shows. Then explain the special significance that the photograph has for you. Attach the photograph (or a photocopy of it) to the final draft of your paper.

3   A Certain Song or Movie.   Is there a certain song or movie that is especially memorable to you? If so, mention the title of the song (the title should be in quotation marks) or movie (the title should be underlined or in italics), and write about the time when the song or movie became so meaningful to you. To be convincing, you will need to include numerous details and clear explanations.

4   A Special Place or Object.   Write a paragraph describing either a place or an object you respond to with strong emotion, such as love, fear, warmth, dread, joy, or sadness. Specific details and vivid description will need to be provided if your emotional reaction is to be understood.

5   A Good or Bad Day in Your Life.   Write in detail about a recent good or bad day in your life—your activities, feelings, and experiences during the day. You might begin by making a list of things that you did, felt, saw, thought, heard, and said during that day. Your aim is to accumulate a great many details that you can draw upon later as you begin writing your paper. Making a long list is an excellent way to get started.

Then select and develop those details that best support the idea that the day was a good one or a bad one. Organize your paragraph using a time order—first this happened, then this, next this, and so on.

6   Directions to a Place.   Write a set of specific directions on how to get from the English classroom to your house. Imagine you are giving these directions to a stranger who has just come into the room and who wants to deliver a million dollars to your home. You want, naturally, to give exact directions, including various landmarks that may guide the way for the stranger, who does not know the area.

To help you write the paper, first make up a list of all the directions involved. Also, use words like *next, then,* and *after* to help the reader follow clearly as you move from one direction to the next.

7   A Helpful Experience.   Write an account of an experience you have had that taught you something important. It might involve a mistake you made or an event that gave you insight into yourself or others. Perhaps you have had problems at school that taught you to be a more effective student, or you have had a conflict that you now understand could have been avoided. Whatever experience you choose to write about, be sure to tell how it has changed your way of thinking.

8   Hindsight.   Occasionally, we call someone a "Monday-morning quarterback." By this we mean that it's easy to say what should have been done after an event (or game) is over. But while we're in the midst of our daily lives, it's hard to know which is the right decision to make or what is the right course of action. We've all looked back and thought, "I wish I'd done . . ." or "I wish I'd said . . ."

Think back to a year or two ago. What is the best advice someone could have given you then? Freewrite for ten minutes or so about how your life might have changed if you have been given that advice.

Then go on to write a paper that begins with a topic sentence something like this, "I wish someone had told me a year ago to cut back a little on my work hours while I'm in school."

9 **Parents and Children.** It has been said that the older we get, the more we see our parents in ourselves. Indeed, any of our habits (good and bad), beliefs, and qualities can often be traced to one of our parents.

Write a paragraph in which you describe three characteristics you have "inherited" from a parent. You might want to think about your topic by asking yourself a series of questions: "How am I like my mother (or father)?" "When and where am I like her (or him)?" "Why am I like her (or him)?"

One student who did such a paper used as her topic sentence the following statement: "Although I hate to admit it, I know that in several ways I'm just like my mom." She then went on to describe how she works too hard, worries too much, and judges other people too harshly. Another student wrote, "I resemble my father in my love of TV sports, my habit of putting things off, and my reluctance to show my feelings." Be sure to include examples for each of the characteristics you mention.

10 **A Time for Courage.** Write about a time when you had to have courage. Think of an action that frightened you, but that you felt you needed to take anyway. Perhaps you were afraid to ask someone out on a date, or to say no when someone asked you to do something you felt was wrong, or to perform a dangerous activity. In your paper, describe the frightening situation that faced you and how you made the decision to act with courage. Then tell what happened—the actions that you took, the responses of those around you, significant things people said, and how things turned out.

For example, you might begin with a statement like this:

- When I was in junior high, it required courage for me to resist the temptation to shoplift with my favorite cousin.

That passage would then continue with a description of what the cousin did and said, how the writer found the courage to say no to the idea, how the shoplifting cousin reacted, and how the writer felt throughout the whole process.

As you describe the incident, use time transition words to make the sequence of events clear, such as "At first I didn't think I could do it. Later, however, I had an idea."

11 **A Key Experience in School.** Write a paragraph about one of your key experiences in grade school. Use concrete details—actions, comments, reactions, and so on—to help your readers picture what happened. To select an event to write about, try asking yourself the following questions:

- Which teachers or events in school influenced how I felt about myself?
- What specific incidents stand out in my mind as I think back to elementary school?

Once you know which experience you'll write about, use freewriting to help you remember and record the details. Here is one student's freewriting for this assignment.

In second grade, Richard L. sat next to me, a really good artist. When he drew something, it looked just like what it was meant to be. He was so good at choosing colors, the use of crayons, watercolors. His pictures were always picked by teacher to be shown on bulletin board. I still remember his drawing of a circus, acrobats, animals, clowns. Many colors and details. I felt pretty bad in art, even though I loved it and couldn't wait for art in class. One day the teacher read story about a boy who looked at the mountains far away, wondering what was on the other side, mountains were huge, dark. After reading, it was art time. "Paint something from the story" teacher said. I painted those mountains, big purple brown mountains with watercolor dripping to show uneven slopes and coloring of sunset, a thin crooked slice of very blue sky at top. Next day I sat down at my desk in the morning. Then I saw my picture was on the bulletin board! Later teacher passed by me, bent down, put hand on my shoulder and whispered good job, lovely painting. Made me feel capable, proud. The feeling lasted a long time.

Once the details of the experience are on paper, you will be free to concentrate on a more carefully constructed version of the event. The author of the above freewriting, for instance, needed to think of a topic sentence. So when writing the first draft, she began with this sentence: "A seemingly small experience in elementary school encouraged me greatly." Writing drafts is also the time to add any persuasive details you may have missed at first. When working on her second draft, the author of the above added at the end: "I felt very proud, which gave me confidence to work harder in all my school subjects."

Before writing out your final version, remember to check for grammar, punctuation, and spelling errors.

12 Finding Time for Reading. A number of authors have described how a parent or teacher has helped them become regular readers—and how that habit of reading then led to enormous positive changes in their lives. Most of us, however, don't have someone around to insist that we do a certain amount of personal reading every week. In addition, many of us don't seem to have a great deal of free time for reading. How can we find time to read more? Write a paragraph listing several ways people can add more reading to their lives.

A good prewriting strategy for this assignment is list making. Simply write out as many ways as you can think of. Don't worry about putting them in any special order. You will select and organize the strategies you wish to include in your paper after accumulating as many ideas as you can. Here is an example of a prewriting list for this paper:

Ways people can increase the amount of time they spend reading

— on the bus to and from work/school

— while eating breakfast

— instead of watching some TV

— choose motivating materials (articles, books about hobbies, problems, etc.)

Feel free to use items from the above list, but add at least one or two of your own points to include in your paper.

13 A Fear of Looking Foolish. Write a paragraph about how the fear of looking foolish affected your behavior in grade school or high school. Choose an example of a time you acted in a particular way because you were afraid of being ridiculed. Describe how you behaved, and be sure to explain just what kind of embarrassment you were trying to avoid.

Your paragraph might begin with a topic sentence like one of the following:

- Not wanting other students to turn on me, I joined them in making fun of a high-school classmate who was very overweight.

- My mother's idea of how I should dress caused me a great deal of embarrassment in school.

- Because I didn't want to admit that I needed glasses, I had a lot of problems in fifth grade.

14 Feeling Out of Place. Write about a time that you felt out of place, as though you didn't belong. Maybe you found yourself in a foreign country. Or maybe you were in a new school, a new neighborhood, a new job, or a new group of people. To think about how to develop this paper, ask yourself questions like these:

- What brought me into the situation?
- What about the situation made me feel like an outsider?
- What did the people around me do or say?
- What did I imagine other people were thinking about me?
- What thoughts and emotions were running through me?
- How did my feeling like an outsider affect the way I acted?

As you write this assignment, be sure to include plenty of concrete details to help the reader understand your experience. Tell exactly where the incident took place, who else was there, what you and others did and said, and what thoughts and feelings you were experiencing.

15 A Special Person. Who has helped you the most in your quest for an education? Write a paper explaining who this person is and how he or she has helped you. Here are some possible topic sentences for this paper:

- My best friend has helped me with my education in several ways.
- If it weren't for my father, I wouldn't be in school today.
- It was my aunt who impressed upon me the importance of an education.

To develop support for this paper, try listing the problems you faced and the ways this person has helped you deal with each problem. Alternatively, you could do some freewriting about the person you're writing about.

Final Matters

Essay Writing in a Nutshell

WHAT IS AN ESSAY?

Like a paragraph, an essay starts with a point and then goes on to provide specific details to support and develop that point. However, a *paragraph* is a series of **sentences** about one main idea or point, while an *essay* is a series of **paragraphs** about one main idea or point—called the *central idea* or *thesis*. Since an essay is much longer than one paragraph, it allows a writer to develop a topic in more detail.

Here are the major differences between a paragraph and an essay:

Paragraph	Essay
Made up of sentences.	Made up of paragraphs.
Starts with a sentence containing the main point of the paragraph (*topic sentence*).	Starts with an introductory paragraph containing the central idea of the essay, expressed in a sentence called the *thesis statement* or *thesis sentence*.
Body of paragraph contains specific details that support and develop the topic sentence.	Body of essay contains paragraphs that support and develop the central idea. Each of these paragraphs has its own main supporting point, stated in a topic sentence.
Paragraph often ends with a closing sentence that rounds it off.	Essay ends with a concluding paragraph that rounds it off.

THE FORM OF AN ESSAY

Introductory Paragraph

> Introduction
> Thesis statement
> Plan of development:
> points 1, 2, 3

The *introduction* attracts the reader's interest.

The *thesis statement* presents the central idea of the paper.

The *plan of development* is a brief statement of the main supporting details for the central idea.

First Supporting Paragraph

> Topic sentence
> (first point)
> Specific supporting
> evidence

The *topic sentence* presents the first supporting point for the thesis.

The *specific evidence* in the rest of the paragraph develops that first point.

Second Supporting Paragraph

> Topic sentence
> (second point)
> Specific supporting
> evidence

The *topic sentence* presents the second supporting point for the thesis.

The *specific evidence* in the rest of the paragraph develops that second point.

Third Supporting Paragraph

> Topic sentence
> (third point)
> Specific supporting
> evidence

The *topic sentence* presents the third supporting point for the thesis.

The *specific evidence* in the rest of the paragraph develops that third point.

Concluding Paragraph

> Summary,
> final thought,
> or both

A *summary* is a brief restatement of the thesis and its main supporting points. The conclusion may also provide a *final thought* or two as a way of ending the paper.

AN EXAMPLE OF AN ESSAY

Cheryl, the writer of the paragraph about a terrible roommate (page 148), was later asked to develop her topic more fully. Here is the essay that resulted:

A Terrible Roommate

Introductory paragraph

One night when I got off work I went out to eat all by myself. After that I stopped at a mall and walked for miles, looking at items I had no interest in buying. When the mall closed, I drove around until I found an all-night coffee shop. Sitting there drinking some bitter coffee, I had lots of time to think about the reason I didn't want to go home: my roommate. I had made the mistake of sharing my apartment with Dawn, a roommate who created too much noise, lacked a sense of privacy, and had too many visitors.

First supporting paragraph

The first thing that bothered me about Dawn was the constant noise she made. She never seemed to stop talking, whether to me or someone on the phone or to one of her many visitors. Even when she wasn't talking, she managed to be noisy. When she ate, she made loud smacking noises and rattled her silverware on her plate. When she talked on the phone, she would whoop and holler and talk so loud that I couldn't help listening to every word. She never just closed a door or a drawer; she slammed it. When she slept, she often snored so loudly that I could hear her through the bedroom wall. Worst of all, she never only watched TV or listened to a CD. She did both at once. I'd walk into the apartment with my hands clapped over my ears, turning off the first noisemaking machine I reached. Immediately she would cry out, "I was listening to that!"

Second supporting paragraph

In addition to being noisy, Dawn was inconsiderate about my privacy. Without so much as a knock, she would come into my bedroom whenever she felt like it. When I got angry about her walking in on me half-dressed, she acted as if I were making a big deal about nothing. If she felt like chatting, she would find me wherever I was, even appearing and sitting down on my bed as I was taking a nap. She even walked into the bathroom once when I was in the tub. If she happened to pick up the second telephone while I was on a call and she knew the person on the other end, she'd sometimes join in the conversation. And I soon realized I could never bring a date back to the apartment when she was around. Instead of staying in her bedroom, she'd sit down on the living room sofa and insist on being social.

Third supporting paragraph

But the worst part of having Dawn as a roommate was the endless supply of relatives and friends that came with her. The girl had more cousins, sisters, and friends than I could count—and it seemed as if they were all too ready to stay over with us. Some nights when I returned from an evening out, I'd stumble over people sleeping on the living room floor. When I got out of bed in the morning and walked into the kitchen, I never knew when I'd find a stranger there, helping herself to the last of the milk or orange juice. And Dawn's visitors were all too ready to stay for days. As I waited in line to get into my own bathroom or use my own telephone, I grew angrier and angrier at the whole situation.

Concluding paragraph

After my moment of truth in the coffee shop, I realized that I couldn't go on putting up with such a terrible roommate. I needed more quiet, more privacy, and fewer visitors. The next day I gave Dawn the news that she had to move out. The experience taught me to be far more cautious in making decisions that are going to affect my life.

WHAT ARE THE PARTS OF AN ESSAY?

When Cheryl decided to expand her paragraph into an essay, she knew she would need to write an introductory paragraph, several supporting paragraphs, and a concluding paragraph.

Each of these parts of the essay is explained below.

Introductory Paragraph

A well-written introductory paragraph will often do the following.

1 **Gain the reader's interest.** On pages 197–198 are several time-tested methods used to draw the reader into an essay.

2 **Present the thesis statement.** The thesis statement expresses the central idea of an essay, just as a topic sentence states the main idea of a paragraph. Here's an example of a thesis statement:

> As a child, I was terrified of the dark, of getting lost, and of not being accepted by others.

What is the thesis statement in Cheryl's essay? Find that statement on page 195 and write it here:

_____

_____

You should have written down the last sentence in the introductory paragraph of Cheryl's essay.

3 **Provide a plan of development.** The plan of development is a brief statement of the main supporting details for the central idea. These supporting details should be presented in the order in which they will be discussed in the essay. The plan of development can be blended into the thesis or presented separately. Here are examples of both kinds of development:

Blended into a thesis statement:

> As a child, I was terrified of the dark, of getting lost, and of not being accepted by others.

> Shop class should be required for all students because the skills taught there make people more confident, save them money on home repairs, and can even prepare them for a career.

Presented separately:

> As a little boy, I struggled to overcome childhood fears. I was terrified of the dark, of getting lost, and of not being accepted by others.

> A manual skills course should be required of all high-school students. The skills taught there can make people more confident, save them money on home repairs, and even prepare them for a career.

Note that some essays lend themselves better to a plan of development than others do. If you omit a plan of development, your introductory paragraph must still gain the reader's interest and present the thesis statement.

What is the plan of development in Cheryl's essay? Find the sentence on page 195 that states Cheryl's plan of development and write it here:

_____

_____

You should have written down the last sentence in the introductory paragraph of Cheryl's essay.

Four Common Methods of Introduction

1 **Begin with a broad statement and narrow it down to your thesis statement.** Broad statements can capture your reader's interest while introducing your general topic. They may provide useful background material as well. If Cheryl had used this method of introduction, here is how her introductory paragraph might look:

> I consider myself a person who is pretty easy to get along with. Among my large group of coworkers, there is not one person whom I really dislike. I love most of my many relatives dearly, and I can easily tolerate the ones that I'm not crazy about. If there had been a "Miss Congeniality" award at my school, I would have been a contender because I always had loads of friends, both male and female. But there is one person I simply could not learn to get along with: Dawn. I had made the mistake of choosing a roommate who created too much noise, lacked a sense of privacy, and had too many visitors.

2 **Present an idea or situation that is the opposite of what will be written about.** One way to gain the reader's interest is to show the difference between your opening idea or situation and the one to be discussed in the essay. If Cheryl had used this method of introduction, here is how her introductory paragraph might look:

> When Dawn first appeared at my door, I just knew we were going to get along well. This peppy brunette with the infectious laugh seemed like just the bright, upbeat roommate I was hoping for. Within minutes, we had discovered that we loved the same musicians, the same movies, and the same fiery Mexican food. I was so excited I quickly called the newspaper and told them to cancel my ad. I wish the story ended there, with my having found the perfect roommate. But the fact is that within thirty days I would have paid Dawn to get out of my apartment. Despite the good first impression she made, Dawn turned out to be a really terrible roommate.

3 **Tell a brief story.** An interesting incident or anecdote is hard for a reader to resist. In an introduction, a story should be no more than a few sentences, and it should relate meaningfully to—and so lead the reader toward—your central idea. The story you tell can be an experience of your own, of someone you know, or of someone you have read about. This method of introduction is the one Cheryl uses for her essay:

One night when I got off work I went out to eat all by myself. After that I stopped at a mall and walked for miles, looking at items I had no interest in buying. When the mall closed, I drove around until I found an all-night coffee shop. Sitting there drinking some bitter coffee, I had lots of time to think about the reason I didn't want to go home: my roommate. I had made the mistake of sharing my apartment with Dawn, a roommate who created too much noise, lacked a sense of privacy, and had too many visitors.

4   Ask one or more questions.   The questions may be ones that you intend to answer in your essay, or they may show that your topic relates directly to readers. If Cheryl had used this method of introduction, here is how her introductory paragraph might look:

Getting a new roommate is always an adventure. Will the two of you become lifelong friends? Will you be like serious study partners—polite, but not really close? Will you drive each other crazy because of different tastes in music (or food, or videos, or friends)? Will you look back on the day you met your roommate as a happy memory, or will it be a memory you'd love to erase? My most recent roommate adventure falls into the "love to erase" category. But because I can't forget it, I'll describe it here. Of all the roommates I've ever had, Dawn stands out as the worst.

Supporting Paragraphs

The traditional essay has three supporting paragraphs. But some essays will have two supporting paragraphs, and others will have four or more. Each supporting paragraph should have its own topic sentence that states the point to be developed in that paragraph.

Notice that each of the supporting paragraphs in Cheryl's essay has its own topic sentence. For example, the topic sentence of her first supporting paragraph is "The first thing that bothered me about Dawn is the constant noise she made."

What is the topic sentence for Cheryl's second supporting paragraph?

_____

_____

What is the topic sentence for Cheryl's third supporting paragraph?

_____

_____

In each case, Cheryl's topic sentence is the first sentence of the paragraph.

Transitional Sentences

In a paragraph, transitional words like *First, Another, Also,* and *Finally* are used to help connect supporting ideas. In an essay, transitional sentences are used to help tie the supporting paragraphs together. Such transitional sentences often occur at the beginning of a supporting paragraph.

See if you can find and write down the one transitional sentence used in Cheryl's essay:

_____

_____

Cheryl's second supporting paragraph begins with this transitional sentence: "In addition to being noisy, Dawn was inconsiderate about my privacy." In this sentence, the words "being noisy" remind us of the point of the first supporting paragraph, while the words "inconsiderate about my privacy" tell us the point to be developed in the second supporting paragraph.

Concluding Paragraph

The concluding paragraph often summarizes the essay by briefly restating the thesis and, at times, the main supporting points. It may also provide a closing thought or two as a way of bringing the paper to a natural and graceful end. Look again at the conclusion of Cheryl's essay:

> After my moment of truth in the coffee shop, I realized that I couldn't go on putting up with such a terrible roommate. I needed more quiet, more privacy, and fewer visitors. The next day I gave Dawn the news that she had to move out. The experience taught me to be far more cautious in making decisions that are going to affect my life.

Final Activity

Choose one of the writing assignments on pages 188–192 and develop it into a five-paragraph essay, consisting of an introductory paragraph, three supporting paragraphs, and a concluding paragraph. Be sure to follow the guidelines in Chapters 9 and 10 when preparing your paper. In particular, do the following:

1. Use prewriting techniques such as freewriting, questioning, and list making to develop your ideas.
2. Make sure you have a clear point and different kinds of support for that point.
3. Outline your essay, using the form that follows.
4. At some point, read your essay out loud. If it does not flow smoothly, rewrite until it does.

The form on the next page will help you plan the essay.

Form for Planning an Essay

Introductory Paragraph

Opening remarks _____

_____

Thesis statement _____

Plan of development _____

_____

First Supporting Paragraph

Topic sentence _____

Supporting details _____

_____

_____

Second Supporting Paragraph

Topic sentence _____

Supporting details _____

_____

_____

Third Supporting Paragraph

Topic sentence _____

Supporting details _____

_____

_____

Concluding Paragraph

_____

_____

Research in a Nutshell

At times in school, you'll need to do research. Research can give you the information you need to study, speak, or write about a particular topic. If you have a school research assignment, here is a good way to proceed.

1   USE A COMPUTER SEARCH ENGINE

Use a computer to do some quick research on your topic on the Internet. You can do this with the help of a *search engine*, which will go through a vast amount of information on the Web to find articles about your topic. One very helpful search engine is Google; you can access it by typing:

www.google.com

A screen will then appear with a box in which you can type one or more keywords. For example, if you are thinking about doing a paper on bullies, you could type in the keyword *bullies*. Within a second or so you will get a list of over 80,000 articles on the Web about bullies!

You should then try to narrow your topic by adding other keywords. For instance, if you typed *bullies in schools*, you would get a list of over 20,000 items. If you narrowed your potential topic further by typing *solutions to bullies in schools*, you would get a list of 2,500 items. Then click on the items that sound most promising to you.

2   USE A COMPUTER TO LOOK FOR MAGAZINE AND NEWSPAPER ARTICLES

Use a computer to access an online search service that can quickly make available to you countless newspaper and magazine articles. One good online resource is Electric Library:

www.elibrary.com

Your school may subscribe to Electric Library or some other online search service such as EBSCOhost or InfoTrac. If you are using a home computer, you may be able to get a free thirty-day subscription to Electric Library, or you may be able to enroll on a monthly basis at a reasonable cost. Electric Library contains millions of newspaper and magazine articles as well as many thousands of television and radio transcripts. After typing in one or more keywords, you'll get long lists of articles that may relate to your subject. When you click on a title that sounds interesting, the full text of the article appears. If it fits your needs, you can print it out right away on a printer.

3 SEE WHAT BOOKS ARE IN YOUR LIBRARY

You may also want to see if there are books on your topic. Go to your library and look for *bullies* in the subject section of your card catalog. You will then get a list of books that your library has on that topic. In addition, you will probably get a list of topics related to bullies. That list may suggest to you more limited topics, helping you narrow your general topic.

4 KEEP THE FOLLOWING HINTS IN MIND

Finally, keep several things in mind when preparing a research paper:

a If you cannot find much information on your topic after doing a quick search, then see if you can choose another topic. You do not want to choose a topic that will be too hard to research. For instance, if there are no books on your topic and your instructor wants you to cite at least two books, look for a topic for which books are available.

b Chances are you will be asked to do a research paper of about five to twelve pages. You do not want to choose a topic so broad that it could be covered only by an entire book or more. You goal is to come up with a limited topic that can be adequately supported in a fairly short paper. Keep looking, then, for ways to limit your general topic.

c As you search on the Internet, your challenge will probably be getting too much information rather than too little. Keep looking for ways to limit your search, as with the example for bullies above. You might also try more than one search engine. In addition to Google, you could use **www.yahoo.com**.

A Brief Note on Fitness

Here are two quick recommendations for staying energized and healthy—and more resistant to the colds, flus, and other viruses that often sweep through schools and colleges and interfere with study.

EXERCISE

Exercise promotes health and provides energy. One of the simplest ways to get exercise is to walk a lot. Don't always ride when you can walk; don't take an elevator when you can climb the stairs.

DIET

Eat a reasonable breakfast. Which is the best way to start the day?

____ Eat nothing; get up just in time to make your first class; have a big lunch.

____ Turn on your body's engine with a cup of coffee and a cigarette.

____ Get a bag of Doritos and a soda from a school vending machine.

____ Pick up a box of sugar doughnuts for yourself and your friends.

____ Have a bowl of cereal and some fruit juice.

You know the answer to the above question, but you may not know the following—taken from a nutrition textbook:

Of all possible ways to eat, the worst is skipping breakfast and then eating a big lunch. You're probably aware that going without breakfast is bad for you, but you probably don't know that a big midday meal doesn't even the score. Lunch is not a pick-me-up; it actually pulls your energy down. A recent study found that a group of people who ate a large lunch lost as much efficiency when they returned to work as if they'd gone without a whole night's sleep. On the other hand, a separate ten-year study found that eating breakfast increases efficiency. Another study, of adolescents, found that kids do better in school when they eat breakfast. Why is breakfast so important? When you wake up in the morning, you probably haven't eaten for eight to twelve hours. Your blood sugar and stored carbohydrates are low, and you may be short of other nutrients as well. You need a solid breakfast that supplies protein, such as a whole-grain cereal with milk. Your morning meal "breaks" the "fast" and replaces the calories and nutrients you need to help keep you going all day.

Dr. Ben Carson

Dr. Carson: "*I try to eat healthily, and I try to take the stairs rather than the elevator. Even at times when I don't have time to exercise* per se, *just by a lot of walking you get quite a significant cardiovascular workout. I try to drink pure substances as opposed to substances that require the body to do a lot of work to get rid of the impurities. Drinking sodas that work the devil out of your kidneys doesn't really do any good as opposed to drinking a bottle of pure water.*"

Jennifer: "*I try to eat at least two good balanced meals a day, with plenty of vegetables. I drink too much soda, and I know that's not good for me. The caffeine in many sodas keeps me awake, and not being able to sleep at 2 a.m. when I've got a full day of classes coming up is not good. Also, I notice that soda doesn't quench my thirst the way milk or water does.*"

Jennifer McCaul

Kenyon Whittington

Kenyon: "*I deliberately try to eat well. If I have a good solid breakfast, I can skip lunch. You must feed your body or it's going to feed off you. A good breakfast for me is orange juice or apple juice, wheat bread, and Total or raisin bran cereal.*"

Zamil: "*Breakfast is my most important meal of the day. I'll have things like blueberry pancakes with eggs, a bowl of cereal, fruit punch, chocolate milk, and an English muffin. I'll also grab a banana or apple or orange to eat as a quick lunch. I notice that a lot of students who ordinarily skip breakfast do have breakfast the day of a test. They say it helps them think better and gives them more energy. And I'm thinking, 'Why not do this every day?'*"

Zamil Ortiz

A Skill for Living Well: Kindness

Until now, this book has dealt with key skills for *learning*. This final section focuses on a key skill for *living*—a skill that, if practiced, can make your pursuit of learning much more rewarding.

In his book *The Big Picture,* Dr. Ben Carson devotes an entire chapter to the idea that people should "be nice." He comments, "It is is such an elementary concept, but I probably get as much reaction to this topic as anything I speak about—whether from an audience of corporate executives or of inner-city kids. The reaction just underscores the importance of this seemingly simple idea."

Why be nice, or kind? One reason, according to Dr. Carson, is that "you can get more done by being nice." If you're kind to other students and to your instructors, they're more likely to be considerate to you. That can make your academic life more productive and satisfying.

A second reason for being kind, again according to Dr. Carson, is that "everyone is worth it." Dr. Carson comments: "We like to think of America as a classless society, but if we are honest, we have to admit that we are divided into many categories—ethnically, economically, educationally, socially, geographically, and in other ways. Being nice to everyone is the simplest way I know to effectively lower the artificial barriers human beings have erected." All of us—regardless of our age, the color of our skin, our income, or our physical appearance— share a common humanity. Being kind to one another is a way to recognize that our shared humanity is more important than the individual differences between us.

A third reason for treating others with consideration was expressed many centuries ago by the Greek philosopher Philo of Alexandria. In an observation that has endured through the ages, he wrote:

Be kind, for everyone you meet is fighting a great battle.

I showed this statement to a number of students while I was interviewing them for this book. Here are some of their responses.

Michelle: *"Philo's words are as true as the air we breathe. We're always dealing with something. You may think people are mean or nasty, but you don't know what's going on inside. We can't read people; we don't know their hearts. It's the heart that causes everything. We're always so concerned about our own situation; we're always so worried about ourselves. We have to allow for what's inside others. A kind look, a word, a hug can completely change the course of how a person is feeling."*

Michelle Miller

Ryan Klootwyk

Ryan: *"Amen. If you haven't fought a battle, you will. Lots of people have hurdles you don't even know about. Everybody is struggling; everyone has issues. Life is not a la-di-da walk through the park. Life isn't easy. We have to care for one another."*

Jasmin: *"All of us are fighting the battle of survival. Everyone is trying to get by, and we should do our best to remember this."*

Jasmin Santana

Aaron Benson

Aaron: *"It's like the saying about walking a mile in another person's shoes. It means giving people the benefit of the doubt. The more you learn about them, the more you can understand them. You don't know what happens to people right before you encounter them. You really never know what people are going through."*

Paul: *"Be a good person, be respectful, because you don't know what people are dealing with. They're having their own problems. You don't want to be judgmental, because you haven't lived that person's life. Being kind is a virtue. And when others see you being kind, they'll treat you so in return. It's infectious."*

Paul Blocker

It may help to think of kindness as a muscle, just as all the learning skills in this book can be seen as muscles. Kindness has to be practiced to become effective and strong and natural. Practicing this human skill, like practicing the learning skills, can make you a better, happier person.

ACTIVITIES

1. Most people agree that it is important to try to be kind, but they become distracted by the hectic nature of everyday life and often forget to work at kindness. Describe someone you know who does an exceptional job at being kind. What is your own attitude about kindness? Do you make a conscious effort to give people the benefit of the doubt? If you don't, do you think you should?

2. Try this experiment: Make a deliberate effort to be kind to at least three different people in the course of the next day. Your behavior can be as simple as listening carefully, smiling, holding open a door, or doing a small favor. Afterward, comment on what it was like—how people reacted and how you felt.

3. Another observation that has endured through the ages comes from the Talmudic scholar Rabbi Hillel over two thousand years ago:

   If I am not for myself, who will be for me?

   And if I am only for myself, what am I?

   And if not now, when?

   What do you think Rabbi Hillel meant? How do his words relate to the importance of personal responsibility? How do his words relate to the importance of kindness?

Biographical Notes
and Acknowledgments

Note: Each student's school affiliation is given the first time his or her photograph appears.

Floyd Allen (pages 47, 91, 97, 174, and 183) is a recent graduate of Wilkes College. Floyd had gone to Wilkes on an athletic scholarship with hopes of someday playing in the National Football League. But at the insistence of his mother, he did not neglect his studies. He chose to major in business administration, with a concentration on marketing and finance. "I always wanted to work with numbers and money," Floyd says, "but I had no idea how much I would enjoy it." He is now working as an options investigator at the Philadelphia Stock Exchange. "A football career could last only a few years," Floyd says, "but I can use my education a lot longer."

Aaron Benson (pages 81, 97, 98, and 206) is a student at West Chester University majoring in journalism.

Aaron recalls his days in high school, when "it really mattered where you fit in." Being popular and having a busy social life become a top priority for too many students during that time, Aaron explains. Even worse was the stigma attached to being "too smart" or "too brainy," a stigma he knew quite well.

Aaron was a student who sat in the front of the classroom, raised his hand to answer questions, and stayed after class in order to get help from his teachers. Aaron remembers how he sacrificed popularity in favor of concentrating on his studies. "Sometimes it was really tough," he admits, reflecting on the feelings of alienation he experienced as a result of his decision not to follow the crowd.

"I made the choice to sit in the front of the classroom, even though I knew there would be comments coming from the back." The students who sat in the back rows were relentless with their ridicule, he recalls. "They made fun of the kids up front, calling us 'nerds' and laughing at us whenever we raised our hands to answer questions. A lot of people were intimidated."

Being accepted seems so important at that age, Aaron explains. "But it's really the wrong thing to pursue. You realize that later in life." How much later you realize it has a lot to do with your own personal growth, Aaron believes, and the goals you set for yourself.

Taking his knocks as a high-school student, Aaron always tried to remain focused on what was important. He knew he was going on to college and a better life for himself. "It was easier to handle the name-calling if I just looked ahead. There was nothing worth giving up my education and the chance to improve my life."

Caren Blackmore (cover, pages 35, 159, 168, 170, and 171) is a student at Oberlin College majoring in theater.

Asked for advice she'd give to high-school students, Caren says, "What I'd like to emphasize, 100 percent, is listen to the advice you're getting! When I was in high school people would be saying, 'This is what college will be like,' and I would be thinking, 'OK, whatever, I've heard that a million times.' But oh, do you need that advice. Once you get to college, you're totally on your own. You wish you had all that advice back.

"And read! In college, you have to do so much of it. If you get into the habit in high school, college will be much easier for you."

Paul Blocker (cover, pages 47 and 206) is an engineering major at Villanova University.

Krystal Buhr (pages 1, 91, 151, 159, 168, and 170) is a student at Bucknell University majoring in secondary education; she looks forward to teaching high-school social studies.

Krystal recalls how in high school, she had found the work so easy that she didn't apply much effort and still achieved success. "In high school, I never did my homework at home. I would do it during lunch periods and study halls, and if we had a substitute teacher, I'd do it right there in class."

She got an early warning that college would be different during an orientation class in her first days at Bucknell. "The lecturer said that we were expected to study between twenty and thirty hours a week!" Krystal exclaims. "At first I didn't believe it because I had never studied, and I'd done well so far. But in college I do in fact have to study as much as thirty hours a week."

When Krystal's English professor tore up her first college paper, she was given more dramatic evidence that college would not be a repeat of high school but would be a whole new world.

Krystal was determined to make it, even though that meant studying and working harder than she had ever dreamed she would have to do. She remembers going back to the professor who had torn up her English paper. "He told me that I hadn't turned in a structured paper," Krystal explains, "and I didn't really know what he meant." So she searched for and found a book on how to write college papers. The book showed her ways to organize and unify her ideas in a formal paper. By the semester's end, her writing had improved to the point that her final grade was an A.

Andy Cao (pages 91 and 113) was born in Vietnam and came to this country with his family in 1981. He is a junior studying information systems at Drexel University.

Andy's advice to high-school students is, "Get organized while you're in high school. Learn how to manage your time, and get into the habit of keeping ahead of deadlines. There are so many deadlines in college, and if you get behind it won't only hurt your grade; it will also affect you mentally, affect your self-confidence."

Maria Cardenas (pages 48, 56, 59, and 62) left Rio Verde, Mexico, for the United States at age seven. With the rest of her family, Maria traveled with the harvest as a migrant worker. Laboring like an adult in the fields, she often attended three or four schools each year and by age sixteen had to drop out of school. More than a decade would go by before she could resume her schooling. Now a junior at Florida Gulf Coast College, Maria Cardenas has maintained a 3.5 GPA and plans to graduate with a B.A. in elementary education. Her story is featured on pages 56–62 of this book.

Dr. Ben Carson (pages 8, 25, 48, 50, 52, 54, 79, 115, 141, and 204) is professor and director of pediatric neurosurgery at the Johns Hopkins Children's Center and the author of three best-selling books, *Think Big, Gifted Hands,* and *The Big Picture.*

He is also the president of a nonprofit organization, the Carson Scholars Fund, which he cofounded with his wife Candy. The Fund recognizes and rewards students in grades 4–12 with $1,000 awards invested for college. Students are nominated by their schools; this helps to elevate academic excellence to the level it deserves. Schools with awardees also receive a large trophy for their display cases.

Dr. Carson is a widely respected role model who shares motivational insights with inner-city kids and corporate executives alike. The story of how he went from being the "class dummy" in grade school to a scholarship student at Yale University is featured on pages 49–54 of this book.

Tynara Chappelle (pages 11, 113, and 181) is a graduate of West Chester University. She is currently working as a parole officer in Philadelphia while saving the money she'll need to go on to law school.

Growing up in a tough inner-city neighborhood, Tynara was no stranger to the sounds of gunfire or the blaring sirens that screamed from police cars and ambulances in the middle of the night. "I grew up in a place where nearly everybody fell victim to the environment," she continues. "The drugs, the crime, and the rest of it were just a *dead end* to me."

Even when the other students at her high school would tease her for always having her nose in books, Tynara kept in mind her goal: college. "It was the saddest thing. People were selling drugs, getting locked up, and having baby after baby," Tynara remembers. "It just wasn't going to be my way to live."

When she chose West Chester University in Pennsylvania, Tynara braced herself for yet another struggle. To deal with the financial obstacle of college, she worked straight through college, sometimes holding down two jobs to cover living expenses and school expenses.

"I used to resent that other students could spend so much time socializing in between classes," admits Tynara, who would often leave a class and go right to work. "Everybody seemed to be so carefree. There were times when I wanted to put my responsibilities aside and do the same thing." But her father was always there with advice: "'All the things you want right now will be there when you're done doing what you need to do,' he'd say."

In her present job as a parole officer, Tynara doesn't at all regret the struggles that she endured for the sake of her education. She meets in court some of very people from the neighborhood where she once lived. Tynara says that it's tough to see them still caught in a dead-end life. But there is also a bright side.

"What's so nice for me to see is how happy these people are for me," Tynara says. "They see somebody from the neighborhood who made it out and found a completely different life. It makes me feel proud when they say that I've made something of myself."

To give something back to the community that she left, Tynara has become a mentor of a high-school student. "What I keep telling her is that you need to set a goal for yourself and make getting there the *number one* objective. Education is the key to this."

Joe Davis (pages 6, 125, and 127), a married graduate student at the University of Pennsylvania, is earning his master's degree in social work. He works as a therapist at the John F. Kennedy Mental Health Center in Philadelphia. He is also coordinator of Think First, a program of Magee Rehabilitation Hospital that sends speakers who have suffered spinal-cord and head injuries into local schools. There they share their personal stories, making their audiences aware of the possible consequences of high-risk behavior.

The story Joe shares with Think First audiences involves years of crime and drug use, behavior that finally resulted in his being on the receiving end of a .22 bullet. The shooting left Joe paralyzed from the chest down. After a long and rocky rehabilitation, marked by continued drug use and an eventual suicide attempt, Joe took a good look at his life and was sickened by what he saw. He enrolled in a vocational rehabilitation program and got his first real job. Then he signed up for a university math class. He didn't do well. Refusing to give up, he enrolled in basic math and English courses at a local community college. Bit by bit, inch by inch, week by week, he struggled to acquire the academic skills he'd never cared about before. "It was *hard*. It still *is* hard," Joe says today. "But it's worth the work."

At a presentation at a disciplinary school outside Philadelphia, Joe speaks to an unruly crowd of teenagers. He tells them about speedballs and guns, fast money and bedsores, even about the leg bag that collects his urine. At first, the kids snort with laughter at his honesty. When they laugh, he waits patiently, then goes on. Gradually the room grows quieter as Joe tells them of his life and then asks them about theirs. "What's important to you? What are your goals?" he says. "I'm still in school because when I was young, I chose the dead-end route many of you are on. But now I'm doing what I have to do to get where I want to go. What are *you* doing?"

He tells them more, about broken dreams, about his parents' grief, about the former friends who turned away from him when he was no longer a source of drugs. He tells them of a continuing struggle to regain the trust of people he once abused. He tells them about the desire that consumes him now, the desire to make his community a better place to live. His wish is that no young man or woman should have to walk the path he's walked in order to value the precious gift of life. The teenagers are now silent. They look at this broad-shouldered man in his wheelchair, his head and beard close-shaven, a gold ring in his ear. His words settle around them like gentle drops of cleansing rain. "What are *you* doing? Where are *you* going?" he asks them. "Think about it. Think about me."

Ed Hamler (page 139) is a student at Philadelphia University majoring in fashion design.

Teron Ivery (cover, pages 107, 139, and 151) will be graduating from Millersville University with a degree in elementary education. He has completed his student teaching experience and is looking forward to his first full-time job teaching young children.

Teron recalls struggling with peer pressure when he was in high school. "School is about social life to a lot of people," he says. "It's about keeping up with the Joneses, you know—having the newest clothes and keeping up with the latest music and trying to be part of the crowd."

Being "part of the crowd" often involves drugs and alcohol, and Teron briefly gave in to that pressure. "I experimented with drugs," he says frankly. "It was 'the thing to do,' and I did it. But I soon realized what a stupid thing that was, and I quit." Stopping his drug use had its price—he cut his ties with the friends who had done drugs with him. As Teron sees it, the price of that friendship was too high. "They weren't bad people," he says. "But they wanted to continue that life, and I did not. I had to make a choice."

The choice was a no-brainer for Teron. "All I had to do was walk down the street to see the effects of drugs on people's lives," he said. "I saw people on the streets, families broken up, people unable to hold jobs. And when I thought of my future as a teacher—drugs just didn't have a place in that. I couldn't be an example to my kids and use drugs."

Ginger Jackson (pages 16, 80, 95, 170, and 171) is a student at Muhlenberg College; she intends to become a teacher.

Lamel Jackson (cover, pages 77, 98, and 115) a student at Haverford College, plans to study engineering.

Keziah Johnson (cover) is a student at Indiana University of Pennsylvania majoring in political science.

David Killingsworth (page 111) is a student at West Chester University.

Ryan Klootwyk (pages 35, 48, 64, 66, 69, 91, and 206) is a recent graduate of Grand Valley State University, where he earned a degree in secondary education. After he completes a job practicum, he will start teaching high-school history. Ryan grew up amid the chaos of heroin addiction, drinking, and abuse at the hands of his mother's vicious boyfriend. He spent his last three years of high school "bouncing between the normal school and the alternative school for troubled kids." After barely earning his degree, he went to work as a manual laborer. More than ten years would go by before he returned to school. His story is featured on pages 64–70 of this book.

May Lam (cover, pages 47, 81, and 107), the recipient of a Gates Scholarship, is a student at Temple University majoring in biology; she then plans to go on to medical school.

Take school seriously, and ask for help when you need it. That's the advice that May Lam has for high-school students. "It's all about your own efforts," says May. "There's always somebody there to help you, but you've got to take the initiative and ask."

Asking for help hasn't always come easily to May. "I'm an 'I can do it; no problem' kind of person," she says. "But there's a difference between working hard, which I've always done, and refusing to ask for help when you need it. If I'm stubborn about asking for help, I can burn out. I've learned to ask for assistance *before* that happens."

Important sources of help for May have been her teachers as well as adults she's met through the mentoring organization Philadelphia Futures. They've helped bridge the gap that sometimes exists between May and her own family.

"My family is poor, and no one has much education," she explains. "I'll be the first in my family to attend college. Because of that, it's really important to my parents that I do well, and they put a lot of pressure on me. A grade of C was just unacceptable to them, and I'd get into trouble at home.

"When I wasn't doing well in a math class, for instance, I couldn't really talk to my parents about it. They'd just get down on me for not doing better. But I sought help and then decided that I could make it using a tutor."

May has also reached out for help with a problem that affects many students. "Peer pressure!" May says. "Peers are so important to teenagers. They affect how we learn. Sometimes I'd get influenced the wrong way by my friends. And that was something I absolutely couldn't talk to my parents about. They'd just say, 'You're hanging with bad people!' and want me to never see them again. But I could talk to my mentor about it."

When May finds herself in danger of "burning out" academically, she makes herself go—quickly—to her teachers for help. "If I wait until the last minute, it's too late," she says. "But if I act in time, just admitting to the teacher that I need help relieves the pressure I feel." In response, some teachers are more helpful than others. "If it's a teacher who sincerely cares for her students, yes, she'll be helpful," May says. "But if not, then, well, I go somewhere else. That's what you've got to remember: Even if the first thing you try doesn't work, you can always find another teacher or a counselor who will give you the help you need. What you can't do is give up."

"You're in school to make something, make some*body* of yourself," May concludes. "If you're not going to make the effort to do that, you might as well stay home."

John Langan (page 1), the author of this book, taught developmental language skills courses at Atlantic Cape Community College after earning master's degrees in reading and writing. He is the author of a number of college reading and writing skills books published by McGraw-Hill. He also writes skills textbooks for Townsend Press, the educational publishing company that he started more than ten years ago. His books have sold over seven million copies.

Marcos Maestre (cover, pages 80 and 93) is a student at Millersville University majoring in marketing with a minor in accounting; his long-term goal is to have his own business.

Jhoselyn Martinez (pages 91, 95, 135, 151, 168, and 181) is a recent graduate of Chestnut Hill College. Today, she works as the producer of a Spanish-language radio program for the Archdiocese of Philadelphia. She hopes to move on to a job in television production.

Jennifer McCaul (cover, pages 79, 113, 135, 159, and 204) is a student at Alvernia College majoring in marketing.

Michelle Miller (pages 35, 77, 95, 169, and 205) is a marketing major at Temple University. She is currently working as a teller at Mellon Bank while saving the money she needs to return to complete her degree.

Michelle Nguyen (page 181) is a student at Temple University studying for a degree in nursing.

Born in Vietnam, the youngest of three children, Michelle came to this country as an adolescent and had to learn English as a second language. "The language barrier made everything difficult," Michelle says, explaining the struggles she has faced with her schoolwork. "Writing and reading classes were tough for me because I was still learning how to use the words properly. I didn't think I could do it."

Having to act as a translator for most of her family members, Michelle knew early on that learning English would be crucial for her. The language barrier made everything so difficult that she often found herself discouraged and wanting to give up.

When it came time for college, Michelle knew that her struggles with English in high school would be doubled. She estimates that she has to work "double or triple" as hard as a native-English speaker. Although she is often tired, she refuses to give in to discouragement. "You just do what you have to do," she said. "If I get a C on a test, yes, that makes me feel bad. But in order to finish what I've started, and to have the career I want to have someday, I have to learn from that and study harder next time." Michelle hopes that other ESL students will especially benefit from her story of achievement. "I think the key is not to get down on yourself," she says. "You don't gain anything by giving up."

Terry Oakman (cover, pages 35, 47, 93, 95, 107, 115, 127, 149, 173, and 183) is a student at Temple University majoring in psychology; he plans to go right on to earn his master's degree. Among the career options he is considering is becoming a high-school guidance counselor.

Terry reports that a "moment of truth" occurred when he was in seventh grade. Two of his teachers sat him down and asked, "What are you going to do with yourself? What do you want your life to be?" Their questions made him become reflective, and he decided in a conscious way to take charge of his life instead of drifting passively along like too many other students he knew. He worked actively to pull up his grades and began to read widely. Among the books that helped him discover the pleasure and power of reading were *The Catcher in the Rye, The Call of the Wild,* and *Animal Farm.* Perhaps because he was part of the football and wrestling teams in high school, no one bothered him about doing well academically, and he maintained a near A average.

Zamil M. Ortiz (pages 15 and 204) is a student at Haverford College; she is considering a major in Spanish or in a social science such as history or anthropology.

Helen Rowe (pages 77, 80, and 124) is a student at the University of Pennsylvania majoring in women's studies.

Helen recalls how she took a year off after high school. "I worked in a bagel store. There, I got a taste of life on minimum wage. I had bosses who treated me and the other employees like we were worthless. That year gave me a good perspective. I realized that I should never take my education and the opportunities it provides for granted."

For Helen, her year in the bagel store only confirmed what she already knew: College was a necessity for her. "My friends warned me, 'If you don't start college right away, you'll never do it,' " she remembers. "I knew they were wrong. What the year off *did* do was make me more determined than ever to get everything I could out of school."

Jasmin Santana (cover, pages 47, 113, 124, and 206), the recipient of a Gates Scholarship, is a student at Drexel University. Her goal is to finish her business degree at Drexel and then attend law school.

Jasmin recalls how, just out of high school, she wondered what she was going to do. "Who was going to hire me and pay me a good salary? Should I take some dead-end job and waste my life? Or move ahead to new challenges?"

Jasmin has seen plenty of her old friends and neighbors take the "dead-end" route. She understands why.

"If you don't know anything but your own environment, it's hard to envision another way of life," she explains. "And without that little bit of vision, it's difficult to decide what you want and figure out how you're going to get there. Coming out of North Philly, I didn't know that anything else was available. But then I saw someone's apartment in Center City, saw the life she was living, and it was nice. Nicer than anything I'd ever seen. I thought, 'I want that. I can't get that here.' "

She realized that college was a key to that better standard of living. "I began to look at the people I knew who had and hadn't gone to college, and compare their level of satisfaction with their lives. There wasn't any contest."

Knowing she'll be the first college graduate in her family gives Jasmin extra motivation. "My family is so happy about what I'm doing that it helps keep me going. I also think about the little ones I might have someday. I want them to be proud of me."

Rod Sutton (pages 6 and 141) is currently a teacher in Philadelphia. Back when he was a thirteen-year-old student, he was expelled from his junior high school in Newark, New Jersey. He had been suspended fifty-two times during his troubled public-school career, which finally ended when the 190-pound youngster got into a shoving match with a teacher who was encouraging him to move along to class.

Rod then enrolled at a Catholic boys' school in Newark. He soon got into a violent, chair-throwing fight with another student that shattered windows and, Rod believed, his chances for remaining at the school. But the compassionate response from the headmaster— he handed Rod a broom and dustpan, told him to clean up the mess, and never mentioned the incident again—had a powerful effect on Rod. He determined that he was going to succeed in school.

Along the way, he faced clear choices. He remembers how for a time his hero was a neighborhood man named Lonnie. "Lonnie represented what I wanted at that time," Rod says. "He had lots of girls. Lots of gold. Flashy cars. I romanticized him. I wanted that career path. I wanted to walk down the street and hear people say, 'Don't mess with him.' "

But Rod was also attracted to another example. Lonnie's brother, Mark, was a lawyer. "Mark was the complete opposite of Lonnie," Rod says. "He had a good job. He had a home in the suburbs. My mother was in love with Mark and all he stood for. He'd ease over to speak to me, ask what I was up to. There was a tug-of-war between those two images in my mind. Mark had the suit, the home, the family, the job. Lonnie had all that flash."

Today, Lonnie is doing prison time for rape. Rod still sees Mark from time to time. "Mark tells me he is proud of me. He didn't think I was listening to what he had to say. He was part of the chain of caring adults who pulled me along. They tried to help me handle the twists and turns of life."

Rod did just that, eventually earning a B.A. in education. He then became an elementary teacher in Camden, New Jersey, where he designed a program which provided positive direction to at-risk boys. He has since moved on to teach at Leeds Junior High School in Philadelphia and recently completed his graduate work at Eastern College for a master's degree in education. He is married, a homeowner, and the father of two treasured children.

Kenyon Whittington (cover, pages 11, 46, 77, 93, 97, 115, 151, 183, and 204) is a political science major at Hampton University in Virginia. As a high-school freshman, he ran into a situation that exemplified his refusal to just go along with the crowd.

"I was sitting at the cafeteria table with my friends," he recalls. "We were doing our immature freshman thing, talking and laughing and checking out girls. Then a group of huge, hulking seniors walked up to us. They said, 'Y'all. From now on, every day at lunch, you'll give us your cash.'"

Kenyon was astounded. "I thought, 'This kind of stuff only happens on TV!'" He was even more amazed to see his friends meekly sliding their dollars and change down the table. Kenyon was the only holdout.

"They all stared me down and one said, 'Hand over your money!'

"I said, 'No WAY am I handing over my money!' My mom and my aunt had always told me you just don't go along with something that's wrong, and this was *crazy* wrong."

One of the thugs smiled at Kenyon. In his teeth, he held a razor blade. "Tomorrow, you'll give me your money or else I'll cut you," he promised. Then the gang moved away.

In astonishment, Kenyon looked at his friends. "You guys are PUNKS! I thought you had more heart that that!" he exploded. They mumbled excuses about not having any choice. Kenyon didn't buy it. He went straight to the dean's office and wrote a full report of what had happened. "My aunt had always told me, 'If you want results, put it in writing.'" His complaint was taken seriously, and the next day the thugs were pulled out of school.

Michelle Wimberly (pages 97, 107, 111, 113, 159, 169, and 181) is a graduate of Wesleyan University in Connecticut, where she earned a degree in sociology. Her friendship with a fellow student from Nigeria has led to her plan to spend several months working in an AIDS education program in that African nation. She presently works as a law office program administrator and director for the Youth Leadership Foundation, and she hopes to go on to graduate school to prepare for a career in international relations.

Michelle remembers how her struggle to excel brought her some unwanted attention at school. "I was very skinny and shy and didn't dress well," Michelle remembers. "I had just four friends that I really talked to, and otherwise I stayed quiet and did my work. It seemed like I was surrounded by girls who always had new clothes and could get their hair done every two weeks. I didn't have any of that. But I had a goal." A gang of girls took notice of Michelle's quiet and studious ways and decided she was "uppity." "They said I was 'acting white,'" says Michelle. "It's such a mess—African American kids get pressure *not* to succeed because it's not a 'cool' thing to do, it's a 'white' thing." The girls taunted Michelle, even threatening to beat her up. Michelle just kept on working. At home, with no private place to do her homework, she frequently locked herself in the bathroom to study.

During her senior year in high school, the pressure started to get to Michelle. A close friend died in a car crash. The girls who were bothering her became even more aggressive. She began to dread going to school. She already had her letters of acceptance from several colleges, including Wesleyan. "I stopped thinking about the future and just let myself concentrate on how bad things were right then," Michelle admits. She began skipping school, lots of it. But then she learned that her admission to college was not guaranteed— that she had to keep up her good performance until graduation. She pulled herself together and returned to school, where she graduated fifth in a senior class of over five hundred.

ACKNOWLEDGMENTS

I am grateful to all the people named above for their insights and experiences. In particular, I thank Maria Cardenas, Joe Davis, Ryan Klootwyk, and Rod Sutton for sharing their stories, and I owe special thanks to Dr. Ben Carson for taking time out from his demanding schedule to participate in this book. I am also grateful to Philadelphia Futures, an outstanding mentoring organization founded by Marciene Mattleman and now directed by Joan Mazzotti. Philadelphia Futures has helped change the lives of hundreds of students in the Philadelphia public schools, including many students featured in this book. I also appreciate the help provided by the photographer Paul Kowal and by the Townsend Press staff, especially Janet Goldstein, Beth Johnson, Eliza Comodromos, Devan Blackwell, and George Henry.

John Langan

Index